Advan [illegible] similated

"Davi [illegible] ilderness, cautic [illegible] Chinese ambi [illegible] to thwart them [illegible] list alarm that confronting China is as [illegible] it will be taxing, given how long an unprepared and naïve America has underestimated Chinese talent, strategic thinking, and persistence. A realistic wake-up call from an American patriot, polymath scholar, and international financial analyst who knows China all too well."

—Victor Davis Hanson, author
The Second World Wars, The Hoover
Institution, Stanford University

"China is our enemy. President Trump knows it. David Goldman knows it. Read *You Will Be Assimilated* if you want to know how serious the threat is. And how America can win."

—Sebastian Gorka, Ph.D., Former Strategist
to President Trump, Host of America First

"David Goldman has lived in, visited, watched, and interpreted China for decades. An economist and a polymath, he predicted long ago the things about China that the rest of us are beginning to see. In this master work, he tells a terrible story, and he shows how to redeem that story from its possible end in disaster. If you want to know where the world is going and how to stop it, read this book."

—Larry Arnn, President of Hillsdale College

"David Goldman's book is an urgent wake-up call for America. He details China's comprehensive plan to replace us as the world's most powerful country and dominate global technology, security, communications, and trade within the next few years. There is still time for America to regain the initiative, but only if we act wisely and quickly. If you read just one book about how China plans to make the 21st century theirs and what we can do about it, read You Will Be Assimilated."

—KT McFarland, Former Deputy National Security Advisor and author of *Revolution: Trump, Washington and "We the People"*

YOU WILL BE ASSIMILATED

CHINA'S PLAN TO SINO-FORM THE WORLD

DAVID P. GOLDMAN

BOMBARDIER
BOOKS

A BOMBARDIER BOOKS BOOK
An Imprint of Post Hill Press
ISBN: 978-1-64293-540-0
ISBN (eBook): 978-1-64293-541-7

You Will Be Assimilated:
China's Plan to Sino-form the World

Cover art by Cody Corcoran

Post Hill Press
New York • Nashville
posthillpress.com

Published in the United States of America

To my teachers. For my children.

CONTENTS

INTRODUCTION

EVERYTHING YOU'VE HEARD ABOUT CHINA IS WRONG (OR NOT RIGHT ENOUGH)

The late Elizabeth Kübler-Ross described five stages of grief—denial, anger, bargaining, acceptance, and depression. Her model applies to America's response to the rise of China as a global power. For the past decade, we have been in denial. We couldn't believe a country that for generations had been a byword for poverty could compete with us. With the election of Donald Trump in 2016, we have transitioned to anger. As matters stand, we will be bargaining before long.

China's national champion, Huawei, is rolling out the next, or fifth, generation of mobile broadband across the whole of the Eurasian continent, from Vladivostok, Russia, to Bristol, England, despite a full-court press by the Trump Administration to stop it. In January 2020, America's closest ally, Great Britain, brushed off President Trump's personal intervention to allow Huawei to build out part of its 5G networks. The European Community announced that it would take no measures to exclude the Chinese giant. Washington tried to strangle Huawei by slapping export controls on US components for its 5G equipment and smartphones, to no avail. Huawei achieved self-sufficiency in chip production and continues to expand with Chinese and other Asian components. Former House Speaker Newt Gingrich deplored this outcome as "the greatest strategic disaster in US history." At stake is not only the sinews of the new industrial age, but scores of spinoff applications that will transform manufacturing, mining, healthcare, finance, transportation, and retailing—virtually the entirety of economic life—in what China calls the Fourth Industrial Revolution.

The year 2019 was a watershed. As matters stand, the United States will be overtaken by a resurgent China in the next several years. The consequences for American living standards and national security will be dire. This book explains what China is, what it wants to become, and what we can do to ensure America's pre-eminent place in the world.

I wrote this book because everything you've heard about China is wrong—not entirely wrong, but not right enough. However bad you think things are, they're a lot worse.

The coronavirus epidemic was China's "Chernobyl moment."

During February, the phrase "Chernobyl moment" became a byword for China's predicament in the first phase of the epidemic. A month later, when the count of new cases in China dropped to near zero, dark rumors circulated on social media that China had intentionally propagated the virus in a plot to undermine the West. For one brief hopeful moment, the entirety of the Western commentariat believed that China's ascendancy had come to a sorry and sudden end. Contempt for China in the United States has turned into anger. As this book goes to press, the media is full of demands to "hold China accountable" for the coronavirus. There are few practical suggestions, though, about how that might be accomplished. The fact remains that China has repeated the benefit of its massive investment in artificial intelligence and the communications infrastructure that supports it. That is a far greater challenge for the United States than the coronavirus epidemic itself.

China's weaknesses, but even more, its strengths, were evident in the coronavirus pandemic of 2020. The first response of provincial officials in Wuhan City to the appearance of the virus was to cover it up and intimidate physicians who tried to raise the alarm—notably Dr. Li Wenliang, who died of COVID-19, and to whom the government later gave a "solemn apology." China's rigid hierarchy typically responds to bad news by killing the messenger. But when China mobilized to stop the epidemic, it reduced the rate of new infections to effectively zero by the week of March 16, 2020. The full story remains to be written, although I sketched the basics in Asia Times.[1] Chinese government algorithms can estimate the probability that a given neighborhood, or even an individual, has exposure to COVID-19 by matching the location of smartphones to known locations of infected individuals or groups. The authorities use this information to use limited medical resources more efficiently by, for example, directing tests for the virus to high-risk subjects identified by the artificial-intelligence algorithm.

All smartphones with enabled GPS give telecom providers a precise record of the user's itinerary. Smartphone users in the United States and Europe can access their own data, but privacy laws prevent the government from collecting this data. China has no such privacy constraints, and telecom providers have used locational data for years for advertising.

The government required individuals to download the Health Code app hosted on the software platform of Alipay, the electronic payments system owned by China's e-commerce giant Alibaba. A smartphone attachment read each person's body temperature and other vital signs, and uploaded the data to the cloud. Big data analysis matched locational data, coronavirus test results, and vital signs to identify clusters of infection and the path of transmission. Facial recognition software confirmed that the bearer of the smartphone was the registered account holder. An artificial-intelligence algorithm determined when the individual no longer was at risk, and transmitted a "green page" to the phone, required for admittance into all public spaces. It sounds like science fiction, but it was the result of years of planning and development. As I report in chapter two, China envisions a radical transformation of healthcare through artificial intelligence powered by 5G mobile broadband. The coronavirus epidemic has turbocharged China's campaign for world leadership in the field.

Demonstrations against Beijing's absentee government paralyzed the city of Hong Kong during 2019, in what Western observers read as a challenge to the authoritarian rule of China's Communist Party. But the demonstrations had no reverberations on the Chinese mainland, and the Beijing regime responded with a cautious, ruthless, and relentless war of attrition. The power of China's imperial center of China has always been fragile, but Hong Kong will not destabilize the Communist dynasty.

You've been told that China is stealing intellectual property.

That's true. But what really ought to worry you is that China is developing its own intellectual property in key areas, and a lot of it is better than ours—artificial intelligence, telecommunications, cryptography, electronic warfare, among other fields. In other key fields like quantum computing, which might be the Holy Grail of 21st century technology, it's hard to tell who's winning, except that China is outspending us by a huge margin.

You've been told that China has stolen jobs from the American manufacturing industry.

That's true. But much worse is the likelihood that China will create most of the jobs in cutting-edge new industries powered by artificial intelligence, with breakthroughs in communications and computation.

You've been told that Huawei, China's national champion in telecommunications, and the world leader in fifth-generation mobile broadband, plans to steal the world's data.

Maybe. Although, breakthroughs in cryptography will soon make it impossible for anyone to steal large amounts of data. But Huawei doesn't think it needs to steal the world's data. It plans for the world to give away all of its data for free. Even worse, 5G mobile communications will contain security features that will prevent the United States from stealing the world's data. America's massive signal intelligence capability will become worthless in a couple years.

You've been told that China's economy is prone to collapse under a giant debt bubble.

A popular book appeared in 2001, under the title, *The Coming Collapse of China*. Since then, China's per capita gross domestic product has risen fivefold. Chinese cities that were Third World slums in 2001, have blossomed into steel-and-glass behemoths that look like sci-fi movie sets—not just Shanghai, Shenzhen, or Guangzhou, but cities deep in the interior like Chengdu and Chongqing, each with thirty million inhabitants. China's growth has slowed to only 6 percent a year, or about three times America's growth rate. China's debt burden is the same size as America's relative to GDP.

You've been told that China has "a secret strategy to replace the US as the Global Superpower."

There's nothing "secret" about China's high-tech military buildup. And you've been told that China is pursuing "unrestricted warfare" against the United States. That's the title of quirky, kooky treatise by two low-level Chinese colonels that the Chinese leadership ignored. As I show in chapter seven, China got the jump on America in the Western Pacific by doing the opposite of what "unrestricted warfare" proposed. Not surprisingly, our military leaders are loath to admit that they were asleep at the switch.

You've been told that China is challenging American military power in the South China Sea.

"Challenge" is a euphemism in this case. The combination of Chinese rocketry, submarines, electronic countermeasures, and air defense makes American military assets in the Western Pacific sitting ducks. We lost the South China Sea years ago. We need to play catchup with the next generation of defense technologies.

You've been told that China is manipulating its currency to sell its goods cheaply in the United States.

That one isn't true at all. What ought to worry you is that China plans to replace the US dollar as the world's reserve currency. That means we won't be able to borrow trillions of dollars from abroad to finance our trillion-dollar-a-year federal budget deficit.

You've been told that China is ruled by a totalitarian clique in the form of the Communist Party, oppressing a billion and a half people who yearn for American-style democracy.

In fact, China has been ruled by an emperor for thousands of years, and the present dynasty—ruled by a committee of bureaucrats, rather than a flesh-and-blood royal family—is an updated version of the imperial system that has revived itself again and again throughout the millennia. A raft of recent books on China—by Michael Pillsbury,[2] Graham Allison,[3] former House Speaker Newt Gingrich,[4] General Robert Spalding (ret.),[5] and veteran defense writer Bill Gertz[6]—rehearse the same ritual denunciations of the wicked Communist Party of China, with its totalitarian surveillance state and ideology of world conquest. American strategists think we are dealing with the Soviet Union of the 1980s. If it were only that easy!

There are More Marxists in Cambridge, Massachusetts Than in China

Communism is a bankrupt ideology, an "ism" that became a "wasm," a miserable failure at social and economic organization. China is something entirely different. The Soviet Communists told their most talented scientists, *Invent something new, and we'll give you a medal, and maybe a dacha*. China says, *Invent something new, launch an Initial Public Offering, and become a billionaire*. As of the end of 2019, there were 285 billionaires in China, including Alibaba's Jack Ma, who is also a member of the Communist Party of China, like many of his fellow billionaires. There are more Marxists in Cambridge, Massachusetts than in the whole of China. I met one professed Marxist over dinner in Beijing a couple of years ago, a pleasant fellow who taught Marxist-Leninist doctrine at the Communist Party's cadre school. His daughter had just graduated from a top American university, and he asked me if I could help her get a job on Wall Street.

We aren't up against drunken and corrupt Soviet bureaucrats; we're up against Mandarin elite, cherry-picked from the brightest university graduates of the world's largest country. America faces something far more daunting than moth-eaten Marxism: a five-thousand-year-old empire that is pragmatic, curious, adaptive—and hungry. China's regime is cruel, but no crueler than the Qin dynasty that buried a million conscript laborers in the Great Wall. China always was and remains utterly ruthless.

We are at a Great Turning Point in History

We stand at the cusp of one of history's great turning points. For thousands of years, China's internal weaknesses—natural disaster, famine, plague, civil unrest, and foreign invasion—kept China's attention turned inward. We are now at the greatest turning point in Chinese history since the unification of China in the 3rd century B.C.E. China is turning outward and looking hungrily at the world. And we look like a protein source. China doesn't want to rule you. It wants to assimilate you, like the Borg in *Star Trek*.

If you want to see this in action, look at China's first great multinational company, Huawei. Huawei bankrupted its competition and hired its talent. It dominates research and development (R & D) in the game-changing field of mobile broadband, in part, because its fifty thousand foreign employees do most of the basic research. For the first time in its long history, China has succeeded in assimilating a critical mass of the West's scientific and engineering elite and harnessing them to its global ambitions. Mobile broadband is just the beginning. China's goal is to own the "control points" in every sphere of economic life, and dominate what it calls the Fourth Industrial Revolution during the remainder of this century. Think of industrial robots that talk to each other over 5G networks and employ artificial intelligence to design production techniques without human input. Imagine medical diagnostics drawing on continuously updated vital signs and genetic histories of a billion people, mining robots directed by white-coated technicians with virtual reality visors, and a dozen other disruptive technologies made possible by the marriage of broadband and AI.

Trump Reverses Sixty Years of Wishful Thinking About China

President Donald J. Trump reversed nearly sixty years of American policy towards China. After President Richard Nixon and his then National Security Advisor, Henry Kissinger, opened diplomatic relations with China in 1972, America viewed China as a counterweight to Russia during the Cold War. After Deng Xiaoping's economic reforms of 1979, and the fall of communism, the American foreign policy establishment thought China would join the procession towards the end of history and turn into a liberal democracy. Meanwhile, the US lost economic ground to China. Trump, to paraphrase William F. Buckley, bestrode history, shouting, "Stop!"

In his February 2019 State of the Union Address, Trump declared:

> We are now making it clear to China that, after years of targeting our industries and stealing our intellectual property, the theft of American jobs and wealth has come to an end. Therefore, we recently imposed tariffs on $250 billion worth of Chinese

> goods, and now our Treasury is receiving billions and billions of dollars.
>
> But I don't blame China for taking advantage of us; I blame our leaders and representatives for allowing this travesty to happen. I have great respect for President Xi, and we are now working on a new trade deal with China. But it must include real, structural change to end unfair trade practices, reduce our chronic trade deficit, and protect American jobs.[7]

President Trump is magnificently right to insist that America's status quo with China cannot continue. But thus far, he has addressed symptoms rather than causes. The trade war with China has settled into an uneasy truce as of the end of 2019, with modest damage to both economies but no clear winner.

China has begged, borrowed, and stolen the technology that made its economy as big as America's. China pays $36 billion a year in royalties for intellectual property, but its bill should be much bigger. Some of it is stolen outright. For example, the plans for Boeing's C-17 military transport aircraft, phished by Chinese hackers and used to build a Chinese knockoff, the PLA's Y-20 transport.[8] Some of it is lifted by Chinese engineers working for Western companies who learn their employers' technology and walk out the door with the skills to duplicate it. And a great deal of it is handed over to China, eagerly, by Western companies who want access to the Chinese market and are happy to give away the family jewels in return for the privilege. That might be bad for the competitiveness of these companies in the long term, but good for the CEO's stock options at a five-year horizon.

China is Dangerous Because it's Adopted the American Idea of a Science Driver for Growth

But the most important thing that China appropriated from the United States is the one big idea that made America the world's only superpower after the collapse of the Soviet Union. That idea is to drive fundamental R & D through the aggressive pursuit of superior weapons systems, and let the spinoffs trickle down to the civilian economy. China is like a two-stage rocket. The export-driven, cheap labor economy that turned China from an impoverished rural country into a prosperous urbanized giant after the Deng Xiaoping reforms of 1979, was only the booster. China began to discard it ten years ago. The next stage is what Huawei calls the Fourth Industrial Revolution, driven by artificial intelligence, robotics, the internet of things, and massive big data applications to supply chain management, transportation, healthcare and other fields.

I wrote this book because America's response to China's global ambitions is a failure. There are two big reasons for this failure. First, we chronically underestimate China's capabilities and ambitions. Second, we need to address our own problems. China envisions a virtual empire in which game-changing technology dominates production, purchasing, finance, and transportation. It puts massive resources into basic research, science education, and infrastructure. America's commitment to basic research and science education has shrunk to roughly half its size during the Reagan Administration. Just 5 percent of our college students major in engineering, compared to one-third in China.

Since 2001, I have written the *Spengler* column for *Asia Times*, which by 2019 had become the largest pan-Asian news platform by readership. In 2016, I joined the investor group that acquired Asia Times, and serve on the board of directors of its holding company.

As head of debt research for Bank of America in the mid 2000's, I traveled to China and spoke extensively to Chinese officials and business people. Then in 2013, a Hong Kong investment banking boutique, Reorient Group, asked me to take a fresh look at China's economy and prepare a presentation for prospective investors. What I saw turned my world inside-out.

It was already evident six years ago that China was poised for a technological breakout that would challenge America's leadership in the decisive new industries of the 21st century. The Belt and Road Initiative was in gestation, and China's global ambitions had already peeked through the mist of China's isolation. I accepted a partnership at Reorient Group and got an insider's view of what China was doing.

Reorient was later acquired by Jack Ma's private equity company and re-named Yunfeng Financial. Working for a Chinese firm took me to the other side of the looking glass. I had the vantage point to see economic and strategic issues through Chinese eyes. Among other things, I worked with senior executives of Huawei, China's national champion in the telecommunications space, and public enemy number one for America's security establishment. I've been inside the belly of the dragon.

At the same time, I served as an adviser to a non-governmental organization that promotes Israeli-Chinese relations. In that capacity, I participated in numerous off the-the-record consultations with senior Chinese officials, including many from the military and national security sphere. Prior to my tenure at Reorient Group, I also consulted for the Defense Department's Office of Net Assessment, the internal think tank then directed by the legendary Andrew Marshall. When the Trump Administration took office, I informally advised then White House strategist Steve Bannon.

China is Overtaking the US in Key Technologies

For the past six years, I have warned that China was overtaking the US in key technologies. In 2013, I wrote in The American Interest (with Dr. Henry Kressel):

> Economies do not exist in a vacuum. If American technological innovation comes to a halt for a prolonged period, other countries with cheaper production costs will learn to do what American industries can do, and American manufacturers will continue to lose market share. China already boasts the world's largest telecommunications equipment firm, Huawei. China is already producing nuclear power plants with Westinghouse technology under license from Toshiba, Westinghouse's majority owner. Fear of Chinese competition is an important factor—probably the most important factor—in the sharp decline in venture capital commitments to high-tech industry during the past ten years.…China remains behind the United States with 1.8 percent of GDP devoted to R & D compared to our 2.8 percent, but it is catching up fast. China is now more concerned with acquiring existing technologies than inventing new

> ones. Nevertheless, it is educating a new generation of university students on a scale never before seen, with uneven quality, but with pockets of impressive strength. If China bests us at innovation some time during the next generation, the world will look radically different just three or four decades hence.
>
> If U.S. innovation continues to attenuate, the weapons technology deployed by China and other potential adversaries will converge on America's. The longstanding American technological edge is already eroding as other nations acquire airframe, avionics, and stealth technology.[9]

In 2013, that sounded alarmist. But China advanced much farther and faster than anyone expected in 2013—in semiconductors, telecommunications, artificial intelligence, computation, missile technology, and other key fields.

The West Consistently Underestimates Asians

China's ambitions and capacities were evident to anyone who chose to look, but we refused to believe our own eyes. Our failure to respond to China's sudden emergence as a world power falls into a sad pattern of Western underestimation of Asian rivals. Historian Andrew Roberts reports that Winston Churchill said, just after Pearl Harbor, that "in the event of war, the Japanese would 'fold up like the Italians,' because they were 'the wops of the Far East.'" Churchill was the greatest Western statesman of the 20th century, but he also was guilty of one of century's worst strategic blunders.

He wasn't alone. In 1904, Czar Nicholas II of Russia, encouraged by his cousin Wilhelm II of Germany, determined to push Japan out of Manchuria. In two catastrophic naval engagements, Port Arthur in 1904, and the Tsushima Straits in 1905, Japan deployed a newer, mainly British-built fleet and destroyed virtually the whole Russian navy. Japanese commanders who were born in an agrarian society before the Meiji Restoration of 1868, proved superior to their Russian counterparts. The shock of Russia's loss brought on the 1905 Revolution and marked the beginning of the end for the Romanov dynasty. The West chronically underestimates Asians, as the Russians found out at Port Arthur, the Americans at Pearl Harbor and the Yalu River, the British at Singapore, and so forth.

Five Myths About China's Economy

China's economy is like the bumblebee that shouldn't be able to fly, but does. American commentators have trouble explaining China's economic success, so they pretend it isn't there, or if it is there, it won't be for long. American misperceptions of China's economy clump together in five myths.

Myth #1: America's Economy is Bigger Than China's

President Trump tweeted on July 30, 2019, "China is doing very badly, worst year in twenty-seven....Our Economy has become MUCH larger than the Chinese Economy in the last three years."

It's true that China's growth rate of 6.1 percent in 2019 was the lowest in three decades, as the president said, but it's also about triple America's 2019 growth rate of 2.2 percent. Whether America's or China's economy is the biggest depends on how you measure it. In US dollar terms, America's economy is much bigger. But if you figure in the relative cost of goods and services, China's economy is about $4 trillion bigger than America's, according to the World Bank's measure of purchasing power parity. That accounts for the fact that domestic Chinese prices are much lower than US prices. A half-hour taxi ride from Chengdu Airport in August 2019, cost me RMB 35, or about five US dollars. In any American city, it would have been fifty to seventy dollars. In terms of current US dollars, China's GDP in 2018 was about $13 trillion versus over $20 trillion for US GDP. But purchasing power parity is a more informative measure.

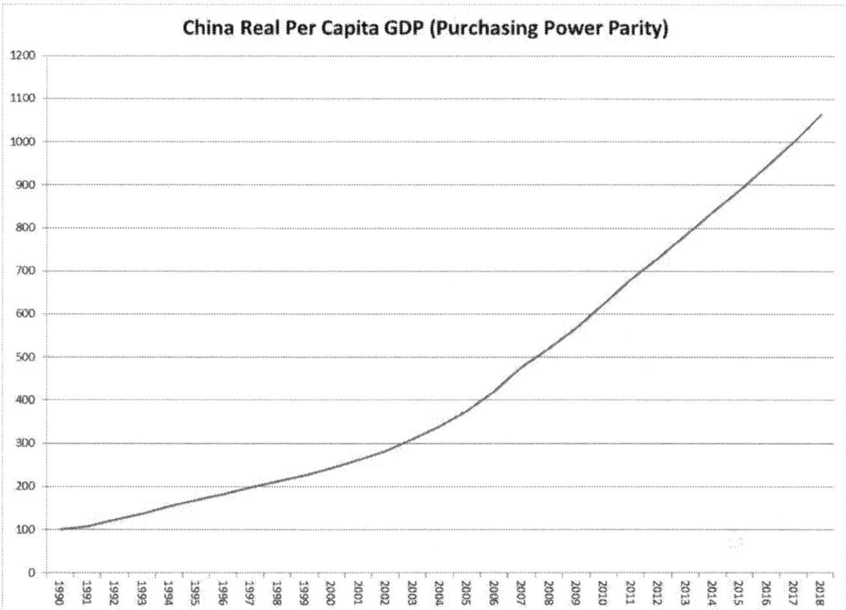

Myth #2: "China is a Poor and Backward Nation"

That comment came from Professor Michael J. Hicks of Ball State University, in 2018. "China is a large, poorly led nation with a military that is decades away from the expertise of Saddam's army and an economy that is more than a century behind ours," Professor Hicks declared. "When you hear a politician telling you that China's economy is just a few years away from surpassing ours, he is simply lying to you. No one living now will see the Chinese standard of living catch up to ours, and I would wager they won't equal America's current standard of living in the balance of this century."[10]

Professor Hicks notes that he served as a U.S. Army officer in Japan and "squared off against Chinese tanks" in Iraq, but I doubt he has spent much time in China lately. A ten-minute walk around any of China's big cities might change his mind. A thirty-year-old Chinese person consumes not quite ten times as much as the previous generation. Accounting for the fact that consumption in China today is about 40 percent of GDP, compared to 50 percent of GDP in 1990, consumption per person has risen about eight-fold.

In other words, the Chinese who grew up in homes with dirt floors and outhouses now live in apartments with central heating and indoor plumbing. Chinese who scrimped to buy a bicycle now can afford a car. Are Chinese government data faked to make things look better? Don't count on it. Basic indicators of economic activity, such as electricity production, freight traffic, and production of key industrial items, are verifiable and they track reported GDP growth fairly closely. In the meantime, China has built the world's longest highway system (about ninety thousand miles), the world's largest high-speed rail network (about eighteen thousand miles today, growing to twenty-four thousand miles by 2025), and enough housing to move nearly six hundred million people from the countryside to cities. None of this was there thirty years ago. China's infrastructure is the wonder of the modern world. Compared to China's airports, roads, and rail lines, most of the United States looks like a Third World country.

China now graduates more scientists and engineers than the United States, Europe, Japan, Taiwan, and South Korea combined, and six times as many as the United States alone. During the past ten years, moreover, the quality of Chinese scientific education has risen to world standards. Mao Zedong's Cultural Revolution of the 1960s nearly destroyed China's university system. Thanks to American graduate schools, Chinese universities have assembled a world-class scientific and engineering faculty. Four out of five doctoral degrees in computer science and electrical engineering are awarded to foreign students, of whom Chinese are the largest contingent. Only 5 percent of American undergraduates major in engineering, which means that there aren't a lot of available faculty positions available for recent doctorates. Most of the Chinese foreign students at US universities go back to China after receiving their degrees, as Texas A&M Distinguished Professor of Engineering Edward Dougherty explains:

> China and India are recruiting some of their best citizens and former citizens to come home, both at the senior and junior levels. For senior people, the inducement goes beyond salary. Research requires

> resources, which can be expensive, both for research staff and laboratory facilities. An offer is especially attractive when it provides secure funding for fundamental work, a rarity in the United States. When a leading scientist returns to his home country, there is a shift of research capital from the United States to a competitor. Given the fact that, in numerous areas, major contributions come from a small group of research teams, even a single shift can have a significant impact.
>
> For recent PhDs, the disparity in incentives between remaining in the United States and returning home can be even greater, and top graduates are being targeted. One alternative for them is to remain in a U.S. university, go through two to five years of postdoctoral work earning $50,000 per year, then apply for one of the few good open faculty positions. If fortunate, these promising scientists will then suffer through a six-year pre-tenure period writing grant proposals of meager scientific value in an environment where the main interest of the department head and dean is the number of dollars they bring in. The other alternative is to return to one's homeland and receive an immediate faculty position at a top university, with funding to build a laboratory and support students. [11]

It's hard to measure the relative quality of STEM education in China versus the rest of the world. The Times Higher Education Supplement includes eight Chinese universities in its ranking of the top fifty engineering and technology schools in the world.[12] Executives of Chinese tech companies have told me that they prefer not to hire Chinese graduates with a bachelor's degree from an American university. Chinese programs are more rigorous, they argue, and Chinese students who go overseas probably are the children of well-to-do families who didn't score well on China's university entrance exam.

China also awards twice as many doctorates in STEM fields as the United States. That's not counting all the Chinese students who earn doctorates in the United States and then return to China.

Myth #3: "China Can't Innovate"

A Google search for the phrase "China can't innovate" brings up ten thousand hits. China spent most of the past forty years copying Western technology—that's what you do when you are starting from scratch. But in the past five years, China has produced the world's best 5G equipment, some of the world's fastest supercomputers, hypervelocity strategic missiles, computer chips that rival the best that America can design, and an un-hackable cybersecurity technology, quantum cryptography. A Chinese robotic spacecraft made the first soft landing on the dark side of the moon in 2019. That's just the beginning.

China now spends about 2.2 percent of GDP on research and development, compared to 2.8 percent in the United States. But China's economy is somewhat larger than America's in terms of purchasing power parity—it costs a lot less to higher an engineering graduate for a tech startup in Chengdu than it does in Silicon Valley, for example. It's fair to say that China's R & D spending in absolute terms is about the same as America's. A big difference is in the composition of spending. Most American R & D seeks incremental improvements in existing products—an upgraded laundry detergent or a less salty can of soup. China's R & D, as the Pentagon explained in its 2019 assessment of China's military capabilities, concentrates on dual-use civilian technologies as well as military applications. In critical areas, China spends much more than we do. In 2019, Hudson Institute analyst Arthur Herman wrote, in *The Wall Street Journal*:

> Beijing is America's chief quantum-computing rival. It spends at least $2.5 billion a year on research—more than 10 times what Washington spends—and has a massive quantum center in Hefei province. China aspires to develop the code-breaking "killer app," which means protecting U.S. data and networks from quantum intrusion is a vital security interest.[13]

Huawei, the world industry leader in mobile broadband, spends more on R & D than its main rivals, Nokia and Ericsson, combined.

Chinese government support for artificial intelligence "dwarfs" the American effort, according to Babson College Professor Thomas Davenport:

> In 2017, [China's] national government announced it wanted to make the country and its industries world leaders in AI technologies by 2030. The government's latest venture capital fund is expected to invest more than $30 billion in AI and related technologies within state-owned firms, and that fund joins even larger state-funded venture capital funds. One Chinese state alone has said it will devote $5 billion to developing AI technologies and businesses. The city of Beijing has committed $2 billion to developing an AI-focused industrial park. A major port, Tianjin, plans to invest $16 billion in its local AI industry.
>
> These government programs will support ambitious major projects, startups and academic research in AI. The national effort also includes using AI in China's defense and intelligence industries; the country's leaders are not reluctant to use AI for social and political control. For example, both AI-driven facial recognition, even to catch jaywalkers, and "social credit"—an AI-driven credit score that factors in social behaviors—are already in use.
>
> U.S. investment plans, mostly in the defense industry, are dwarfed by the Chinese effort. DARPA, the Defense Department's research arm, has sponsored AI research and competitions for many years, and has a $2 billion fund called "AI Next" to help develop the next wave of AI technologies in universities and companies. It's not yet clear how much real progress its efforts have made.[14]

Myth #4: "China's Economy Will Be Crushed by a Mountain of Debt"

Some analysts claim that China's economy will suffer a debilitating debt crisis. The numbers don't support this view.

According to the Bank for International Settlements, China and America have about the same debt burden. Total credit to government, households, and nonfinancial corporations stands at 261 percent of GDP in China and 249 percent of GDP in the United States. The big difference lies in who owes the debt. Central government debt is about half of GDP in China, but about 100 percent of GDP in the United States. By contrast, private corporate debt is only about 75 percent of GDP in the US, compared to about 150 percent of GDP in the United States.

China's financial system has plenty of inefficiencies and imbalances. It is overly dependent on giant state banks who are accustomed to handing out loans to state-owned companies without asking questions. This encourages inefficiency and corruption. The Chinese authorities are allowing private companies to fail rather than encouraging banks to paper over their problems. Seventeen billion dollars of Chinese corporate bonds defaulted during the first eleven months of 2019, a small number compared to the overall $4.4 trillion onshore corporate bond market.[15] Most Chinese corporate debt, though, funded infrastructure which can support the debt burden.

China's way of funding infrastructure spending explains most of the difference in the concentration of debt. In the United States, federal, state, and local governments fund infrastructure spending out of tax revenues or borrowing. But in China, state-owned companies borrow from state-owned banks to fund infrastructure.

In a 2017 study for *Asia Times*, I calculated that two-thirds of the net debt owed by non-financial companies in China's benchmark equity index, the Shenzhen 300, was owed by only twenty-two companies. Almost all of them are involved in basic infrastructure—energy, communications infrastructure, shipping, airlines, or metals. Ten percent of the net debt of non-industrial SHSZ300 companies is owed by the oil giant PetroChina alone. This suggests that a great deal of Chinese corporate indebtedness should be viewed as "public works" investment by the Chinese sovereign.[16]

After borrowing roughly the same amount relative to the size of their respective economies, what did China and the United States get in return? America's national debt rose above $20 trillion, not counting an estimated $46 trillion more in unfunded liabilities of the Social Security and Medicare systems. The United States spent most of the money on transfer payments. China used its debt to move 550 million people from countryside to city and to build the world's newest and biggest infrastructure. At the end of the day, it appears that China got the better deal.

Myth #5: "China has Devalued its Currency to Gain Unfair Advantage in Trade"

In August 2019, the US Treasury designed China as a "currency manipulator." That designation was rescinded after the US and China struck a "phase one" trade deal in December 2019, but it was wrong to begin with. According to the official statement, "China has a long history of facilitating an undervalued currency through protracted, large-scale intervention in the foreign exchange market. In recent days, China has taken concrete steps to devalue its currency, while maintaining substantial foreign exchange reserves despite active use of such tools in the past. The context of these actions and the implausibility of China's market stability rationale confirm that the purpose of China's currency devaluation is to gain an unfair competitive advantage in international trade."[17]

There's a problem with this statement, namely that China's currency has doubled in relative value against its competitors during the past twenty-five years. The "real effective change rate" adjusts the nominal price of a currency by the difference between its inflation rate and the inflation rates of its trading partners.

Of course, it's hard to determine the true exchange rate of an inconvertible currency. If China were to lift exchange controls tomorrow and allow its people to buy foreign currency with their RMB deposits, the exchange rate of the RMB almost certainly would fall. That might lead one to assert that the RMB is artificially overvalued, or that China is manipulating its currency upward rather than downward, contrary to the finding of the U.S. Treasury. On the other hand, a dollar buys more in Mainland China than it does in the United States. That's why the Chinese economy looks considerably larger when measured against purchasing power parity. The fact remains that China's currency has been rising rather than falling for most of the past quarter-century, and today is worth twice as much as it was in 1994.

The Myth of a Chinese "Secret Plan"

American denial has faded into American anger, but the quality of America's strategic thinking remains abysmal. In place of contempt for a weak and ineffectual China, many American commentators evince paranoia about China's intentions. Michael Pillsbury's 2015 book, *The Hundred Year Marathon,* claims that China has a "secret plan" hatched by a group of Chinese "hawks" to "replace us, just as America replaced the British Empire, without firing a shot."

President Trump's public nod to Dr. Pillsbury has given enormous weight to his book. That is unfortunate. Pillsbury is wrong on both of his principle counts. First of all, China has no intention of replacing the United States, just as the United States had no intention of replacing the British Empire. The global order that the United States built after the Second World II had little in common with the British

Empire, just as the global role that China envisions for itself has little in common with the global role that the United States played during and after the Cold War.

Contrary to Pillsbury, there is nothing secret about China's intentions. China's plan for global economic supremacy was advertised on the Huawei website starting in 2011, and proclaimed with great fanfare and considerable expense at every telecommunications conference for the past ten years. The military dimension of China's ambitions is important, but subordinate to an economic and technological vision so vast and ambitious that American analysts have lacked the intellectual bandwidth to perceive it.

Graham Allison's Thucydides Claptrap

We use the word "empire" to describe China, evoking memories of military conquest and colonial occupation. But China is an entirely different entity; it aims for assimilation and indirect control rather than imperial rule. It avoids the imperial overreach of foreign military commitments, and seeks to lock in its influence through dominance in trade and technology. Professor Graham Allison of Harvard University won a year's worth of notoriety in 2017, with his "Thucydides Trap" thesis, warning that established powers—in this case, the United States—typically go to war against rising powers—in this case, China. As I show in the chapter below, entitled "Thucydides Claptrap," Allison is barking up the wrong tree, and the wrong tree is in the wrong forest to begin with. China's enormous high-tech military buildup is not designed to win a war with the United States, but to make war with the United States unlikely. China controls its borders and its coastal waters out to a couple hundred miles, to such an extent that the United States cannot bring its military to bear. Allison shoehorns ill-fitting historical examples into his thesis, which are as wrong as his reading of the present.

Don Quixote Charges at the Communist Party of China

American anger has given birth to a dangerous delusion, that the United States can engineer the overthrow of the Communist Party of China. As the New York Times reported, on July 20, 2019:

> In a ballroom across from the Capitol building, an unlikely group of military hawks, populist crusaders, Chinese Muslim freedom fighters and followers of the Falun Gong has been meeting to warn anyone who will listen that China poses an existential threat to the United States that will not end until the Communist Party is overthrown.
>
> If the warnings sound straight out of the Cold War, they are. The Committee on the Present Danger, a long-defunct group that campaigned against the dangers of the Soviet Union in the 1970s and 1980s, has recently been revived with the help of Stephen K. Bannon, the president's former chief strategist, to warn against the dangers of China.

The founders of the Committee on the Present Danger prevailed on me to join the group, and in April 2019, I shared a podium with Steve Bannon and other China hawks at New York's Regis Carlton Hotel. Steve tried to convince me that President Trump's tariffs on Chinese products would lead to mass unemployment, street demonstrations, and the downfall of Chinese President Xi Jinping. I told him that he was deranged. Later in 2019, I disassociated myself from the Committee, which I had hoped would promote an American response to China in the form of crash R & D efforts to maintain superiority in key technologies.

There is no easy way for American to respond to China, no quick fix, no short cut. The world has seen nothing like China's breakout onto the global stage. It will transform the lives of every inhabitant of this planet, including that of Americans. The Russian revolutionary Leon Trotsky said—perhaps apocryphally—that you may not be interested in war, but war is interested in you. The same is true of China.

What does this mean for you personally? If China comes to dominate the key technologies of the 21st century, you as an American will be poorer and less secure. After World War II, Americans got paid simply for being Americans. The whole world had to come to us. We had the only deep capital markets, the only venture capitalists, the only national defense establishment able to put massive resources behind basic R & D, and the only skilled workforce ready to turn innovations into products. We invented every component of the digital age: semiconductors, displays, sensors, lasers, networks, and the internet itself. American companies enjoyed natural monopolies in dozens of fields. Our goods and services sold at a premium. The US dollar was king. When I lived in Germany during the first Reagan Administration, American soldiers on German bases could afford BMW's on Army pay.

In 1960, America produced 40 percent of the world's GDP. Now it produces just 24 percent. Even more important is the decline of America's share of high-tech industrial production. According to the World Bank, our share of high-tech exports fell from 18 percent in 1999, to just 7 percent in 2014, while China's share rose from 3 percent to 26 percent.

America's commitment to high-tech manufacturing collapsed with the tech bubble of 2000, never to recover. By no coincidence, the income of US households barely grew during the next twenty years.

If China surpasses the United States, we will fade into second-rate status, much like Britain did during the 20th century. We will be poorer, weaker, and less secure.

China's challenge is formidable. We are competing with 1.4 billion intelligent and industrious people. Chinese schoolchildren turn up at 7:30 a.m. and leave at 5:00 p.m. Ten million Chinese teenagers take the college entrance exams each year and prep twelve hours a day for two years to gain acceptance at a good university. The Asian work ethic explains why 28 percent of students at America's Ivy League colleagues are Asians, although Asians comprise just 5.6 percent of the US population. The difference is that America has eighteen million Asians, and China has 1.4 billion. Foreign students earn four out of five doctorates candidates in computer science and electrical engineering at American universities, and Chinese students are the biggest cohort. Most of them return to China. We have educated a world-class engineering faculty for Chinese universities, the best of which are at par with the best American universities.

But we are well past the point where a one-to-one comparison of Chinese and American technical capacity can explain the strategic balance. As I will explain, China has recruited scores of thousands of the best Western scientists and technicians to its plan for technological leadership in the 21st century. Huawei, the focus of Washington's concern, has created a business model unique in Chinese history, with fifty thousand foreign employees and research centers in two dozen Western countries. It is not a Chinese company, but an imperial company, a sort of technologically-driven horde that produces a snowball effect. As it grows, it crushes the competition and absorbs their talent.

The fall of Baghdad to the Mongols in 1258, offers an object lesson. The city of a million people sheltered behind eighteen-foot walls, and the Abbasid Al-Musta'sim rejected Mongol demands for tribute. The Mongols were lightly armed horsemen, the Abbasids believed; what could they do against the vast fortifications of Baghdad? But the Mongol chieftain Hulagu Khan brought with him one thousand Chinese artillery experts, according to a contemporary Persian account. It is not known whether they employed cannon or catapults, but it took the Chinese engineers three weeks to breach the walls, after which the Mongols made a giant pyramid of the heads of Baghdad's inhabitants. Today's Chinese are not the Mongols, but the analogy holds to in that the Chinese have acquired the technical means from the West to ruin us. China's critics complain that it has stolen Western technology. Far more dangerous is the fact that China has assimilated some of the West's best talent.

Can America remain the world's most powerful, productive, and inventive country? I wrote this book to answer that question with a resounding yes. It won't be easy. China is the first challenger we have faced whose economy is as big as ours. Surpassing China will take all of our resources, inventiveness, and national spirit. We can do it. But we have been losing time, and time is getting short.

CHAPTER ONE

AN EMPIRE OF EMPERORS: WHAT IS CHINA, AND WHY YOU SHOULD WORRY ABOUT IT

Lyndon Johnson apocryphally told Israeli Prime Minister Golda Meir that it was hard to be president of three hundred million Americans. She replied, “It’s harder to be prime minister of three million prime ministers.” Xi Jinping might add that it is even harder to be the emperor of 1.4 billion emperors. We tend to think of the West as individualistic and China as collectivist. In some ways that’s true, but the notion can also be misleading. As individuals, the Chinese are the most ambitious people in the world. Ambition is the sinew that holds together the sprawling, multi-ethnic, polylingual empire that China has been since its founding. For five thousand years, China’s ambition has been constrained by the limits of nature. The great flood plains of the Yellow and Yangtze Rivers supported a larger population at higher living standards than any other part of the pre-modern world. But China’s riparian civilization was also fragile, subject to periodic drought, famine, and flood, leading to civil unrest, barbarian invasion, and prolonged periods of chaos.

All this compelled China to turn inward. Its forays into the broader world were brief and abortive. No more; China can feed itself and control natural disasters. It has turned outward to the world and is seeking its place in the sun. This is a grand turning point in world history. For most of the past five thousand years, China has been the world’s most populous and wealthiest civilization in the world, but largely indifferent to events outside its borders. Now its ambitions are turned outward. Its 2,500-year-old system of elite formation now embraces the ten million students who take the annual college entrance exam. It has absorbed tens of thousands of the best Western scientists and engineers into its project for technological dominance, above all through Huawei, its bridgehead in the world market. And it proposes to extend its imperial principle of assimilation through infrastructure to the whole of the Eurasian continent, through the Belt and Road Initiative.

Western observers often attempt to draw a bright line between the good Chinese people and the nasty Chinese government. That is an unsubtle form of condescension, and wholly misguided. The character of China's state is shaped by the ambitions of the Chinese people. Sadly, the distinction between "good people" and "bad state" is a misjudgment on which America's China hawks and China doves agree. Since the late Chinese premier Deng Xiaoping introduced market reforms in 1979, the liberal foreign policy establishment has argued that economic liberalization inevitably would lead to political liberalization. That didn't happen. The China hawks argue that the Chinese people will rise up and overthrow their Communist overlords if the United States applies sufficient pressure, by placing tariffs on Chinese imports to the United States. That won't happen, either.

The Liberal Illusion That Prosperity Promotes Political Reform

China doves promised that China's economic success inevitably would lead to political reforms. Prominent among them is former Goldman Sachs President John L. Thornton, now a professor at Tsinghua University in Beijing and chairman of the board of trustees at the Brookings Institution, Washington's oldest and best-funded think tank. In 2009, Thornton told the Congressional-Executive Commission on China that China was making progress towards democracy:

> Premier Wen Jiabao consistently advocates for the universal values of democracy. He has defined democracy in largely the same way as many in the West would. "When we talk about democracy," Premier Wen said,

> "We usually refer to the three most important components: elections, judicial independence, and supervision based on checks and balances."
>
> Premier Wen's emphasis on universal values of democracy reflects new thinking in the liberal wing of the Chinese political establishment. He likely represents a minority view in the Chinese leadership, but like many other ideas in China during the past three decades, what begins as a minority view may gradually and eventually be accepted by the majority.
>
> Now let me move to the second issue: new and far-reaching economic and socio-political forces in present-day China. Let me briefly mention three such forces, the first is the new and ever-growing middle class, the second is the commercialization and increasing diversity of the media, and the third is the rise of civil society groups and lawyers. These new players are better equipped to seek political participation than the Chinese citizens of 30 years ago....
>
> Political participation through institutional means remains very limited. Yet, the ongoing political and intellectual discourse about democracy in the country, the existence of a middle class, commercialization of the media, the rise of civil society groups, the development of the legal profession, and checks and balances within the leadership are all important, contributing factors for democratic change in any society. In all these aspects, China is making significant progress.[18]

China remains quite as authoritarian as ever it was, and technology has vastly increased the ability of its government to monitor and control the details of everyday life. The government of China knows where every smartphone is at all times, and can verify that it is carried by its registered owner through a vast network of facial recognition cameras. Soon it will require Chinese citizens to log on to the internet through facial recognition to police the online activity of the whole of society.

American hawks have argued that the Chinese political system is fragile and that the Communist Party can be toppled by outside pressure.

Prominent among them is Gordon Chang, whose book *The Coming Collapse of China* appeared in its first edition in 2001. "The People's Republic is a paper dragon," Chang argued. "Peer beneath the veneer of modernization since Mao's death, and the symptoms of decay are everywhere: Deflation grips the economy, state-owned enterprises are failing, banks are hopelessly insolvent, foreign investment continues to decline, and Communist party corruption eats away at the fabric of society." That was eighteen years ago. In the meantime China's per capital GDP has quintupled. Chang continues to provide newspaper and television commentary predicting the imminent collapse of the Chinese system.

Hawks and doves are both wrong because they share the same false premise: For a society to succeed, they both believe, it must look and act like the United States of America. The doves thought that China would evolve into something like a Western democracy and succeed, while the hawks thought China would remain authoritarian and collapse. In fact, China remained authoritarian and deepened its economic success. Hawks and doves suffer from a sort of narcissism. They cannot conceive that a society so radically different from ours can flourish.

China is in a Golden Age

But China has flourished. As Francesco Sisci observes, China is in a Golden Age, the first time in his history that no one need fear going hungry. Since 1986, household consumption in China has risen seventeen-fold—that is, 1,700 percent. That isn't a fabrication of Communist Party statisticians. Chinese now in their thirties, spent their early childhood in homes with dirt floors and outhouses. They now live in newly built apartments with central heating, air conditioning, and indoor plumbing. In 1986, just 3 percent of Chinese had access to universities or professional schools. That proportion grew to 50 percent by 2017. One-third of new labor force entrants have university degrees, and one-third of those are engineers. The Chinese buy four hundred million smartphones a year and twenty-five million automobiles. Chinese commute to work in Shanghai on high-speed trains that reduce the distance from Wilmington to New York City to a forty-five minute interval. We will take a closer look at China's economy in another chapter.

We have to stop viewing China through a half-silvered mirror that reflects our own image back at us, and understand China on its own terms. It isn't a pleasant picture, but we need to take a hard look at it.

China's Emperor as Capo di Tutti Capi

China has had thousands of years to develop a unique and distinct culture, and a unique and distinct political system. Over the long centuries, Chinese culture and Chinese governance have shaped each other. It is a delusion to believe that the "good Chinese people" will rise up and overthrow the "wicked Communist Party." For millennia, China has been ruled by an imperial caste of administrators selected by standardized exams. The Communist Party is simply another incarnation of the Mandarin caste. The character of China's government corresponds to the character of its people. The emperor is not a revered demigod on the Japanese model, or an anointed sovereign claiming divine right, but simply the emperor whose job it is to prevent all the other emperors from killing each other. He is Lucky Luciano, the *capo di capi,* whose function is to keep the peace among the predators who fear him more than they fear each other. The Chinese don't love him any more than rank-and-file Mafia soldiers love the *capo*. They say cheerfully, "Without an emperor, we'd kill each other." And that is just what they have done in the tragic periods when imperial dynasties collapsed. Civil war, foreign invasion, famine and plague often reduced China's population by one-tenth to one-fifth, until a new dynasty sorted itself out.

America isn't competing with the government of China or China's Communist Party, but rather with 1.4 billion Chinese. To compare China to the Mafia trivializes the question; there is a world of difference between building the world's longest-enduring civilization and hauling trash in Brooklyn. But one strains for comparisons within the Western experience for an identity that is so radically different from anything we encounter in the West. If you want to understand China, put down this book and get on a plane and see for yourself. If that isn't convenient, please bear with me as I explain.

The emperor who unified China and gave it his name was Qin Shi Huang, who famously entombed himself with thousands of terracotta soldiers to serve him in the afterlife. He built the Great Wall and stupendous water management systems still in use today, but at terrible cost. When he began the Great Wall around 200 B.C.E., perhaps four hundred thousand conscript workers died. The records of the 6th century C.E. Sui dynasty claim that a further five hundred thousand people died in its construction.[19] The stupendous structure earned its designation as the largest cemetery on earth. Qin Shi Huang's history has passed into legend mainly because the Qin emperor burned the records of the kingdoms he conquered and killed hundreds of scholars who embodied the living memory of the past. Terrified of death, he searched for magic elixirs and sorcerers who would enable him to live forever, but had to settle for interment with soldiers of baked clay.

Qin Shi Huang appears in modern popular culture as a shape-shifting monster that rises from the tomb in the 2008 horror film *Tomb of the Dragon Emperor*. It's not a flattering portrait of China's founding ruler. The Hollywood incarnation of Qin Shi Huang, played by Kung Fu star Jet Li, rules with magical powers and buries masses of his enemies in the Great Wall. He is tricked by a sorceress who turns him and his soldiers into clay. Western archaeologists—the "Mummy" crew—inadvertently wake the immolated emperor, who then sets out to conquer the world. After a lot of computer-generated special effects, he is killed by a magic dagger. The plot is silly, although it adopts some elements of Chinese legend.

One might have expected hostility on the part of the government of the People's Republic of China to this portrayal of China's founding emperor. On the contrary, China not only allowed director Rob Cohen to film on location, but also dispatched cultural advisers to help the filmmakers reconstruct the language and court ceremony of the Qin dynasty. The film became a modest box-office hit on the Chinese mainland. Screendaily.com reported: "On the first day of release, the film grossed more than $2.05 million (RMB14m), similar to the opening gross of *The Forbidden Kingdom*, with $2.33 million (RMB16m), and of last year's local blockbuster *Assembly*, with $2.19 million (RMB15m)."[20] Living memory still evokes the image of emperor as monster: The first Communist emperor, Mao Zedong, starved to death more than 50 million Chinese during the "Great Leap Forward" of 1958–1962, a horrendously failed experiment in state economic management. The founder of the new China was a monster, like the founder of the old China.

Cruelty is the Norm in Chinese Governance

"Overall, Chinese historiography for two thousand years has consistently looked back at Qin with fear and loathing. The greatest villain is the First Emperor himself," reports historian Steven Sage.[21]

All of China's governments have been cruel in a way that boggles the Western imagination. Chiang Kai-Shek's Kuomintang founded the democratic government of Taiwan under American tutelage after the Communist Revolution of 1949, but in war it displayed a ruthlessness unmatched in Western history. In June 1938, as the Japanese Army approached the city of Wuhan in Henan Province, Chiang ordered his generals to blow up the dikes containing the Yellow River near Huayuankou, hoping to slow the Japanese advance. Chiang knew that the resulting deluge would flood a region inhabited by twelve million of his own citizens. Nearly nine hundred thousand Chinese drowned.[22] This was "the largest act of environmental warfare in history"[23] and the most wanton in disregard for human life. The flood disrupted Henan province's irrigation network, and a further two to three million Chinese died in the consequent Henan famine of 1942–1943.[24] Western governments have shown unspeakable cruelty to enemy civilians, but there is no comparable incident in Western history in which a government deliberately sacrificed the lives of millions of its own citizens to gain a temporary military advantage. By the standards of Chinese leaders, Chiang Kai-Shek was not particularly cruel. On the contrary, Chiang's subsequent regime in Taiwan was one of the most benevolent that any part of China has enjoyed. But under duress, he displayed more traits in common with Mao Zedong or the Dragon Emperor than with any Western leader.

At a closed-door conference in Beijing with senior government advisers not long ago, I asked the Chinese group if they felt nostalgic about any of their past rulers. After all, the Jews pray thrice daily for the return of King David's dynasty. Medieval British romances call Arthur "the once and future king." Similar tales are told about the German emperor Frederick Barbarossa, Charlemagne, and others. Folklorists call this motif the "king asleep in the mountain," and it is encountered from Portugal to Japan—but not in China. None of the Chinese officials in attendance could name a government they would like to see return. On the contrary, the Chinese are happy to see the back of every one of their dynasties. They tolerated them when they were useful and turned on them when they became corrupt or weak, which takes a couple centuries in the best cases, and a couple of decades in the worst. The present Communist regime is also a dynasty, although it is founded on a self-perpetuating elite rather than a biological family. A Foreign Ministry official praising present regime told me with enthusiasm, "This dynasty will last three hundred years!" That would set the longevity record for a Chinese dynasty, and sounds like high praise. But if you told an Englishman that his monarchy would last three hundred years—the British crown celebrated its thousandth anniversary in 1973—he would be insulted. If you told an American that his Constitution would endure for three hundred years—that is, until 2087—he would be aghast. Chinese civilization is eternal in the understanding of the Chinese. Governments are passing arrangements.

China is a country that remembers its founding emperor as a monster, but for millennia worshipped the emperor's chief civil engineer as a god. I will return to the apotheosized engineer below. This dichotomy holds the key to China's political character.

China is a Polyglot Empire, Not a Nation

China is utterly unlike the United States, and it is difficult to make sense of the difference without knowing the country and its history. Try to imagine that all the immigrants to the United States had never learned English, but spoke German, Italian, Spanish, Dutch, Gaelic, Yiddish, Swedish, Finnish, and so on. Of course, it is impossible to imagine America without assimilation into American culture. That's what makes people Americans. Because America successfully assimilates people from so many cultures, Americans assume that everyone really is like them. People who abandon their cultures and decide to become Americans really are like other Americans. Those who stayed home and embraced their own culture aren't necessarily like Americans at all. There are 3.8 million Chinese-Americans, whose values and outlook are as American as those of any other immigrant group. Among China's 1.4 billion people, there are tens of millions who might like to become Americans, and who would assimilate into American culture as easily as other immigrants have. These are the exceptions. In the main, the Chinese really are different.

Not until the present generation has a majority of Chinese understood even the rudiments of a common spoken language. Even today, few Chinese can converse in the official dialect. The Chinese government estimated in 2014 that only 70 percent of its people speak basic Mandarin, but that only one out of ten Chinese citizens speak it fluently.[1] Six major languages and two hundred eighty minor ones still are spoken. Variations among China's languages aren't minor. A Mandarin speaker from Beijing and a Cantonese speaker from Guangzhou won't understand a word the other is saying. The two languages are as different as French and Finnish. Sixty million people speak Cantonese, about as many as speak Italian. Neither of them will understand much Sichuanese, spoken by one hundred twenty million people in China's southwest. Sichuanese is a gentler, less guttural language than Mandarin, with more muted intonation. Another eighty million people speak Hakka, although Hakka migration to other parts of China is eroding the number of Hakka speakers. That's more than the number of Europeans who speak German or French. Hakka sounds a bit like Cantonese, with its singing intonation, but the vocabulary is so different that the two languages are mutually unintelligible.

---

1 "The national language ability is the most important part of the composition of national language ability. It is not only related to national unity, national unity, economic development, cultural heritage and social progress, but also the most vivid and intuitive reflection of the comprehensive quality of people. The dream of human growth, talent, success and comprehensive development has an important fundamental role. Considering that 30% of the population in China still do not speak Mandarin, and only 10% of the other 70% of the population can communicate smoothly with standard Mandarin, the task of promoting Mandarin and improving the national language ability of the country is still very difficult." http://old.moe.gov.cn/publicfiles/business/htmlfiles/moe/s8316/201409/174957.html

No Chinese mother has ever sung her baby to sleep in "Chinese." Mandarin is the Beijing court dialect, a *Kanzleisprache*, not a national language. The Chinese language is not spoken but drawn in characters that that derive from pictograms. When Chinese meet who speak mutually unintelligible languages, they communicate in writing. In the West, cultural identity is inseparable from sound. The deep roots of culture begin with oral tradition, with songs and stories that were memorized and chanted, from the epics of Homer in Greece and the Norse sagas to the Hindu Vedas. Nationality in the West is inseparable from language. Dante's Tuscan language became Italy's national language, and Luther's Bible translation created standard German, just as the King James Bible promulgated English. The first nation-state was the kingdom that united the twelve tribes of Israel at the start of the first millennium B.C.E., on the premise that all Hebrew speakers should belong to the same polity. At the time, that was an innovation. Six hundred years later, Aristotle still argued that the ideal size of a city-state was a thousand or so households.[25] No Greek thinker until Polybius in the 2nd century B.C.E proposed that all Greeks should belong to the same polity. Israel became the model for the Western monarchies, which appropriated the idea of kingship by divine right as a foundation for legitimacy.[26]

Children born into Western nation-states absorb their national identity with nursery rhymes. Chinese children learn the characters, the ideograms that unite China into a single culture, in a marathon of acculturation that is unlike anything Western children undertake, with the possible exception of traditional Jewish religious education. After two years of primary education, they will be able to write about eight hundred characters, and about twenty-five hundred after four years. At the end of six years of primary school, they will know thirty-five hundred characters, enough to read a newspaper and most books. The standard Chinese dictionary has fifty thousand characters, but knowledge of thirty-five hundred qualifies for basic literacy. Even fewer are required to read the Chinese classics; the *Analects* of Confucius has only fourteen hundred.

To learn to read and write, Chinese children begin school at 7:30 a.m. and leave at 4:00 or 5:00 p.m., and then practice for hours at home with brush and inkpot. The discipline and effort required for

Chinese children to become Chinese is hard for Westerners to imagine. The inherent difficulty of the characters also explains why the smartphone has transformed China. Ideograms are based on roots, or "radicals," overlaid with additional brushstrokes. Smartphone apps ask the user to draw the first one or two brush strokes, to bring up a menu of the characters that derive from them. Smartphones make it easier and faster for the Chinese to communicate.

The system of characters is an artifact of empire. Its origins go back at least to 1,200 B.C., when the first surviving ideograms were written on bronze vessels and oracle bones. The present system of characters, though, was not standardized until the Tang Dynasty in the 8th century C.E.[27] The Tang dynasty brought to its present frontiers, defined by the deserts to the north and west and the Himalayas to the south—except for the later conquest of Tibet and the whole of Xinjiang. China began as a set of small kingdoms in the Yellow River Valley and extended its reach by a unique process of cultural extension. Neighboring peoples were conquered and invited to become Chinese—to learn the characters, to adopt Chinese dress, and absorb Chinese customs—while preserving their local languages. It took the unification of China under a single dynasty to make the characters standard across China.

Between the Tang, Zhou, and Song dynasties, China entered a golden age. It invented gunpowder, clocks, mechanical gear systems, paper, moveable type, and printing. It raised literacy levels and expanded the civil service examinations to draw on a larger pool of candidates. Civil service examinations in China began in 165 B.C.E., but the Tang dynasty standardized the system that still selects China's governing caste. The grandsons of the Mongol conqueror Genghis Khan defeated the Song Empire in 1279.

Along with infrastructure, imperial meritocracy holds China together. Not until 212 C.E. when the Roman Empire had long been in demographic decline, did the Emperor Caracalla issue the Antonine Constitution that gave Roman citizenship to all free men in the empire. China, by contrast, built its empire by creating citizens as it expanded. Even more, it created a caste of leaders by offering the most ambitious among its new citizens a path to power and wealth through the imperial examination system. The Taoist and Confucian classic texts comprised the whole of the curriculum for the imperial examinations. This established a unified imperial culture that resisted the centrifugal forces of the ethnically and linguistically disparate provinces. Confucius according to the texts and commentaries that have come down to us taught a sort of virtue ethics that some Chinese scholars have compared to Aristotle.[28] Aristotle was no more successful in teaching moderation to his pupil Alexander the Great than the Confucian texts succeeded in inculcating moderation into Chinese emperors.

Ambition is the glue that holds the polyglot, ethnically mixed Chinese empire. Napoleon invented the modern mass citizen army, saying that each of his soldiers kept a field marshal's baton in his rucksack. That is, he awoke the ambition of the downtrodden peasants of France and made of them a force that crushed the professional armies of the European monarchs.

The Chinese are more practical than the French. The 14th century *Romance of the Three Kingdoms* occupies a place in the Chinese canon comparable to Homer, Shakespeare, Machiavelli, and Clausewitz combined. In a superficial Western reading, it might seem like a blend of *The Sopranos* and *Game of Thrones*, with its 800,000-word narrative of power struggles and betrayal during the decline of the Han Dynasty during the first two centuries of the Common Era. Above the violent and sometimes sordid events it recounts, its attributed author, Luo Guanzhong, offers a philosophical conclusion about Chinese statecraft: "It is a general truism of this world that anything long divided will surely unite, and anything long united will surely divide." More specifically, "The empire long united must divide, long divided must unite; this is how it has always been."

China is not a nation-state, but rather an imperial structure composed of highly diverse peoples and tongues, always subject to centrifugal pressures which in time of crisis have led to the division of the empire at frightful human cost. The object of every dynasty, including the committee of Mandarins that constitutes the Chinese Communist Party, is to forestall the eruption of these centrifugal forces. As I explain in chapter six, Beijing threatens war over the South China Sea to demonstrate, a fortiori, that it will go to war over Taiwan, because one breakaway province may lead to many breakaway provinces and the dissolution of the empire.

The Boundless Ambition of the Chinese

Every Chinese carries, as it were, a copy of *The Romance of the Three Kingdoms* in his back pocket, or in contemporary terms, a study guide for the *Gaokao*, China's formidable university entrance examination taken by 9.7 million Chinese in 2017.

As Francesco Sisci reports, "Right at the end of Tiananmen Square, next to Zhengyangmen ('the Midday gate') and two hundred meters from Mao's mausoleum, there is a spot where people can take pictures of their children dressed as little Manchu emperors and sitting on a throne. The place is symbolic: the ancient gate once opened on the *nei cheng* (the inner city) and the buildings of the imperial government. Every day, there is a line of parents, mostly from the countryside, holding their children by the hands and waiting to take the picture as a sign of good luck. Each parent wants his or her only child to be successful—to become, in his or her way, an emperor."[29]

The Chinese don't like their emperor to begin with, and they certainly do not want to die for him in Japanese fashion. To the extent that the Chinese empire succeeds, it does so because it offers individual Chinese a platform for the achievement of individual ambition. If it fails to do that, the Chinese will ask, *What is it good for?* When the emperor lost the "mandate of heaven," that is, the capacity to satisfy the ambitions of its most demanding subjects, Chinese rebels routinely allied with foreign invaders against the imperial throne. We will return to the tragic cycle of dynastic rise and fall, and explain why Chinese history in our generation has taken an entirely new direction.

Israel is the most ancient nation, which united all Hebrew speakers into a single polity with a single ruler and a single cult. It is also the only nation of the ancient world that survives today. China is the most ancient empire, and the only empire that survives today. Although the roots of China's civilization extend back five thousand years, Chinese in recognizable form begins with the Zhou Dynasty at the beginning of the first millennium B.C.E., contemporaneously with the kingdom of

David. Centuries before the territory of ancient Israel had been divided among eleven of the twelve tribes. The tribe of Levi had no land of its own, but rather was dispersed among the other tribes, dependent on sacrifices brought by the other tribes. The Levites became a national tribe, whose self-interest lay with the nation and the cult, and thus a pillar of national cohesion. Levite status depended exclusively on ancestry, and Levite loyalty was to the national religion. A smaller number of the Levites were priests (Kohanim). The priestly caste balanced the power of the kings. The prophet Nathan confronted King David over his adultery with Bathsheba and his murder of her husband Uriah, and caused David to repent; ancient history knows no comparable story of the humiliation of an oriental monarch. The separation of church and state in ancient Israel instituted the first checks and balances in recorded history, although not the only ones in the ancient world. Paul Rahe has shown how the complex Spartan constitution created such checks and balances a few centuries later.[30]

China's Mandarins also constituted an imperial caste; selected and promoted by the empire, their interests lay with the emperor, rather than their home province. Unlike the priestly caste of ancient Israel, the imperial bureaucracy did not counterbalance the emperor. On the contrary, the Mandarins are the instruments of the will of the emperor, who was also head of the imperial cult, responsible for conducting the annual sacrifices. Rather than counterweights to the emperor, the Mandarins were emperors in miniature. Francesco Sisci observes:

> China for many is an opportunity to make their fortune. But apart from a strong sense of a common culture and the opportunity to build wealth, they have little affection for, or a sense of protection from the Chinese state or its laws. In China there is a perception often that power without impartial laws and without responsibilities is capricious. On the other hand, a population accustomed for centuries to the unrestrained exercise of imperial power will have little sense of responsibility or duty towards the common good of the country represented by the institutions of the state. There is no fabric of civic rights and responsibilities which delimit the action

> of the state, so that the risk always remains present that the state can run amok with the exercise of naked power.

China is a ruthless meritocracy. Americans say, *No child left behind*, but the Chinese say, *Only the exceptional survive.* A high school student with a top score on the *Gaokao* will attend Peking University, Tsinghua University, or another elite institution, with a clear path to a top career in government or business. University admission depends only on examination scores. Top officials and billionaires can buy admission to Harvard for their children, but not to Peking University. Fingerprints are required as proof of identity at examination centers. The occasional paid exam-taker sneaks in with a latex slip-on fingerprint to take a test for a rich but stupid student. Such exceptions are rare. There is plenty of corruption in China, and the relatives of senior government officials get rich with sickening regularity. But the *Gaokao*, the filter through which China selects its political elite, is the Holy of Holies in Chinese society. That is the decisive event in the lives of ambitious and intelligent young Chinese, their opportunity to turn their ambition into power and money. Whatever other forms of corruption infest Chinese society, the selection of China's elite remains sacrosanct, because ambition is the currency with which the Chinese state buys the loyalty of its most capable citizens.

Chinese parents borrow money to pay for tutoring and cram schools for their children, starting in elementary school. According to a one study, 93 percent of Chinese parents have paid for private tutoring (compared to 47 percent in the US).[31] In 2018, the *South China Morning Post* reported:

> "Tutoring classes have risen [in popularity] against conventional schooling," Gu Mingyuan, head of the Chinese Society of Education, which is affiliated with the Ministry of Education, told news site Jiemian.com.
>
> "Parents send their kids to six hours of extra tutoring per week at an average cost of 120,000 yuan per year, and that can rise to 300,000 yuan per year. Parents are also feeling very helpless."[32]

One hundred twenty thousand yuan a year is roughly what the average white-collar employee in Beijing earned in 2018. When their child comes of age to prepare for the *Gaokao*, ambitious parents will sacrifice a full year's income to maximize his or her chances for success. Chinese parents pay for more than exam preparation. There are between thirty and fifty million piano students in China, and more than ten million violin students. China produced 376,000 pianos in 2013 (and a similar number of digital pianos). That's about as many as America produced in 1909; by 2009, the total had fallen to just thirty thousand.[33] Chinese parents believe, with good reason, that the discipline and concentration required in classical music will hone their children's academic performance. Children under eighteen, meanwhile, are restricted to two hours a day of video games, a limit enforced by facial recognition programs and other identity checks.[34]

The Chinese Communist Party is simply the old Mandarin bureaucracy in a new guise, with one important difference—rather than relying on a particular family to furnish China with rulers, the Communist Party selects China's leaders. Like the old Mandarin system, though, the Communist Party rules from the top down. Western society is dense with bottom-up activity—churches, charities, political associations, sports leagues, parent-teacher associations, and other organizations that ask nothing from the government and fund their activities privately. China by contrast runs on strictly vertical hierarchies. The empire selects its Mandarins through a unified system of exams and then assigns them to supervise every social function.

A peculiar consequence of the ferocious competition among Chinese for the top slots and the concentration of power in the bureaucracy is that the Chinese have few friends. The notion of political friendship in Aristotle's sense among citizen-peers in a Greek city-state simply does not apply. There are no deliberative bodies, no voluntary associations, and no opportunities to form peer relationships to begin with. But the dearth of friendship has deeper roots. "Here in China we don't have friends. When you're in elementary school, you size up your classmates and figure out whom you're going to walk over," a young Chinese economist explained. He had done the number crunching for a study of Chinese banks that I published in 2014, at Reorient Group, a Chinese-owned investment banking boutique in Hong Kong, and I put his name on the published report.

"Why did you do that?" he asked.

"That's normal in the business," I said. "It's called mentoring."

"No one in China does that," he said, with incredulity.

Of course, my young colleague exaggerated to make a point: the Chinese have friends. But the winner-take-all competition and prevalence of vertical hierarchies rather than peer relationships makes things different.

Amoral Familism

What the Chinese have is family. Sociologist Edward Banfield coined the term "amoral familism" to characterize the behavior of southern Italians who displayed loyalty to their family but to nothing else.[35] That fits well with the Mafia analogy that introduced this discussion, but to leave the matter there would be a gross distortion. Unlike the lethargic southern Italians, the Chinese derive irreplaceable benefits from their state, which has provided a broad platform for the ambitious and talented. However much of their energy and enthusiasm might be devoted to the state, their first loyalty is to family. Westerners are prone to the false impression that the Chinese are reserved, even cold. Nothing could be further from the case. The Chinese keep up their guard in the public square, but are spontaneous and relaxed with their families. For thousands of years, the extended family farm was the basic social unit of Chinese society. The economies of ancient Athens and Rome were founded on *latifundia*, plantations worked by slaves. Rather than masters and slaves or lords and serfs, the Chinese were bound by ties of kinship. Francesco Sisci writes, "The ideal family in the 19th century was unchanged from the times of Confucius, some two thousand years before—three generations under one roof. The older man had many wives, even more children. Each male heir also had many wives and children all living together harmoniously in a large courtyard, resembling a small village of dozens of people....Each relative had a name indicating his precise relationship to the speaker. There were no vague appellations like 'aunt,' 'uncle' or 'cousin.' There were terms such as 'uncle, first younger brother of my father' (da shushu) or 'uncle, second brother of my mother' (er jiujiu), and so on. Cousins also bore different names, accordingly. It was an intricate cobweb of relations in which each individual had his or her precise place."[36]

Manual labor was held in contempt by the gentleman of Athens, and was unthinkable for a Roman emperor, but China's emperor from ancient times ploughed a furrow with his own hand as a demonstration of "sincerity," as described in the *Book of Rites* (Liji), one of the Confucian classics that dates from the Zhou dynasty in the first millennium B.C.E.:

> The son of Heaven himself guided the plough in the southern suburb, to provide the grain for the sacrificial vessels; and the queen looked after her silkworms in the northern suburb, to provide the cap and robes of silk. The princes of the states guided the plough in their eastern suburb, also to provide the grain for the sacrificial vessels, and their wives looked after their silkworms in the northern suburb, to provide the cap and robes of silk. This was not because the son of Heaven and the princes had not men to plough for them, or because the queen and the princes' wives had not women to tend the silkworms for them; it was to give the exhibition of their personal sincerity.[37]

The ceremony continued in abbreviated form until the fall of the Qing Dynasty in 1912. I do not mean to minimize the extreme cruelty that Chinese emperors; a million men among the conscripts who built the Great Wall are said to have been buried there. Nonetheless, the emperor dramatized his position as *pater familias* of the empire, and his status as exemplary farmer, by putting his own hand on the plough. Athens and Rome collapsed when the slave systems that supported them ceased to be viable. The Chinese empire rested on the families of China, and survived.

The Chinese family has changed, but its paramount position in society has not. The Chinese undertake the largest mass migration in history each year at the Lunar holiday, when three billion Chinese take long-distance journeys to be reunited.[38] The hierarchical character of the

Chinese imperial state is an amplification of the hierarchical character of the Chinese family. The Confucian virtues of benevolence and moderation are those of the *pater familias,* who rules the household absolutely. As Francesco Sisci observes, China understands loyalty to superiors and benevolence towards inferiors, but not the rights and obligations that define the relationship of citizen and state in the West. It is a civilization that knows nothing of checks and balances, separation of church and state, constitutional guarantees, or restrictions of any kind on the whim of the ruler. The will of the *pater familias,* or his avatar the emperor, has no constraints except those of filial charity. Often in Chinese history, the unconstrained power of rulers has worked wonders. In the 3rd century B.C.E., the Qin State civil servant Li Bing enlisted tens of thousands of laborers for twenty years to build the Dujiangyan irrigation system, which for the past two millennia has watered two thousand square miles of the Sichuan plain and made China's southwestern province the country's breadbasket. The infrastructure of today's China is a wonder of the modern world. With tragic regularity, though, China's rulers have inflicted terrible suffering on their people, from Qin Shi Huang's burning of the books and immolation of the scholars, to Mao Ze Dong's Great Leap Forward.

China's Unique Natural Circumstances and the Character of its State

I do not believe that nature dictates the character of states, but the rise of Chinese civilization on the flood plain of the Yellow River helps explain its magnificence, as well as its fragility and cruelty.[2] China's rivers are

---

2 The German American historian Karl Wittfogel proposed a materialist reading of "Oriental Despotism" in his celebrated book *Oriental Despotism: A Comparative Study of Total Power* (Yale University Press, 1957). Wittvogel argued that the need for flood control and riparian agriculture gave rise to large states dominated by a central bureaucracy. Among his examples are Imperial China, Mesopotamia, Pharaonic Egypt and Incan Peru. This in his view set the precedent for 20th-century Marxist regimes. A more nuanced reading of the same material is found in Steven Mithen's *Thirst: Water and Power in the Ancient World* (Harvard University Press, 2012). Wittfogel's depiction of a proto-totalitarian state founded on water control seems too simple in the case of China. Li Bing enlisted the support of the peasants

its blessing and curse. Flood control prompted the founding of the first of the legendary dynasties of China's prehistory, the Xia. According to the *Records of the Grand Historian*, composed in 94 B.C.E by the Han dynasty courtier Sima Qian, a devastating flood in the Yellow River Valley during the legendary reign of the Emperor Yao brought the tribes of agriculturalists together under the leadership of the hero Gŭn, Count of Chóng, and his son Yu the Great. Traditional sources have Yu declare: "The inundating waters seemed to assail the heavens, and in their extent embraced the hills and overtopped the great mounds, so that the people were bewildered and overwhelmed. I opened passages for the streams throughout the nine provinces and conducted them to the seas. I deepened the channels and conducted them to the streams."[39] The annals add: "...Yu then traveled throughout China, cleaning up the rivers and dredging canals; hence the floods of the rivers were guided to enter the eastern sea. Yu won great respect among the people and henceforth became the leader of all China."[40]

The traditional narrative is embellished with an excavator dragon and an earth-moving giant turtle, but modern archaeologists believe that a catastrophic flood devastated the Yellow River Valley around 1,900 B.C.E. A newsletter of the Archaeological Institute of America explains:

> The researchers, led by Qinglong Wu of Peking University, found that a landslide caused by an earthquake created a natural dam some 650 feet high at the upper reaches of the river. After building up for six to nine months, water broke through, resulting in a "Great Flood," one of the biggest of the last 10,000 years, says Darryl Granger, a geologist at Purdue University. He adds that the inundation would have extended more than 1,000 miles downstream and overwhelmed and rerouted the river's network of tributaries, leading to years of uncontrolled annual flooding.

of Sichuan for his great project and was worshipped thereafter as a divine benefactor—in sharp contrast to the odium attached to the Qin Emperor.

Archaeologists also uncovered an even earlier hydraulic project in the Yangtze Delta. A group of Chinese researchers announced in 2017, the discovery of

> ...one of the world's oldest examples of large-scale and formalized water management, in the case of the Liangzhu culture of the Yangtze Delta, dated at 5,300–4,300 years B. C.E. The Liangzhu culture represented a peak of early cultural and social development predating the historically recorded Chinese dynasties; hence, this study reveals more about the ancient origins of hydraulic engineering as a core element of social, political, and economic developments. Archaeological surveys and excavations can now portray the impressive extent and structure of dams, levees, ditches, and other landscape-transforming features, supporting the ancient city of Liangzhu, with an estimated size of about 300 hectares. The results indicate an enormous collective undertaking, with unprecedented evidence for understanding how the city, economy, and society of Liangzhu functioned and developed at such a large scale.[41]

China's foundational myth of a great Yellow River flood appears to have a foundation fact, just as Noah's Flood may derive from popular memory of a catastrophic inflow of seawater from the Mediterranean into the Black Sea.[42] But there is a radical difference between the flood myth reported in the ancient Chinese annals and the story handed down to the West through the Hebrew Bible. Noah's flood requited the violence and cruelty and mankind, and leads to the establishment of a moral order by the righteous survivor. China's great flood arises from an accident of nature rather than an act of divine retribution, and it leads to the founding of Chinese civilization in the form of the Xia Dynasty. Not divine mercy, but human intervention—in the form of water management requiring the combined labor of the whole population—pushes back the floodwaters.

The geography of the great Chinese flood plains required a central government capable of undertaking massive water management projects.

Chinese civil engineering was the wonder of the ancient world. Sichuan Province became the breadbasket of China and a byword for wealth after the Qin Dynasty split the waters of the Min River (Minjiang) at Dujiangyan, near the modern metropolis of Chengdu. The Qin official Li Bing built an artificial island in 256 B.C.E. to divert the spring floodwaters that frequently devastated the Sichuan plain, and cut a channel through the living rock of a mountain to divert the excess water into canals that still irrigate two thousand square miles of fertile ground. The Dujiangyan hydraulic system has remained in continuous use for nearly two and half millennia, and is one of southwest China's great tourist attractions as a UNESCO World Heritage Site.[3] The uneven depth and slope of the riverbed presented a challenge to hydraulic engineers, even by today's criteria. We do not know how ancient Chinese engineers solved the problem, but the result is one of the great technological achievements of the ancient world, unparalleled in India, Mesopotamia, or Egypt—the other great riparian civilizations. Li Bing's engineers used

3 Shangdong Zhang and Y-Jun Yi, "Hydraulic Principles of the 2,268-Year-Old Dujiangyan Project in China," in Journal of Hydraulic Engineering 139(5):538-546 · May 2013. The authors summarize their thesis: "The Dujiangyan Project is a World Cultural Heritage Site with relevance to water conservancy. It has been operated for more than 2,260 years and still plays an important role in irrigation, urban, and industrial water supply, flood control, and tourism. This paper discusses the hydraulic principles of the project, focusing on the reasons for the longevity of the project. In particular, two aspects of the project are reviewed; namely, the practical engineering design of the project and its outstanding historical significance and time-based maintenance. The project ingeniously used the topography of the terrain in the design of weir structures. The tasks of water diversion, irrigation, and flood control were achieved using a two-step approach. The first step was achieved by utilizing the shifting of streamlines and the bend of flow from the town of Guankou to Fish Mouth (a diversion embankment). The discharge of flow and sediment was further optimized by using the second step of combined control of Feishayan (a sediment and flow spillway) and Baopingkou (an irrigating gate). The bend of flow within the Inner River forces the surface water to flow into Baopingkou, whereas the bottom sediments and pebbles discharge from Feishayan. Dynasties throughout history attached great importance to the management and maintenance of the project. Retrofitting and time-based renovation prevented the abandonment of the project due to sediment accumulation and aging of building materials. Because the maintenance and operation costs were far lower than the economic, social, and ecological benefits the project had brought, the Dujiangyan Project was sustainable over the long term. The study of the engineering design and maintenance rules of the Dujiangyan Project has value for the design and construction of modern hydraulic projects."

firepots and cold water to cut a channel through a mountain to divert the overflow, employing tens of thousands of conscript laborers over eight years of digging. The suffering and loss of life no doubt were extreme for workers, who, year after year, lowered thousands of stone-laden baskets into the river to create the artificial island to split the Min River, and carried firepots to heat rock and water to cool and crack it. Then as now, the Chinese accepted hardship and even cruelty on behalf of collective need. Then, as now, Chinese leaders planned over a horizon of several generations.

Li Bing became governor of the state of Shu, part of what today is China's southwestern province of Sichuan, in 277 B.C.E, after the Qin Shi Huang conquered it. The Shu people venerated the Min River as a cruel deity. "The governor coopted this indigenous belief and made it a Qin state cult by building a temple to the god," reports historian Steven Sage. "Prior to his governorship, a local custom had prevailed whereby two maidens were purchased annually, by popular subscription, to provide sacrifice victims for the river spirit. The sacrificial ceremony had proceeded in the manner of a wedding. Superstition had it that unless propitiated each year with a pair of new brides, the Min might overflow."[43] Li Bing staged a show to convince the credulous locals that he had vanquished the river spirit. "The old, capricious god was vanquished," Sage adds. "In its place, an enduring memorial cult grew around Li Bing. His, probably first, son and successor in the Dujiangyan project, Li Erlang, was also later worshipped. Their efforts might seem to parallel myths of the great hydraulic engineer Yu the Great and his own son Qi."

For centuries, Li Bing was venerated as a demigod, at a temple next to Dujiangyan. China is the only civilization to make civil engineers into gods. The Chinese recall the founding Qing emperor Qin Shi Huang with horror, but venerate the enlightened administrator Li Bing. That encapsulates the difference between Chinese dynastic politics and Chinese civilization. The politicians and generals, at best, are a necessary evil, whereas the tamers of rivers are divine benefactors. The ruins of Egypt's great pyramids, another great instance of ancient engineering, stand today in mockery of the pharaohs' hope for immortality. Li Bing's hydraulic system still tames the Minjiang flood, and waters the Sichuan plain today.

Dujianyan is one of three great hydraulic projects undertaken by the Qin Dynasty. Another was the great Zhengguo Canal, which linked the Jing and Luo Rivers. The historian Sima Qian recounts:

> When the canal did make further progress, it was used to cause the stagnant waters to flow, and irrigate the salty land [on the Guanzhong Plain] over an area of more than 40,000 qing [about 2,700 square kilometers], so that the harvest totaled one zhong [3.2 meters] per mou [667 square meters]. Thereupon the area within the passes was turned into fertile but uncultivated land, and there were no calamitous years, and thus Qin became rich and strong, and in the end unified the feudal states.[44]

The vast improvement of agricultural productivity in Sichuan Province and the availability of military transport by river empowered the Qin to subdue their rivals and establish the first unified Chinese kingdom.

In comparison to the Qin era hydraulic projects, the irrigation canals of ancient Mesopotamia and Egypt were minor affairs. They arose from the urgent need to control the floods which devastated ancient China and periodically afflicted China throughout its history—including the 1931 Yangtze-Huai River flood that killed up to four million people. They demanded innovation on the part of the elite, and enormous collective efforts on the part of the population. Where they succeeded, they bettered the lives of millions of Chinese for centuries and millennia to come. The ferocity of nature demanded centralized rule and collective effort.

How utterly different is the experience of the two cultures of the Eastern Mediterranean—Israel and Greece—that formed the thinking of the modern West. As Deuteronomy 11:10-15 explains:

> 10) For the land, whither thou goest in to possess it, is not as the land of Egypt, from whence ye came out, where thou sowedst thy seed, and wateredst it with thy

> foot [by foot-pumps that brought water from the Nile into irrigation ditches—DG], as a garden of herbs:
>
> 11) But the land, whither ye go to possess it, is a land of hills and valleys, and drinketh water of the rain of heaven:
>
> 12) A land which the Lord thy God careth for: the eyes of the Lord thy God are always upon it, from the beginning of the year even unto the end of the year.
>
> 13) And it shall come to pass, if ye shall hearken diligently unto my commandments which I command you this day, to love the Lord your God, and to serve him with all your heart and with all your soul,
>
> 14) That I will give you the rain of your land in his due season, the first rain and the latter rain, that thou mayest gather in thy corn, and thy wine, and thine oil.
>
> 15) And I will send grass in thy fields for thy cattle, that thou mayest eat and be full.

Agriculture in the Eastern Mediterranean depended on the winter rains and rocky soil that trapped water, favoring crops such as olives and vines that drew on underground moisture. There were no great rivers to tame, and no flood plains to irrigate. The hilly land required terraces that preserved topsoil, best cultivated by smallholding farmers. The social system of biblical Israel was founded on small farmers working their own land, and the prophetic ideal called for every man to sit under his own vine and fig tree. A good deal of the military power of Greece, as Victor Davis Hanson explains, depended on independent farmers who when needed donned armor and fought in the phalanx.[45] That was manifestly not true of Sparta, which lived off the labor of the enslaved helots and trained the whole of its manhood for war starting in early childhood. Nor was it true of Athens, which relied on imports for half its food supply at the height of its imperial power under the Delian League. But it surely was true of Thebes, the first Greek land power to crush the Spartan infantry.

China could not flourish without rule from the top that was capable of undertaking the enormous hydraulic projects on which China's prosperity was founded. The Greek city-states, by contrast, made alliances of convenience against foreign enemies when need arose, but saw no need to create larger political structures that made governance more remote from the smallholder than it needed to be. Ancient Israel regarded the central power of the monarchy with deep suspicion; the prophet Samuel appointed Israel's first king with great reluctance and only after being instructed to do so by God.

I do not claim that West's individualism as expressed either in Athens or Jerusalem is a simple response to natural conditions. Man does not live by bread alone, and the Hebrew and Greek concept of the human spirit comes from above, not from below. The Greek city-states ultimately were overthrown by a unifying emperor, in the person of Alexander the Great, while the ancient Hebrews ultimately could not prevail against the great Babylonian Empire that destroyed the first Jewish Commonwealth in the 6th century B.C.E. The ideas of the Greeks long since migrated to the custody of other peoples, while the Jews lived on in exile with the vivid memory of their ancient state, until they returned in the 20th century.

Nonetheless, the grandeur as well as the cruelty of the Qin Emperor exceed the imagination of the West. No Western ruler of ancient or modern history has wielded the transformative power over the lives of ordinary people that Qin Shi Huang wielded to create the Chinese state.

During the 2,500 years since the founding of the Qin Dynasty, China has wrestled with its unruly rivers, its seismically unstable ground, and its fickle weather. Its five thousand-year effort to tame its great rivers and transform the bane of flooding into the boon of irrigation made China the most powerful country in the world for most of recorded history. But it has frequently failed, with terrible consequences. The five worst floods in modern history all occurred in China, not counting the deliberate flooding of the Huayuankou in 1938, mentioned above.

The End of China's Tragic History

China has an enormous territory, but only 10 percent of it is arable, compared to 25 percent of Europe's land. During periods of plenty, the population rose; in periods of famine, starving peasants became bandits and rebels, and shortage of food turned into civil unrest. No fewer than 1,828 famines were recorded in China from 108 B.C.E to 1911

C.E., or almost one every year. Most of the famines were restricted to one province, although some were widespread and devastating. Tens of millions died in the famines of 1810–1811 and 1846–1849, sapping the strength of the Qing Dynasty just before the British began the two Opium Wars. Famine and plague during the Taiping Rebellion of 1850–1873 killed perhaps thirty million; the famines of 1907 and 1911 in East and Central China killed twenty-five million; and the artificial famine brought about by Mao's blundering Great Leap Forward killed twice as many.

The recurrent phenomenon of famine and its secondary consequences, civil war, foreign invasion and plague, has destroyed the work of past dynasties and forced China to retrace its steps dozens of times in its history. China's earliest dynasties, the legendary Xia (2070–1600 B.C.E.), Shang (1600–1046 B.C.E.) and Zhou (1046–256 B.C.E) are known only from accounts composed centuries afterwards, in part because the Qin Dynasty destroyed all written records of China's preceding history. Starting with the Qin, China has had sixty-nine dynasties (excluding some short-lived upstart or reel dynasties) since the Qin. The longest lasting of these were the Tang (618–907 C.E.) of China's golden age, and the Qing (1636–1912 C.E.) of China's imperial decline. Several lasted less than a dozen years.

After the Mongols conquered China in the 13th century, many of the earlier inventions were forgotten. When the Jesuits arrived in China at the end of the 16th century, the Manchu emperors marveled at the European clocks and other mechanical devices they brought with them, unaware that clocks were invented during the Tang dynasty seven centuries earlier. Again and again in Chinese history, the fruits of Chinese diligence, inventiveness, and ambition were destroyed by natural and political disaster.

Chinese dynasties rose and fell, sometimes quickly, while Chinese civilization demonstrated endurance equaled by no other in history. A comparison to the West is instructive. Roman civilization did not survive the fall of the Roman state. Latin became extinct as a spoken language and barely survived as a language of scholarship and administration through the monasteries. As I noted earlier, the late Roman economy rested on great plantations worked by slaves, for an elite that disdained manual labor, whereas the extended family farm was the fundamental unit of China's economy, under the rule of an emperor who personally ploughed furrows and sowed a crop for the sacrifices.

Brian Ward-Perkins reports, "We are told that during Alaric's siege of Rome in the winter of 408–9 'almost all the slaves who were in Rome, poured out of the city to join the barbarians'; and a few years later, during a similar siege, a slave revolt on a smaller scale occurred in the south Gaulish town of Bazas. These slaves had little to lose, and some of them, in happier times, may have been warriors from beyond the frontiers—it is not surprising that they took advantage of Roman weakness to try and join the invading armies."[46] Some 30 percent of Rome's population were slaves,[47] and their revolts enabled a relative small number of invading barbarians to conquer the much larger population of Rome. It might be argued that both China and Europe eventually assimilated the barbarians who invaded them, but in the case of Europe, it occurred over centuries while the population shrunk to a fraction of its 2nd century C.E. peak. Imperial governance in China has been fragile while its civilization has been robust, perhaps because nature allowed no alternative. China's dependence on its great unruly rivers for sustenance requires, as a matter of survival, a centralized state directed by a well-selected administrative caste. As quickly as China might change dynasties, it has clung to the ways that have worked for so many thousands of years.

What does this mean for China in the 21st century?

Everything has changed in China, and nothing has changed.

The tragic cycle driven by imperfect human efforts to tame nature now has come to an end. China is at a turning point in its history as momentous as its original unification under Qin Shi Huang. For the first time during the five thousand years of Chinese civilization, famine is no longer a threat. China still imports food, but it is self-sufficient in grains. It has significant environmental problems to address, including chronic water shortages in large parts of the country and environmental degradation due to excessive use of fertilizer, but the threat of starvation has been lifted forever, thanks to the productivity of modern agriculture.[48] Starvation—and even cannibalism—remains a living memory for many Chinese above the age of seventy. Many of the living grandparents of today's Chinese remember the death of tens of millions by hunger during the Great Leap Forward. China no longer worries about malnutrition, but about obesity.[49]

The Dragon Awakes and Turns Outward to the World

For thousands of years, China's enormous energies have been dissipated at frequent intervals by famine and war. With nothing to fear from famine or foreign invasion, the Chinese have no natural obstacles to their ambition. The present Communist regime has emulated the Tang Dynasty, which opened the civil service examinations to the lower classes and enhanced the imperial talent pool. It has given young Chinese the skills and opportunity to reach for their own imperial scepters. Nearly eight million Chinese graduated from universities in 2018, double the number in the United States, with six times the number of STEM degrees. One-third of new entrants to China's labor force have university degrees, and one-third of those are engineers. The imperial bureaucracy perfected in the Tang Dynasty unified an ethnically and linguistically heterogeneous empire by offering opportunity to its cleverest and most ambitious men. Today's Communist dynasty has taken steps to unify the empire on a scale not previously imaginable. The higher education gap between China and America is widening. Nearly ten million Chinese high school students take the modern equivalent of the Mandarin examination, the *Gaokao*. To put that in perspective, America colleges have only 8.2 million undergraduates.

Meanwhile, during the past forty years, the government has moved nearly six hundred million Chinese—the equivalent of all of Europe, from the Ural Mountains to the Atlantic Ocean—from countryside to cities, building the equivalent of all the cities of Europe to house and employ them. Although the major regional languages have held their own against the Beijing court dialect, or spoken Mandarin, dialects are dying out. Perhaps one hundred of the empire's two hundred eighty languages are in danger of extinction.[50] Young Chinese who moved to cities often cannot communicate with their grandparents who still live in rural villages, because the grandparents speak only dialect and their grandchildren have learned Mandarin. The unifying capacity of Chinese civilization has never had such a decisive advantage against the centrifugal forces of ethnic diversity.

CHAPTER TWO

YOU WILL BE ASSIMILATED: CHINA'S PLAN TO TAKE OVER THE GLOBAL ECONOMY

Let's invent a genre-bending script for a new James Bond movie, with a sci-fi angle. A global corporation turns all the world's smartphones into data collectors in every aspect of human existence. It starts with a healthcare app that tests toddlers for congenital eye disease and uploads the data to the Cloud, and soon adds remote testing for blood chemistry, metabolism, and lung function. It adds an environmental app that listens to bird calls to check the stability of avian populations. It allows you to pay for any sort of purchase with a tap of your phone, and transmits every purchase record to the Cloud in real time. It analyzes retail payments and business supply chains, urban traffic patterns, social media posts, stock market movements, currency fluctuations, crop yields—every detail of everyday life. This gigantic global brain maintains a profile of every country in the world, with broadband coverage, download speeds, cost of service, physical infrastructure, and smartphone penetration. It plans to assimilate most of the whole world's seven billion people into its web.

This deluge of data is transmitted to servers through broadband connections at hundreds of times today's speeds, and analyzed by a gigantic array of high-speed servers designed to detect the significance of miniscule patterns in the data. The global corporation provides the smartphones, the apps, the sensors, the broadband, the servers, and the artificial intelligence software to mine the data. It links its servers to industrial robots that learn to create their own assembly lines, to shipping terminals, and airfreight fleets that move goods, and to millions of driverless cars and trucks that ferry workers and goods to jobs, stores, and factories. The broadband networks track the location, spending habits and online posts of every person on the planet, and high-definition cameras installed at hundred-yard intervals verify that the smartphone under surveillance belongs to its registered owner. Billions of medical records are matched to billions of genetic profiles, while computers use machine learning to identify genetic flaws and invent new pharmaceuticals.

Do you think we could sell it to Hollywood? The movie moguls would advise us not to quit our day jobs. There's no James Bond villain to boo at—just a vast, persistent, patient, and relentless intelligence that absorbs the people of the world into a network too incredible for movie-goers to imagine.

But we're not talking about science fiction. Everything I described in our film script is happening now, or scheduled to happen within the next ten or twenty years. China has a plan to assimilate most of the world's population into a virtual empire dominated by its telecommunications, computation, manufacturing, and logistics. You can read all about it on Huawei's English-language website, and hear it streamed in the main presentations at Huawei's Connect 2019 mega-conference in Shanghai. There are no secrets here. China is proud of what it has accomplished at home and what it proposes to accomplish globally.

Huawei is employee-owned, according to its managers, but Western analysts claim it just offers profit-sharing to its employees, who have no real control over company management. China's legal system for ownership of non-public companies is murky.[51] Huawei employees act like they own it, however, and put in terrifying hours. When the Trump Administration imposed export controls on US components to Huawei in 2019, the company had ten thousand engineers working around the clock to find ways around the American boycott.[52] Its founder, Ren Zhengfei, owns a reported 1.4 percent of the company, valued at $450 million. Under China's ambiguous legal structure, his executives and workers own the rest. Whatever the ownership structure means, Ren remains an emperor in his own realm, and his word is unchallenged in the company's senior councils, Huawei executives aver.

5G Broadband Changes Everything

5G broadband is the key—the key that unlocks hundreds of doors in the world of 21st century technology. In a 2019 study, the consulting firm Deloitte explained why:

> 5G technology introduction marks the beginning of a new era in connectivity that will impact almost every element of daily life. First-adopter countries embracing 5G could sustain more than a decade of competitive advantage. Countries that were first to adopt prior generations of wireless technology were also rewarded with broader macroeconomic benefits, but 5G has potential for an even larger first-mover advantage. What's different this time? 5G is more than just a new wireless interface protocol offering more capacity and better performance for smartphones. It is that, but it is also a myriad of technology innovation like antenna designs and device communication protocols to standardize both the way licensed and unlicensed networks interact and the way network applications collaborate. With this array of capabilities, 5G technology will influence everything we do.
>
> Instead of just connecting people to people through their smartphones, 5G connects an unlimited number of things to other things, which can communicate all day, every day. As a result, the value that 5G can create is not constrained by the number of people and the amount of time we have for consuming information. The opportunity for technology to influence productivity and automation could have a seismic impact on our macro economy. Network effects, where the value of a product or service is dependent on the number of users, could grant a first-adopter sustained leadership and the potential

> to capture a greater share of the benefits associated with 5G.[53]

As I report in chapter five, US officials warn that Huawei might steal Western data on behalf of China's intelligence services. That really is beside the point. Spy agencies always exaggerate the importance of secrets; after all, they trade in secrets, and they are as eager to talk up the value of their merchandise as anyone else. Whether Huawei has the capacity to steal data or not is a secondary issue. It plans to persuade the world to give up its data for free, the way Tom Sawyer persuaded his friends to whitewash his fence.

Take the case of healthcare, which now comprises 10 percent of the GDP of the world's developed nations and may become the world's single biggest industry as an aging population requires more medical services. Huawei will provide users with a sensor that plugs into a smartphone and slips over the index finger, taking your oxygen level, heart rate, temperature, and blood pressure. Another smartphone sensor will take an electrocardiogram. You will upload your vital signs and heart status to your smartphone, and from there to the Cloud, along with your digitized health records, family health history, and—before long—a genetic analysis of your DNA to detect a predisposition to stroke or heart attack. Huawei's artificial intelligence servers will slice and dice your data and cross-grid your information with hundreds of millions of case histories. Your phone will beep if the risk of heart attack or stroke hits a certain probability, and an optional app will have a car service driver en route to take you to the nearest emergency room. Huawei expects to have half a billion people linked to its Cloud servers within ten years. Why wouldn't you offer up your data? Of course, you will have helped Huawei create a database for medical research that will force every medical research organization in the world to conduct its experiments on Huawei servers.

China's medical application of information technology had a test of fire in early 2020, when the coronavirus epidemic burst out of Hubei province and threatened to engulf the country. According to Chinese business executives familiar with the exercise, the Chinese government and information technology companies matched locational data for hundreds of millions of smartphones to the results of mass testing for infection, in what appears to be the largest artificial intelligence application on record. Chinese government algorithms can estimate the probability that a given neighborhood, or even an individual, has exposure to COVID-19 by correlating the location of smartphones to known locations of infected individuals or groups. The authorities use this information to use limited medical resources more efficiently by, for example, directing tests for the virus to high-risk subjects identified by the artificial intelligence algorithm.

China has had years to prepare for this sort of crisis. In 2015, I toured Huawei's headquarters in Shenzhen, and saw a twelve-by-twelve-foot map of Guangzhou City, with countless small lights. Each of these denoted a smartphone, a Huawei official explained, and the company's data scientists could tell you the foot traffic at the site of a prospective new fast food restaurant. At the time, Huawei could match smartphone location to social media posts and online purchases. During the past several years, the Chinese government has combined smartphone locational data with facial recognition, making it easy to verify that the person carrying the phone is the registered user. China also uses electronic records of medicine purchases to identify sick individuals who may have attempted to flee quarantine.

Tencent's WeChat messaging app allows users to take their temperature and other vital signs and send them to the cloud in real time. Chinese citizens in quarantine were required to use a smartphone app to monitor their medical condition. An algorithm determines when the user is healthy enough to leave isolation, and creates a "healthy status" page that users must display to gain entry to public buildings and shopping malls. South Korea employed smartphone apps to warn users when they were in proximity to a possible source of infection, but the Korean system is not as comprehensive, nor as intrusive.

All smartphones with enabled GPS give telecom providers a precise record of the user's itinerary. Smartphone users in the United States and Europe can access their own data, but privacy laws prevent the government from collecting this data. China has no such privacy constraints, and telecom providers have used locational data for years for advertising. A Chinese bank executive reports that his company purchases locational data from telecom providers. "If you have walked by an auto dealership three times in the last few weeks, we send you a text advertising an auto loan," the executive said. "We wouldn't be allowed to do that in the West."

Big Data will transform medical diagnostics, pharmacology, preventive care, and emergency treatment. It has already transformed public health.

Huawei's "Tom Sawyer" Plan to Get the World's Data

American officials allege that Huawei's broadband technology conceals "back doors" that can steal the world's data. In response, the Chinese telecom giant has offered to submit its hardware and software to international inspection and allow its customers to rewrite the source code if they so desire. All of this is beside the point. Huawei won't need to steal everyone's data, because it will persuade most of the world to give it all the data it wants for free.

Popular culture gives a poor idea of what artificial intelligence entails. No one is going to build robots that think like humans and make their inventors fall in love with them, except perhaps for the geeks who live in their mother's basements and have conversations with SIRI. AI is a giant data mill that allows computers to distinguish between a random mark on a chest X-ray and a tumor, between a harmless variation in blood chemistry and a possible symptom of disease, between a banana peel that goes into the organic bin and a plastic spoon that goes into recycling, and so forth. "Machine learning" doesn't mean that machines will learn to think like humans. It means, rather, that computers need to compare vast numbers of photographs, recordings, statistics, or other data to "learn" to distinguish one thing from another. Facial recognition from the cameras spaced one hundred yards apart in most of China's cities has 90 percent accuracy for Asian faces, but far lower accuracy for Western faces, because China has a vast database of its own citizens' photographs and identities from which the machines can learn, but far fewer for Westerners.

AI has gigantic implications for healthcare. Medical services already comprise 18 percent of America's GDP, compared to 11 percent for manufacturing and 6 percent for housing—and as America's population ages, healthcare's share of the economy will continue to grow. The triad of smartphones, fast broadband, and artificial intelligence will transform medicine in ways we can only begin to imagine.

On September 15, 2019, *The Wall Street Journal* reported that the government of Israel has taken the lead in unifying decades of patient records into a format that computers can scan and analyze:

> The government last year announced a $264 million initiative to begin to combine those millions of records into a giant unified system, one that takes decades of individual patients' information and puts it all in the same format so medical data looks the same across all health-care institutions. Corralling the records and organizing them in ways that maximize their usefulness to AI programs and data analytics, the government hopes, will make the data of even greater value to researchers and health-care companies. And the greater goals, officials say, based largely on the promise of AI technology, are to make health-care less expensive, more effective, and better tailored to individuals everywhere.
>
> AI-assisted machines and programs, with their ability to learn and draw conclusions from the millions of detailed histories, medical tests, and diagnostic results stored in these records, have the potential to help doctors give more preventive care by spotting diseases in earlier stages; tailor more medicine to the needs of specific patients; read diagnostic imagery and lab tests faster and more accurately; and make health-care less expensive.[54]

That experiment is underway in a country with eight million people. Multiply that by hundreds to imagine what it means for China.

In short, you will be assimilated.

The nearest equivalent in popular culture is the Borg of *Star Trek: Next Generation*, except no one will have to implant gears in their face. China has transformed itself in the space of two generations from an impoverished, mainly rural country into an economic superpower dotted with one megalopolis after another bristling with steel and glass towers, thirty thousand kilometers of high-speed trains, one hundred fifty thousand kilometers of highways, and an array of high-tech industries that in some cases have already leapfrogged the West. As China continues to transform itself, it has begun the Sino-forming of the rest of the world.

Huawei Will Be the Equivalent of Google, Facebook, and Amazon in All the World's Industries

In principle, China's virtual empire is just an extension of what Facebook, Google, and Amazon have been doing for years. They don't steal your data, although you may not be aware of how much personal information you hand over to them every day. You give them your data in exchange for services that make your personal life more convenient and your business life more productive. Facebook provides a communication and news platform gratis. Google gives you internet search, email, browsers, access to millions of books published over the centuries, a library of free apps, as well as a smartphone operating system. In exchange, Google and Facebook get your likes and dislikes, your internet searches, your online purchases, your location, and an array of other data. Their computers crunch all the numbers and determine which advertisements are most likely to trigger a purchase.

That's huge business. Google's advertising revenues in the second quarter of 2019, topped $27 billion, while Facebook took in $17 billion. Google's efforts to apply the same methods to other fields than advertising haven't worked out as well. American companies spend $200 billion a year on advertising, the bread and butter of Google's business. But Americans spent almost twenty times as much—$3.65 trillion—on healthcare in 2018, roughly one-fifth of the entire US economy. Healthcare is the Holy Grail of the digital world, but success in the United States remains elusive.

In 2011, Google shut down Google Health, a project to digitize personal health records, because Americans didn't want to turn over their personal data. Wrote Google manager Aaron Brown, "In the end, while we weren't able to create the impact we wanted with Google Health, we hope it has raised the visibility of the role of the empowered consumer in their own care....There has been adoption among certain groups of users like tech-savvy patients and their caregivers, and more recently fitness and wellness enthusiasts, but we haven't found a way to translate that limited usage into widespread adoption in the daily health routines of millions of people."[55] In 2018, Google took a tentative step towards reviving its health platform as more electronic health records became available.[56] Amazon meanwhile is developing software to read and digitize medical records,[57] while Google has filed patents for a proprietary form of electronic health record.[58]

We can barely imagine what could be accomplished with a large database of electronic health records. Think of the way the best doctors diagnose disease. They have treated thousands of patients and read the medical journals, and are alert to slight anomalies in a patient's CAT scans, blood analysis, or MRI's. Their experience and acuity helps them identity medical conditions that less-experienced practitioners might ignore. With artificial intelligence, computers can sort through diagnostic tests, medical histories, and genetic information to compare an individual patient's case to billions of other cases. So-called machine learning, which simply means massive trial-and-error analysis of possible predictors of medical problems, can extract patterns from the data faster than any human physician. The humblest triage nurse in a rural medical clinic would have access to diagnostic tools that would astonish television's Dr. House.

It sounds benign, even beneficial. If the Chinese want to reduce the cost and boost the quality of healthcare, why not welcome them? There's a gigantic catch—artificial intelligence is the crown jewel of 21st century technology; if China dominates AI, it also will dominate all the technologies that spin off from AI.

In a digital world, there are binary outcomes. Either you're Facebook or Myspace, Excel or Lotus 1-2-3, Google or Altavista. Networks' effects dictate that there will be only one winner in each field of digital technology. When everybody farmed, it didn't matter whether your farm was slightly better or worse than your neighbor's. But when the product is software, your offering is infinitely scalable. That is, the cost of adding an additional user is zero. If you had to do research in an old-fashioned library, you would have to keep adding more books, more card catalogues, and more librarians to accommodate more searches. Not so Google: the internet search monopoly might have to add the odd server farm to manage the six billion searches it performs each day, but that is drop in the bucket compared to its revenues. Google exploits a network effect: the more people who search Google, the better Google becomes. China kept Google on the far side of the Great Firewall of China. It did so to allow Tencent, Baidu, and other Chinese companies to come up the learning curve without getting stifled in the cradle by American competition.

The Control Point

Paul Scanlan became Chief Technology Officer of Huawei Technologies in 2016. I met him several years earlier when he ran the company's business consulting division, pitching national broadband networks to prospective Huawei customers. A thirty-year industry veteran, he began his career with telecom providers in his native Australia before joining Huawei in 2009. In his spare time he plays jazz guitar, jamming occasionally in Shenzhen clubs. Malaysia's national broadband network was his first big success as Huawei's advocate. I saw him at work in Mexico in 2015, when I introduced him to senior officials of Mexico's Ministry of Telecommunications. In October 2019, we met in Washington, D.C., where Huawei threw a party for the local press at the W Hotel's rooftop bar. Before the festivities Paul spoke to me about Huawei's ambitions.

China Scoops Up Western Talent by the Tens of Thousands

"Huawei is a multinational company with two hundred thousand employees," I began. "It has fifty thousand non-Chinese employees, most of them engineers. To what extent is Huawei a Chinese company, and to what extent is it a multinational company?"

"It's a Chinese company," Paul Scanlan replied. "None of the actual products are produced outside China. Product engineering is centered in China. We have research centers in twenty-one countries around the world. R & D outside China is more focused on basic research than on development. The focus is longer range. Typically, there will be a handful of Chinese personnel present to help explain the work to the management team in China."

It's no mean feat to enlist the talents of tens of thousands of Western scientists and engineers. That's the first time in its history that China has harnessed a critical mass of elite Western talent to its global ambitions, and it might be Huawei's definitive accomplishment. In Nikkei Asian Review, Sept. 11, 2019, Lauly Li and Cheng Ting-Fang observed that "Huawei's rapid rise is driven by a global talent hunt." According to Li and Cheng:

> Huawei's drive to become the world's largest smartphone maker has been fueled by an aggressive global hunt for science and engineering talent. The company made its first smartphone, running on the Android operating system, a decade ago. In 2016, the year after it enticed dozens of staff from HTC, Huawei shipped 30 percent more smartphones than it did in 2015. In 2017, it sold more than 150 million handsets; in 2018, it shipped more than 200 million.
>
> The company says that it now has 800 physicists, more than 700 mathematicians and 120 chemists working for it. Among those hires are high-profile figures such as the award-winning engineer Tong Wen, and the Italian microwave technology expert Renato Lombardi, who runs a global research facility for Huawei in Milan. Eighty-five thousand of Huawei's employees—44 percent of its total headcount—work in R & D, Huawei spokesperson Joe Kelly told Nikkei, including twenty thousand working on fifth-generation technology alone.
>
> Huawei also sponsors universities to the tune of more than $300 million per year, and maintains a specialist research unit, called the '2012 Laboratories,' which focuses on developing technologies that will give it an edge decades in the future—from DNA data storage to atomic-scale manufacturing and optical computing. The company said that

it invested $1.5 billion in developing artificial intelligence last year.[4]

Huawei wants to lead the Fourth Industrial Revolution

There is nothing secret about Huawei's ambitions. The presentations at the firm's Shanghai Connect conference in September 2019, are available in streaming video with translation on Huawei's website, and they project a vision of a Fourth Industrial Revolution more ambitious than anything we read about in the West. If you look twenty years ahead, I asked Paul, and if everything goes the way you would like it to go, what do you think the world will look like, and what do you think Huawei will have done to change it?

Paul replied, "The Chinese aren't thinking of dominating the world. I think that history shows that. It's not the intention. If you listen to Mr. Ren [Zhongfei, Huawei's founder and chairman], what he said very specifically, it's very important not to take too much market share. That's how this man thinks. It's not about having Chinese competitors. It's about having Western competitors. He made two comments. If you take too much market share, and you're dominant—that is, well over 50 percent, or 60 percent, or 75 percent—you have a problem. If there's no Western competitor, then there's no opportunity for innovation.

"Let me take you through a bit of the history and talk about why he comes to this conclusion. Many years ago, we were a reseller of a product in Hong Kong, a switch by Mytel. We didn't own anything. And we used to sell it in rural China. We didn't go to Shanghai or Beijing—big cities. We had no brand name. We had big competitors—the Ericssons and Siemens of the world, and other companies like this. So we played where we could play. Just think about how the company started up. We didn't own a product, and we played where we could play. A few years later, that product was taken away from us. That's when Mr. Ren and everybody else suddenly realized that we didn't have a product. So what are we? Are we a system integrator? Are we a reseller? That's when he first got the idea that we need to understand and own intellectual property.

4 https://asia.nikkei.com/Spotlight/Cover-Story/Huawei-s-rapid-rise-is-driven-by-a-global-talent-hunt

You could say that maybe a few years later than that, and since it's all been published—and I don't want to name names, because we settled all that issue—maybe we didn't invent things the way we should have."

Paul was referring to a settlement with the American telecommunications giant Cisco. In 2004, Huawei settled a suit by Cisco, then America's dominant provider of telecommunications equipment, for alleged technology theft. Cisco alleged that Huawei stole its technology for internet switches and routers; Huawei agreed to change its product line, and Cisco dropped the lawsuit.[5] More recently, the Justice Department charged Huawei with stealing intellectual property from T-Mobile, but the new allegations involved a low-tech gadget that tested the resilience of smartphone screens through repeated taps.[6] Dubbed "Tappy the Robot," it was the subject of lighthearted T-Mobile adver-

5 "Yesterday's agreement marks the completion of Cisco's lawsuit against both Huawei Technologies its subsidiaries, Huawei America, and FutureWei Technologies, that was pending in the US District Court for the Eastern District of Texas. The completion of the lawsuit comes after a third-party review of Huawei's products, and after Huawei discontinued the sale of products at issue in the suit. Huawei has agreed to change its command line interface, user manuals, help screens and portions of its source code to address Cisco's concerns. Cisco agreed to suspend its patent infringement lawsuit when the third-party review got underway, so the settlement of the lawsuit comes as no great surprise." https://www.theregister.co.uk/2004/07/29/cisco_huawei_case_ends/

6 The Wall Street Journal reported on August 29, 2017: "U.S. prosecutors are looking into additional instances of alleged technology theft by Huawei Technologies Co., according to people familiar with the matter, potentially expanding beyond existing criminal cases against the Chinese telecommunications giant.

Among the situations being examined are episodes in which Huawei was accused of stealing intellectual property from multiple people and companies over several years, as well as how the company went about recruiting employees from competitors, these people said.... Huawei is already contesting one case of trade-secret theft: In January, prosecutors in Seattle issued an indictment accusing Huawei of stealing smartphone-testing technology from its one-time partner T-Mobile US Inc. from 2012 to 2013. The indictment also accused Huawei of launching a bonus program to reward employees who stole confidential information from rivals. Huawei called the charges "politically motivated" in an Aug. 9 motion to dismiss the case." The T-Mobile case involves "Tappy the Robot," a simple device that tests the durability of smartphone screens by tapping them repeatedly.

https://www.wsj.com/articles/u-s-prosecutors-probe-huawei-on-new-allegations-of-technology-theft-11567102622 tising videos that showed employees declaring, "Robots are cool!" and moving their arms robotically.[59]

That was then, Paul maintained. "Today we own almost eighty-eight thousand patents. What's more important is that we own 30 percent of the intrinsic 5G patents. And we have developed integrated circuits, specifically the Kirin processer, not to compete with Qualcomm, for our own products, for our differentiation. The ARM processor brand product doesn't compete with Intel. The AI chips are for our own purposes, not to compete with Nvidia."

Huawei's Threat—a Global Price War in High-End Computer Chips

That's Huawei's velvet glove, for display purposes, but there's an iron fist inside it. After the US Commerce Department placed Huawei on the "entity list" in May 2019, Chinese analysts gamed a possible price war between Huawei and some of its US competitors. With the introduction of the Ascend line of artificial intelligence chips in December 2018,[60] Huawei can compete head-on with Nvidia and other US designers of server processors. And Huawei's Kirin chipset for smartphones, according to a Japanese study, is already "equal to or better than" Apple's competing product.[61] One private Chinese study considered the outcome of a price war in which Huawei cut its high-end chip prices by 30 percent. Nvidia would run out of cash in eighteen months, and Qualcomm would run out of cash in twenty-four months, the Chinese analysts concluded. Huawei clawed its way to top position in the telecommunications equipment market by undercutting its competitors' prices, and might well do the same in chips.

Huawei prefers to speak softly, but the big stick is apparent to industry insiders. Nonetheless, the global ambitions of the Chinese national champion are breathtaking.

If Huawei doesn't want a monopoly, what is it looking for, I asked? Paul Scanlan replied, "We're looking for what's called the control point."

In effect, Huawei has cloned the Google and Facebook business model with its enormous network effect for internet searches and advertising, and applied it to virtually every aspect of economic activity.

Huawei's Shanghai Connect conference in 2019 emphasized the impact of 5G networks, smartphones, Cloud computing, and artificial intelligence on healthcare. Huawei has developed health apps for smartphones that do medical tests—for example, eye examinations for children—and upload the data to the Cloud.

Big Brother is Healing You

"Medical technology is a good example," Paul enthused. Smartphones with inexpensive attachments can take vital signs, and even electro-cardiograms, daily and transmit the data to the Cloud in real time. That will transform healthcare in poor countries. He added, "You can have a rural clinic staffed by a single triage nurse who can do basic bloodwork and other tests, and transmit the data to a medical team thousands of miles away which can diagnose potential problems and prescribe preventative care." Soon, the triage nurse in a remote clinic will be able to do a great deal more.

On January 10, 2019, the *South China Morning Post* reported:

> China has successfully tested the world's first remote-surgery equipment using 5G mobile network technology. In the January 8th procedure, a doctor in the southeastern province of Fujian removed the liver of a laboratory test animal at a remote location, by controlling robotic surgical arms over a 5G connection. The lag time lag was said to be only 0.1 seconds between the doctor's control device and the robot in the surgical room. Researchers said the high-speed can reduce the risk of deadly medical mistakes, and raises hopes that 5G-enabled remote surgery will soon be reliable enough for use on human patients.[62]

That would give Huawei access to the medical records of billions of people, with updates in real time. The implications for medical diagnosis and research would be staggering. Huawei would be able to compare the diagnostics of individuals with billions of medical case histories. Israel is digitizing the medical records of its nine million citizens, and that's spoken of as a breakthrough, but here we are talking about a-billion-and-half Chinese citizens and another couple billion people elsewhere. In effect, all the smartphones in the world become data gathering devices for Huawei.

Again in March 2019, Huawei partnered with Yitu Healthcare to develop an intelligent healthcare cloud backed by AI that can integrate healthcare data into efficiency and effectiveness. At the Mobile World Congress (MWC 2019) this year, Huawei's Deputy Chairman, Ken Hu, disclosed the launch of Huawei's digital inclusion plan, Tech4All, and three key actions: connect, apply, and skill. And he put forward the goal, "five years for 500 million people to benefit from digital technology." In line with this vision, the company has partnered with leading research institute, IIS Aragon and DIVE Medical—a startup, to co-create an AI-powered assessment for early signs of visual impairment. They call it Track.AI, an initiative to provide a unique value for the visual impairment children community to make sure nobody is left behind.

Paul continued, "This is what we mean by the *control point.* We don't want to do everything ourselves. If you are a pharmaceutical company, you won't have to duplicate our investment in AI. You simply rent time on the Cloud, using our AI servers, and obtain access to our data. The key is gathering and porting the data to servers where it can be put into usable form. That's our contribution. We don't want to control everything. We want partners who are best in class in every field."

In 2017, Healthcare Global magazine reported:

> At the end of 2016, Huawei and Philips signed a memorandum of understanding to build a new, cloud-based healthcare solution for deployment in China. The country is becoming home to an increased ageing population and limited resources, which has seen the need for the healthcare industry to become increasingly digital and patient-centric. The use of digital technologies will therefore deliver increased accuracy within diagnostics and analytics and enable the ability for medical professionals to provide exceptional medical treatment surrounding chronic, long-term conditions.
>
> Testing surrounding Huawei and Phillips' healthcare solution has now been completed, at which the

> project is now looking towards a future where cloud and machine-learning will digitalize and disrupt the healthcare vertical with unprecedented speed and reach.
>
> Targeting China's smaller urban centers, the two companies will expand high-quality, cloud-driven healthcare to communities which lack advanced healthcare solutions or physicians with specialist skills.
>
> The use of cloud AI will enable the processing of large volumes of data in a shorter timescale, and deliver greater accuracy than traditional medical professionals. Ludwig Liang, Head of Population Health Management for Philips in China, has explained the significance of this within China's tier-2 cities, as many physicians "don't necessarily have the skills to read image diagnostics like MRI scans and CT scans.
>
> If you ask a doctor to process thousands of images a day, he may miss something. In contrast, AI is adept at spotting patterns in big datasets. For terminal illnesses, machine learning solutions hosted in the cloud can make a real difference in a patient's prognosis.[63]

Huawei will have the advantage in the collection and storage of data. It has built national broadband networks in many countries, starting in Malaysia, and now in Colombia, Brazil, Mexico and numerous other countries. Huawei builds the networks, provides the smartphones, develops the data collection apps, maintains the Cloud, and provide the AI tools to process the data. That turns Huawei into something like Facebook or Google, but with a central role in every field of human activity—not just advertising or internet search.

Everyone else will want to partner with Huawei, Paul explained, making the Chinese firm something like a central hub for the Fourth Industrial Revolution. "We want to make our data available to partners from all over the world," he continued.

So there are two things to focus on. One, is economy; the second, is industry.

Paul Scanlan has spent most of the past ten years on overseas flights. I asked him which countries he would cite as Huawei success stories.

With an Aussie half-smile, Paul replied, "Let's pick two that perhaps the US would not like to consider. But let's pick them, in any case, because they really are exemplary. The first one is Russia. Russia bought one of the companies—they bought an operating system from a Finnish company. Because of all the sanctions on Russia, they've had to do all their own development. And now they've asked Huawei very specifically—they're very keen to have local manufacturing, local production, local innovation, local everything—they've asked Huawei to integrate everything and put that operating system there. We will have a similar challenge in the eco system developing all the apps, which will be Russian apps, which the Russians are quite good at developing. This is an example where the government has said to Huawei, *You want to play ball here, we need localization, we need assembly, we need manufacturing, we need you to integrate our operating system on your platform.* They're pretty good examples of where the government has picked some areas which are practical; they've invested themselves in some components. That's one type of example."

Paul Scanlan was being modest. "Huawei Plays Star Role in New China-Russia AI Partnership," was Dimitri Simes's headline in the Nikkei Asian Review on February 4, 2020.

Simes reported:

> Russia's access to Western technology has been limited by U.S. and European sanctions imposed over the Ukraine crisis in 2014. China has felt a similar squeeze amid the trade war with U.S. President Donald Trump.
>
> But Samuel Bendett, a research analyst at the Washington-based Center for Naval Analyses, thinks the growing Sino-Russian cooperation could chip away at America's edge.
>
> "Both China and Russia are making public their plans to compete for the [world's] best and brightest high-tech workers, seeking to attract this newly emerging AI talent pool to their respective countries," Bendett said. "The U.S., he continued, "has

> an advantage in the near- to mid-term as the country with the biggest financial and educational support for AI development, but Sino-Russian cooperation can erode this advantage down the line."
>
> The Pentagon sees a national security threat, even though Moscow and Beijing have yet to openly collaborate on military AI. In an AI strategy report released in February 2019, the Defense Department warned that growing Russian and Chinese spending on military applications for artificial intelligence threatens "to erode our technological and operational advantages and destabilize the free and open international order."[64]

Despite its much smaller population, Russia graduates as many engineers each year as the United States, because one-third of Russian students major in the subject, the same proportion as in China. Huawei hunts for talent in Russia, as it does all over the globe. In a November 2019 conference, it unveiled a plan for an "AI ecosystem" in Russia by 2025, employing one hundred thousand software developers, according to Simes's report.

Asked to mention some other Huawei success stories, Paul continued, "Another one is Colombia, where I had the privilege of meeting [Colombian president] Íván Duque. He came to Shanghai, and we were talking about security and trust, and he said, 'We trust you. We trust Huawei.' We need you to take all the ideas you have and help me in Colombia. I'm here in Shanghai because I want a direct trade route between Bogota and Shanghai. I need investment.' Second point: I came to Cartagena. What was remarkable about that trip is that it was billed as Colombia and China. The only companies there were Chinese companies. I find those two quite remarkable for different reasons."

To my surprise, Paul added, "Then let's take the UK. The Security Evaluation Centre Oversight Board looked at our source code exhaustively and pointed out some ways we could improve. In fact, they did us an enormous favor by calling attention to less than perfect architecture. We made an enormous investment in improving the software and are confident we will satisfy UK security concerns." He was right; in January

2020, the UK government declared that it would allow a limited role for Huawei in the buildout of Britain's 5G networks, despite the personal intervention of President Trump to dissuade Prime Minister Boris Johnson from doing so.

Huawei has made itself part of the fabric of British telecommunications engineering, starting in 2011, when it hired the Chief Information Security Officer of the British government John Suffolk as the head of its UK business. A senior Huawei executive told me that the company's relationship with the UK is the best of any Western country. GCHQ, the British counterpart of the National Security Agency, spent years critiquing Huawei's code, often demanding improvements that the Chinese firm promptly made.

In 2012, Huawei announced, to the applause of then Prime Minister David Cameron, that it would invest £1.3 billion in the United Kingdom. A Huawei report notes that in 2018, it "invested £112 million in research and development, employing more than 300 researchers in the UK. Huawei also collaborated with 35 universities and research institutes."

Does Huawei Promote Political Repression?

Let me get on to the unpleasantness," I told Paul. "China is widely accused of using technology for social control. The United States banned the export of components recently to twenty-eight Chinese companies, some of whom are involved in facial recognition and other things that have security implications. Do you think that there is a justifiable concern in the West that the technology which Huawei and other Chinese companies are giving to the world will indeed help repressive political regimes?"

The Huawei executive wasn't fazed. "What we do, is we sell products," he said. It's not our job to know what you do with them, or who's going to tell you how to use them, or maybe you told us how you were going to use them. Are we a moral vacuum in that respect in that we sell to those countries? Don't most of the companies on the US stock market sell pretty much everything to China, and to every other country which has what you might call a repressive regime? Everybody sells everything to everybody. You can always say you should have known. Let me give you a different type of analogy. A technology can always be misused. A technology can do a lot of things. I've been now for almost seven years in China, in Shenzhen specifically. There are all electric buses, all electric taxis, all electric anything with two wheels. I was in Singapore not long ago, and they had just passed the fifty percent mark on their buses. That's not the remarkable thing. The remarkable thing is that six years ago, the traffic was all over the place. If you tried to cross at a pedestrian crossing, you probably were going to get run over. Today, pretty much everybody drives in the lane, everybody stops at traffic lights. Pedestrians will stand there and wait even if there is no traffic, because there is a red light—at ten o'clock at night when there's no cars. How did that come about? First, government trying to educate the public. But also, we've got cameras everywhere. And we do see who you are and what you're doing. A classic example is a picture of a guy holding a mobile phone in a truck. He's caught and he's fined. So they're trying to use technology to be able to help enforce rules. It goes even further than this. All the traffic lights are monitored so they are automatically connected according to the flow of traffic, autonomously. So we have a lot of opportunities for society to benefit. Like anything, it can be misused. There are more cameras in London than there are in Shenzhen, and the number in Shenzhen is huge."

Most Western observers take a far less benign view of China's surveillance systems. On February 2, 2018, Anna Mitchell and Larry Diamond wrote, in *The Atlantic*:

> Imagine a society in which you are rated by the government on your trustworthiness. Your "citizen score" follows you wherever you go. A high score allows you access to faster internet service or a fast-tracked visa to Europe. If you make political posts online without a permit, or question or contradict the government's official narrative on current events, however, your score decreases. To calculate the score, private companies working with your government constantly trawl through vast amounts of your social media and online shopping data.

> When you step outside your door, your actions in the physical world are also swept into the dragnet: The government gathers an enormous collection of information through the video cameras placed on your street and all over your city. If you commit a crime—or simply jaywalk—facial recognition algorithms will match video footage of your face to your photo in a national ID database. It won't be long before the police show up at your door.
>
> This society may seem dystopian, but it isn't far-fetched: It may be China in a few years. The country is racing to become the first to implement a pervasive system of algorithmic surveillance. Harnessing advances in artificial intelligence and data mining and storage to construct detailed profiles on all citizens, China's communist party-state is developing a "citizen score" to incentivize "good" behavior. A vast accompanying network of surveillance cameras will constantly monitor citizens' movements, purportedly to reduce crime and terrorism. While the expanding Orwellian eye may improve "public safety," it poses a chilling new threat to civil liberties in a country that already has one of the most oppressive and controlling governments in the world."[65]

The Machines Become Sentient

The combination of machine learning and 5G will allow robots to talk to each other and work out production processes without the help of human engineers, Paul enthused.

"Let's take robotics today," he told me. "5G changes everything. Typically, 5G is spoken about in terms of download speed, but that's not the most important advantage. For industrial processes, autonomous vehicles and other applications, the latency—the time it takes for one device to acquire and respond to a signal from another device—is more important. On a factory floor today, Robot A does its instruction, passes the bit to Robot B, and it's the same thing. Now if we put very low latency inside each of the robots—and they can be robots from different manufacturers—and put them in a room and give them the rules, like Go or like chess, to enable them to connect in real time—milliseconds, lightning fast—then put a bit of plastic in view and say, *I want you to make a plastic cup*, the robots will organize themselves much better than we would have thought. You're going to push the plastic flat, you're going to extrude it this way, you're going to finish it that way—that's the way we think, and that might be the first attempt of the robots. Then afterwards we can talk about cutting down the amount of wastage, or the time it takes to make these things, or other key performance indicators, and they will start to do things differently. What we saw when we did this is collaboration between robots from different manufacturers—ABB, Kawasaki, and others. Connectivity allows you to move from very basic stuff to very sophisticated stuff. This connectivity requires a platform enabled with AI."

Huawei's chief partner in robotics is ABB, the world's largest maker of industrial robots, with more than four hundred thousand machines installed worldwide. ABB's Chief Technology Officer, Bazmi Rizwan Husain, told Huawei's 2019 Shanghai Connect conference:

> ABB is a 130-year-old company which makes a lot of things, primarily two industries. We serve the electrical energy industry and the manufacturing industry. In the automation segment, industrial robots were an innovation that was brought into the market by ABB way back in 1974. We have a history of being ahead of the times. There are major shifts going on. The energy revolution is changing the way that electricity is generated, transported and consumed. On the industry side we are going through the 4th industrial revolution. For this revolution to succeed, we have to go beyond automation. Automation has to be told how to react to every situation it encounters. Given the growing complexity that is developing in industry, we need systems that not only react as they are programmed but are able to handle situations that are not planned. These systems are what we call autonomous. We believe that the cornerstone

technology for moving towards autonomous systems is artificial intelligence.

AI in the past decade has made enormous progress. It has shown superhuman capabilities in some areas, for example games, where it has beaten the best human players. For AI to play the key role that it must for industrial autonomy, it has to learn to deal with unplanned situations. It has to come from the closed world to reality.

I'd just like to highlight some of the key elements that are needed for industrial AI. Today's AI has explainability issues. It makes it very difficult to be used in physical processes, and even more so when the consequence of a wrong action could be dangerous, or expensive, or both. The second aspect is the data. In industry, since the mid-80s, most of the process plants have what is called distributed control systems. There is lots of data available. But industrial data is about a variety of different equipment. If you look at equipment such as a transformer, or a robot, there is very little they have in common. There is a lot of data, but there is a great variety of data. A second aspect is that you can have several years of data. But it is not unusual to find that you have three or four years of data about a robot, but no instance of failure. So it is hard to apply AI to the problem of failure when there is no data about failure. This is equipment that is designed not to fail.

The third aspect of industrial data is that normal operations are not a differentiating factor. It's really looking at an outlier, and making that the new normal. For the deployment part, it is deployed in real time operations in very constrained equipment. If you look at inference times, they are not adequate for real time use. That has to change. That AI has to be deployed all levels, at device level, and the cloud level.

This demonstration has four elements. You've got the conveyor belt on which the garbage is coming, you have the sensor system that detects the presence

> of garbage and sends information to the intelligence unit, and then there is a robot system that picks up the items and puts in the right bin. This was done in collaboration together with Huawei. First, the entire solution that was developed from the ABB side is a China-based team. ABB has seventeen thousand people in China with a very strong R & D capability here. The entire solution was designed and developed in a little over one month. It was done locally and done with speed and an example of great collaboration we have with Huawei.

During the 2016 presidential campaign, Donald Trump held up signs reading "Trump Digs Coal" at his rallies, and promised to increase coal mining employment. Huawei's partners envision an entirely different future for the mining industry. ABB's chief technology officer told the Huawei conference:

> Let me give an example of what can happen in the future, from the mining industry. It's crucial for economies. Mining is not always safe and productive and efficient as it could be. ABB supplies a lot of equipment to improve safety and productivity. Today most mines are operated in island mode. You have extraction and mining that are then fed into the processing site, treated as separate islands. When we look at a mine of the future, it will be a confluence of several technologies. The first thing is to take humans out of harm's way—out of the mines where there is danger. Humans will work in a safe control room above ground through virtual reality, augmented reality—they will be able to see and control the process. In the operations part, humans are replaced by autonomous equipment both for moving the more, for charging the mine for new blasting areas—and if you have a problem, you will use digital diagnostic capabilities. You will be able to fix the fault faster and better.

Sentient industrial robots that design their own production procedures, robo-surgery by remote control, and augmented-reality mining coal may sound like science fiction, but Huawei and its partners—the heavyweights of the medical technology and robotics world—have already built the technology. If we fell into a coma and woke up ten years from now, we wouldn't recognize some basic industries.

The 5G-artificial-intelligence combination will also bring about a revolution in scientific research, Paul continued.

"Another Western company," he said, "is the Square Kilometer Array, built by an Australian gentleman, and they're building a farm of several hundred square kilometers of small antennas pointed to the sky to collect data, in a two remote areas. One is Western Australia, the other is South Africa—quiet areas where there's no interference. We put hundreds of thousands of these antennas to collect data. We did a simulation, and it shows the power of AI equipment. To identify an exoplanet and locate the position of this one particular thing, it took them one hundred sixty-nine days of computing time. It took us ten seconds. And that was remarkable in some ways. What he was trying to show is that collaboration between Western companies in a sphere where there is no competition, where there is no issue of taking jobs away, but is entirely for advancement, for learning. If you have that sort of data, you can crunch it very quickly. It would be a sad case if because of the way the administration is doing things here, that it would delay the rollout of 5G that prevented the gathering of information that could be presented in a form that AI could fix cancer, or fix malaria, or whatever it is. This really improves the world."

Phillip Diamond, the founder of the Square Kilometer Array, was another star presenter at Huawei's Shanghai Connect Conference in September 2019:

> Huawei has been a key partner since inception. Next year we will witness the birth of the Square Kilometer Array Observatory. The SKA will then become an intergovernmental organization similar to CERN and only the second in the world dedicated to astronomy.
>
> To achieve the levels of sensitivity and spatial resolution that we need, the SKA will use many connected antennas known as arrays, that can act together. It will have two such arrays with different

technologies, one in South Africa and the other in Australia, both in remote regions of the world, which allow us to get away from artificially generated interference that would pollute the extremely faint radiations we wish to detect. In South Africa, we will be building close to two hundred large dishes, and in Western Australia there will be more than two hundred thirty thousand smaller dipole antennas.

In fact, we already have hardware on the ground, and before official construction starts in 2021, we have built prototypes. China has led the design of the SKA dishes. When you build an enormous radio telescope, the aim is to gather as much information as possible from the universe.

The data arrays will send a massive amount of data to two supercomputers, one in each of the host countries, where the data will be processed to allow astronomers to undertake their scientific investigations. This will initially require more than fifty petaflops of digital signal processing power going to two hundred petaflops. Each year, we will archive more than six hundred petabytes of data—dwarfing the amounts currently handled by platforms such as Facebook and Google. Major research infrastructures like SKA have a long history of driving innovation.

I'm sure you are all familiar with the fact that CERN in Switzerland developed the worldwide web. Wi-Fi was developed by radio astronomers in Australia who were trying to process signals coming from black holes. I can't predict what the spinoffs will be coming from the SKA, but there's an enormous potential for us to have a similar impact in areas like data visualization, artificial intelligence, and machine learning. In fact, our partners here at the Shanghai astronomical observatory have already been working with Huawei, applying machine learning to such astronomical problems as pulsar searches and radio galaxy detection, using simulated SKA images. AI's ability to speed up data analysis will be invaluable

> when the SKA is operational, when we're dealing with these enormous data volumes.

Huawei is building the world's biggest Cloud computing capacity and racing to design the world's fastest artificial intelligence processors. And behind Huawei stands the Chinese government's massive commitment to supercomputing, and—most ominously—to quantum computing. American companies still may have an edge in quantum computing, but it won't last for long, according to Google's chief quantum computing engineer, Hartmut Neven. Speaking at a January 2020 conference, Neven warned, "We are indeed most worried (about) an unknown competitor out of China to beat us in the race to (such a) machine, because China as a society just has the ability to steer enormous resources in the directions that are deemed strategically important. They plan to have three different labs, and they will actually all be devoted to quantum information (the science at the core of building quantum computers)."

The conversation with Huawei's Paul Scanlan was a blast of cold air. Americans are busy with the valuation of competing providers of streaming video, the relative merits of e-commerce platforms at Amazon and Wal-Mart, and the profitability of the hundred-and-tenth smartphone dating app. The Chinese want to transform the way we live. They do the physics, and we do the apps. We are becoming geeks in a new Roman Empire.

CHAPTER THREE

WORLD DOMINATION, ONE COUNTRY AT A TIME[7]

In 2013, my friend Eduardo Medina-Mora became Mexico's ambassador to the United States. We had known each other since 1988, when I was preparing a study of Mexico's tax and regulatory system for a U.S. consulting firm, and Eduardo was running a small Mexico City law firm after a stint as press officer for the Ministry of Fisheries. We kept in touch over the years. In 2003, when he headed Mexico's foreign intelligence service, the CISEN, and I ran the fixed income research department of Bank of America, we compared notes over dinner in Mexico City. He went on to serve as Attorney General and other senior posts.

Eduardo complained that no one in the Obama administration seemed responsible for Mexico. "We don't even know who to call when a problem comes up," he told me, at his office at Mexico's Embassy on Pennsylvania Avenue, where I called on him to offer my congratulations. "It's easier for [then Mexican President Enrique] Peña Nieto to get the president of China on the phone than Barack Obama. What would you advise me to do?"

A few months earlier, I had joined Reorient Group, a Hong Kong investment banking boutique, as managing director in charge of the Americas. I suggested that we remove the batteries from our BlackBerrys to prevent official eavesdropping. We did so.

7 This, in part, was published first in *Tablet* magazine and is used with permission.

"You can invite the Chinese in to build a broadband network," I then said. "That will get the attention of the Americans."

It didn't. But I did get a look at how China's strategy for global economic hegemony worked from the inside.

A year and a half and many machinations later, I brought Mexican Ambassador Alicia Buenrostro Massieu to the headquarters of Huawei Technologies in Shenzhen. Ambassador Buenrostro, the niece of a former finance minister whom I had known for years, came with as many of her Hong Kong entourage as would fit in a minivan. The trip to Shenzhen took a bit less than an hour, including a stop to pass Chinese customs. The new bullet train from West Kowloon Station in Hong Kong to Shenzhen takes only eight minutes, one more technological wonder among the many that make some Chinese cities look like sets for science fiction films.

The Huawei campus covers five hundred acres and makes Stanford University look dowdy. The executive dining center features an enormous artificial waterfall, young women in traditional costume playing ancient Chinese instruments, and three-star quality Cantonese food. We dined in a small private room with a Huawei executive, whence a guide escorted us to the exhibition hall. We passed thousands of Huawei workers returning from lunch. "They all have a futon under their desks," said our guide. "They take a nap after lunch because they work until ten o'clock."

The Huawei tour took three hours. It might be the largest technology museum in the world, bigger than the Henry Ford Museum in Dearborn, Michigan, or the Franklin Institute in Philadelphia, except it shows only new things. The array of gadgets was breathtaking. Huawei proposes to outfit smart cities with everything from signals for autonomous vehicles, environmental controls for buildings, and smart cameras that can provide instant facial recognition and track the movements of criminal suspects in real time. It manufacturers a box the size of a steamer trunk, for example, that can be parachuted into a disaster zone or a remote mining camp that will provide area Wi-Fi. It also manufactures security. One exhibit consisted of a four-by-six-yard wall map of Guangdong City, glistening tens of thousands of small lights. "Every one of the lights is a smartphone," said our guide. "We can track the location of every phone and correlate position to online purchases and social media posts."

"And what do you use this information for?" I said.

"Well, if you want to open a new Kentucky Fried Chicken franchise, this will help you to find the best location," said the guide.

Yeah, right, I thought. The Ministry of State Security knows where everyone is at all times and whom they are with; if the phones of two Chinese who posted something critical about the government are in proximity, the State Security computers will detect a conspiracy. That was before China installed high-definition video cameras with facial recognition software powered by Huawei chips at one hundred-meter intervals in major cities. This technology gives China unprecedented tools for social control. But it also helped China suppress the coronavirus epidemic.

You, Too, Can Be Like China

At the end of the tour, the Mexicans and I sat on a semicircular bench in a small amphitheater, and a young Chinese man stepped to the podium and turned on a projector. "You Mexicans have a big economy," he said, "but very low broadband penetration." And he showed some charts and graphs to this effect. "Your economy is backward today, but you can become a great and rich economy, just like China. Let us build a national broadband network for you," he said. "Then we will bring in e-commerce and e-finance and create a whole new ecosystem that will make you a modern economy. He sounded vaguely like the Borg: *We will assimilate you. Resistance is futile.*

Ambassador Buenrostro was astonished. After some time, she asked, "How long have you been doing this?"

The man from Huawei said, "Oh, six or seven years."

Buenrostro said, "In Mexico, nothing ever changes."

Not necessarily, though. In 2014 and 2015, I traveled to Mexico to introduce Huawei executives to senior officials of Mexico's Communications Ministry, hoping to land a role for Reorient Group in financing the project. Reorient was a startup created by a Hong Kong entrepreneur whose business acumen and connections were impressive.

He helped to launch an Africa-centered logistics firm headed by Erik Prince, the founder of Blackwater, with backing from CITIC, China's largest financial firm.

Mexico might as well have been on the dark side of the moon where Reorient Group was concerned, but I wanted to follow the red thread and see where it led. Since 2011, Huawei had been promoting the idea of national broadband networks as the centerpiece of a new economic "ecosystem," flanked by the likes of Alibaba, the Chinese e-commerce giant, and other services firms.

Huawei's mantra was the same as I had heard at their Shenzhen headquarters: *Invite us in, and we'll make you rich like China.* That wasn't an idle boast.

Mexico was the first "developing country" I studied as an economic consultant. I would go on to Peru, Nicaragua, Russia, and other countries before leaving the field in favor of relative value research on Wall Street. The main thing you notice about developing countries is that they don't develop—or if they do, only small parts of them develop. Most people work a subsistence plot with poor implements, or they sit all day in a market stall waiting for someone to come along and buy a liter of cooking oil. They barely make enough to eat, and they don't pay taxes, which means that the government has no money to spend on infrastructure or services. More than half of Mexico's employment is what economists euphemistically call "informal"—that is, off-the-book businesses that have no access to capital.

East Asia is different. The Chinese economic model is only a souped-up, bigger and more ruthless version of the Asian model that began with Japan's restoration of Emperor Meiji in 1868, and was replicated by South Korea and Taiwan: move subsistence farmers to the cities and build factories for them to work in. While its per capita GDP rose thirty-five times, China moved five hundred fifty million people from the countryside to the cities, and it built the equivalent of all of the cities of Europe to house them.

Modernization in China isn't the enclave of a middle-class modernity, as in India, but a movement that reaches into the capillaries of society. Entrepreneurs in Chinese villages connect to the world market through mobile broadband, sell their products and buy supplies on the Alibaba platform, and obtain credit from microfinancing platforms. Information and capital flow down to the roots of the economy and products flow back up to the world market.

China Exports Its Economic Model

China now proposes to export its model to Southeast Asia, Central Asia, Latin America, and parts of the Middle East and Africa. This involves a Faustian bargain of sorts; the same technologies that have lifted billions of East Asians out of dire poverty and the ever-present risk of starvation into prosperity and economic security can also give dictatorial regimes previously unimagined tools for social control. China's Belt and Road Initiative (BRI) has a $1 trillion war chest for infrastructure investments and export loans.

In making such offers, Chinese planners are thinking a generation ahead. The scarcest resource in the world is labor, specifically workers who can read an instruction manual, learn skilled or semi-skilled jobs, and show up for work on time. Virtually all the world's population growth during the 21st century will take place in sub-Saharan Africa and the Indian subcontinent—the latter mostly in Pakistan, where the average female has four children, compared with 2.2 in India.

The problem is that the productive parts of the world are all aging together. There are plenty of young people in the world, but low educational levels, abysmal infrastructure, and political instability sideline the regions where population growth is most rapid. The people of aging countries with shrinking populations cannot find enough young people to absorb the investments they need to make to fund their prospective retirements. China's own labor force stopped growing a couple years ago. In 2018, kindergarten admissions in China fell by 740,000, the first decline on record, and the birth rate fell to eleven per one thousand people in 2018, from thirteen per one thousand people in 2016.

The good news is that the prospects are good for a quantum jump in productivity in the developing world. The bad news is that China is acting aggressively to position itself as the dominant equipment supplier, investor, joint venture partner, and technology provider in this revolution. By contrast, the United States is drifting toward the export profile of Brazil, with strength in agricultural commodities and energy but overall weakness in high-technology manufacturing and exports.

When I first worked in Mexico City in 1988, Eduardo Medina-Mora's little law firm employed a secretary who did nothing all day but dial the telephone because it took five or six tries to get through to a local number. By 2015, the system had improved, but Mexico still had the most expensive broadband in the world and one of the lowest penetration rates (in subscriptions per capita) relative to the size of its economy. Scrambling to get to a meeting at the Communications Ministry, I used Waze to direct the taxi driver, who did not use the program, because broadband was too expensive.

In 2015, Mexico announced that it would create a wholesale broadband network, the *red compartida* (shared network), that would lease broadband to any carrier that wanted it. The consortium that won the bid to build the $7 billion network, ATLAN, engaged Huawei and Nokia to build the actual infrastructure. The first elements of the network went live in March 2018. Mexico's broadband usage was expected to rise sevenfold between 2015 and 2020 as a result.[66]

By then, I was out of the picture. In the summer of 2015, Alibaba's billionaire founder, Jack Ma, bought Reorient Group through his private equity firm, Yunfeng Capital. Early in 2016 he fired all of Reorient's Western bankers, and there ended my Forrest-Gump-like observations of great events in the broadband world.

But as the man with the PowerPoint at Huawei headquarters told the Mexican delegation, *It's not about selling a broadband network. It's about the ecosystem.* As Daniela Guzman recently reported in Bloomberg News: "As America recedes into the background, Chinese foreign direct investment in Latin America and the Caribbean has skyrocketed over the last ten years, according to a 2018 report by the Economic Commission for Latin America and the Caribbean. China dropped close to $90 billion in the region between 2005 and 2016. With a growing emphasis on telecommunications, Chinese investment in emerging technology is increasingly the primary fuel behind Latin America's tech boom." She quoted one South American entrepreneur saying, "When you go to China, you see what's going to happen in Latin America in five more years. Today, we look at China. We look at Meituan, at Alibaba and Tencent, to see what we can do in the future."[67]

To get there, Latin American economies will depend on Chinese technology, Chinese software, Chinese e-commerce, Chinese venture capital, and of course, the Chinese market. America's intelligence agencies worry that China will use its dominance in 5G networks to steal data. That may be true, but far more damaging to America's position in the world is the prospect that the most productive countries of the Global South will be hardwired into the Chinese economy.

When I visited Huawei headquarters, I guessed, wrongly, that the man with the PowerPoint presentation about Mexico had worked up the data for the ambassador's visit. In fact, Huawei has a plan for eighty different countries, with detailed recommendations for building information and communication technology (ICT) infrastructure. You can look up each plan on the company's website. It publishes a Global Connectivity Index, led by the United States, with a 2019 score of eighty-five and trailed by Ethiopia with a score of twenty-three. The higher the Global Connectivity Index (GCI) score, the greater the gross domestic product per capita.

Huawei tracks the progress of every country in the world and publishes the results the company website.[68] In countries like Egypt and the Philippines, for example, less than one-third of the population had a smartphone in 2014. By 2017, half to two-thirds of the country owned a smartphone and had a broadband subscription. This is a revolution unlike anything the world economy has ever seen.

Here's a sample of Huawei's country evaluations:

The good news for Adopters and Starters is that countries at every level of development have shown the ability to move up the GCI S-curve by focusing ICT deployment on competitive sectors of their local economy.

The Philippines and Egypt are prime examples in 2018. Both have focused on building out their fundamental ICT infrastructure to expand affordable Internet access and drive greater participation in the economy. From 2014 to 2017, the Philippines boosted smartphone use from 30 percent to 67 percent, extending primary Internet access to a greater portion of the population and fostering new business opportunities. Its GCI score moved up from thirty-four to thirty-five, pushing the Philippines over the threshold from Starter to Adopter status.

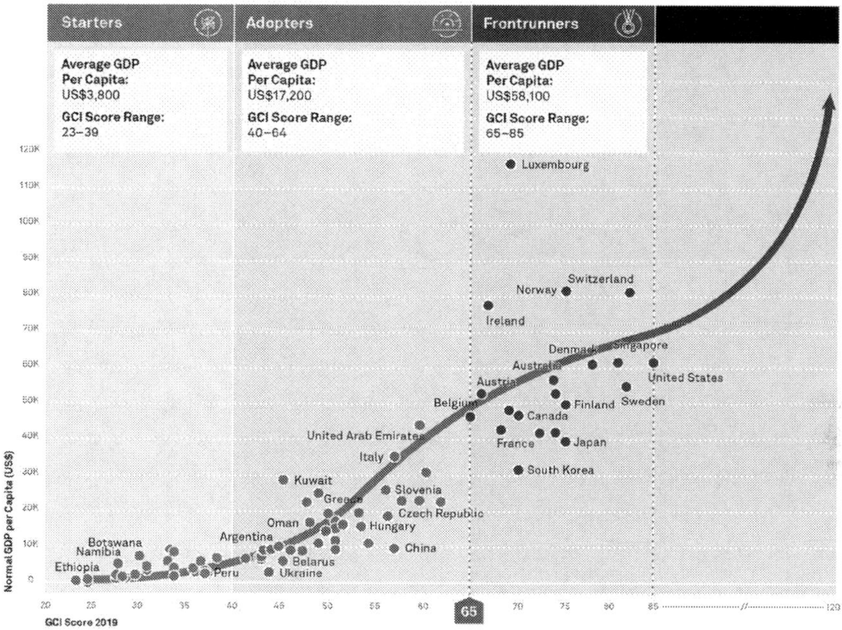

Courtesy of Huawei—Global Connectivity Index

At the same time, concerted efforts by the Ministry of Communications and Information Technology in Egypt saw mobile broadband subscribers jump from 38 percent to 62 percent of the population. Egypt's GCI score also moved up one point in 2018, placing the country at the top of the Starters' cluster. Expanding digital access to a massive number of new computer and smartphone users helped the Philippines climb to the top of the Starter cluster and jump the gap into the Adopters. The Philippines rounded off the year with a GCI score of thirty-five, up from thirty-four in 2017. In the Philippines, like many developing economies, smartphones are the primary gateway to the Internet. Smartphone use in the country expanded from 30 percent of the population in 2014, to 67 percent in 2017. Higher speed 4G coverage, which only reached 2 percent of the population in 2014, grew to 12 percent. Other indicators of digital growth are computer use, which grew from 27 percent to 34 percent, and cloud migration, which accounted for 17 percent of total software investment during the same period—up from 6 percent.

Strong national planning has helped drive this growth. Manila has declared a Cloud First Policy, which highlights its commitment to reduce the cost of government ICT by eliminating duplication and fragmentation. With this policy, the government has upped its cloud adoption and paved the way for the Philippines to move up to the Adopter cluster. Expanding Internet access, the core of the Philippines' Digital Strategy, has largely been driven by private operators, and has succeeded in creating new business opportunities in previously undeveloped areas.

The IT Business Process Outsourcing (BPO) industry also continues to play an important role in the Philippines' digital transformation, enabling micro, small and medium-sized enterprises (mSMEs) to use the Internet as a tool for marketing, innovation and delivery in global markets.

China's GCI score climbed three points, making it one of this year's fastest movers. Beijing's comprehensive, long-term strategy for digital transformation of the economy is paying off. Deployment of key enabling technologies is key to China's advancement. Huge investments in 4G technology have helped increase coverage from 7 percent of the population in 2014, to 69 percent in 2017. Fiber-to-the-Home (FTTH) coverage reached 64 percent in 2017, up from 18 percent in 2014. The growing coverage of both fixed and mobile broadband across China continues to drive e-Commerce, and has equipped entrepreneurs with a solid digital platform for launching small-scale Internet businesses.

> Most notable in the past year was China's announcement of the New Generation AI Development Plan, which sets high investment goals in a bid to become an AI leader by 2030.
>
> Egypt is at the top of the GCI's Starters group. In 2018, its GCI score improved by one point, the result of concerted efforts along three fronts: making fixed and mobile broadband more affordable and accessible, increasing the percentage of people who use smartphones, and boosting Internet access for both the

> public and private sectors. Smartphone use grew from 19 percent in 2014 to 49 percent in 2017. Mobile broadband subscribers expanded from 38 percent to 62 percent from 2014 to 2017, and Internet access grew from 29 percent to 41 percent. Egypt's Ministry of Communications and Information Technology has developed a National Broadband Plan that aims to increase high-speed broadband coverage. Priorities for the program include digital transformation of government operations, job creation, and reducing the now stark digital divide between urban and rural communities. Government initiatives have largely looked to promoting e-Commerce to expand the country's digital economy. Egypt's fast-growing e-Commerce sector has attracted foreign direct investment, especially in electronics and ICT, and has helped the country build a workforce equipped with digital skills.
>
> Egypt represents one of the largest telecom markets in Africa and Arab world, possess great potentiality and necessary assets to surge in the digital era. Current telecom market is highly dynamic with sustainable and steady growth in the demand for various telecom services in general and Broadband services in specific. "eMisr National Broadband Plan" launched by National Telecommunication Regulatory Authority (NTRA)—regulatory arm of Ministry of Communications and Information Technology (MCIT)—is aimed to boost broadband Internet penetration and development of a digital society. The eMisr National Broadband plan is based on three hubs: 1) to provide the service to span a wide geographical area, 2) to increase the prevalence and usage of the service, raising subscribers in the broadband services, 3) to provide citizens in disadvantaged areas with high-speed Internet access, and thus reducing the digital divide in Egypt.

The steam engine powered the first great revolution in economics, and the smartphone will catalyze the second. Talent is the scarcest resource in the global economy, and the spread of broadband through the backwaters of the world economy opens the global market to the talented few. Men and women who till subsistence plots or wait for passersby in market stalls suddenly can sell to the whole world through e-commerce. Capital will find its way into the capillaries of the world economy through e-finance.

The backward economies in which most of the world's people live waste time and grind down the spirit. In so-called emerging markets, between one-third and two-thirds of the workforce spend most of their time doing little or nothing. The proportion of workers outside the formal economy ranges from 32 percent in Turkey to nearly 60 percent in Nigeria.

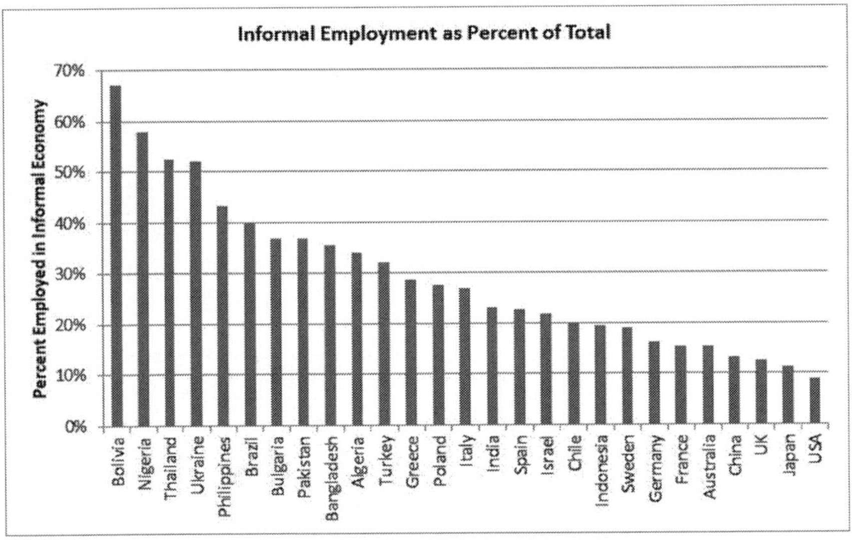

Everyone has a hustle, but no one has access to capital, nor rights to property, nor security from the arbitrary intrusion of the authorities. Men work seasonal construction jobs for cash payments, and women find things to sell. No one pays taxes; there is no way to collect them, and "informal" workers couldn't afford them in any case. In turn, governments provide paltry services and accumulate debts. An inbred elite milks the state budget and manages monopolies.

China is the first emerging country to fully integrate the informal economy into the formal economy, and it has done so through smartphones and electronic payments. China is on the way to becoming a "cashless society," in which virtually all transactions are electronic and therefore transparent to the tax authorities.[69] Turkey, which has the same rate of smartphone penetration as China, plans to become a cashless society by 2023.[70]

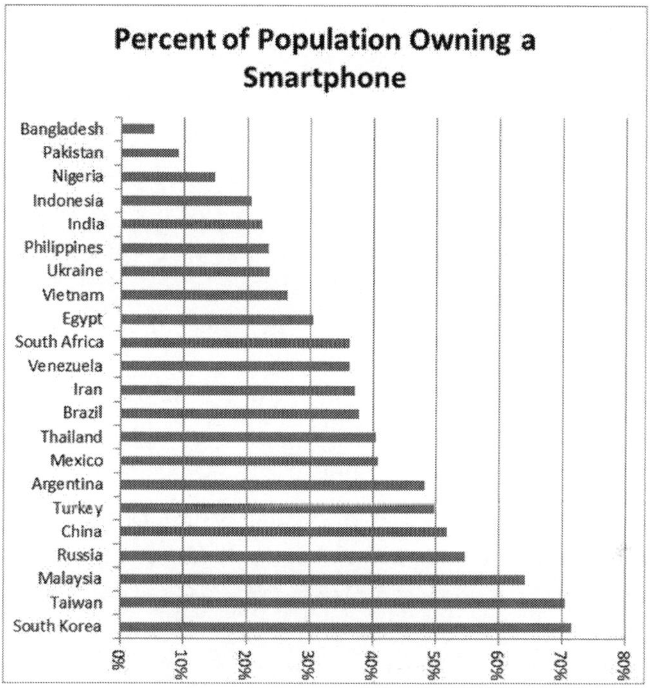

China is also investing aggressively to stay ahead of the technology curve. By 2025, IBS estimates there will be 655 million smartphones operating on the new 5G standard, with an order of magnitude greater download speed than existing smartphones. The impact of extremely fast mobile broadband on a variety of industries will be earth-shaking. Of these 655 million 5G phones, IBS adds, 431 million will be manufactured by Chinese companies. "In addition to the 5G smartphone market, China will be the leader in establishing 5G communications infrastructure. There is the potential for over two million 5G base stations in China in 2022," IBS adds.

Empire Is Infrastructure: The Belt and Road Initiative

China will spend over US$1.3 trillion during the next eight years[71] to connect the Eurasian continent through a network of railroads, broadband, energy pipelines, and ports through the overland Silk Road Economic Belt and the Maritime Silk Road. The scale of the project leaves Western analysts stumped for superlatives. "China's overall ambition for the BRI is staggering," declares a 2019 Council on Relations Briefing. "To date, more than sixty countries—accounting for two-thirds of the world's population—have signed on to projects or indicated an interest in doing so. Analysts estimate the largest so far to be the $68 billion China-Pakistan Economic Corridor, a collection of projects connecting China to Pakistan's Gwadar Port on the Arabian Sea. In total, China has already spent an estimated $200 billion on such efforts."[72]

China has turned its imperial principle outwards to the world, and its object is to bring all of Eurasia into its economic sphere. That is what China's founding emperors did to bring disparate peoples speaking hundreds of different languages into the Chinese Empire. For the first time in its history, China has the confidence and the resources to extend its reach to the whole of the Eurasian landmass. In scope of ambition, it is the grandest imperial project in human history. Some analysts are bullish. "This massive uptick in investment and construction activity bodes well for Chinese companies and countries with an economic link to the China. Long term, the initiative could accelerate China's transformation into a high-income economy and cement the country's position as a global economic power," Morgan Stanley analysts argued, in a 2018 report.[73]

Xi Jinping announced the grand design in 2013, but in a larger sense, the project began in the 5th century B.C.E., when the warring State of Wu struck northward at the State of Qi. King Fuchai of Wu ordered construction of a canal for military and trading purposes. In 486 B.C.E., ground was broken for the Han Conduit, which would link the Yangtze and Huai Rivers. An earlier canal, the Hong Gou, linked the Yellow River to the Bian and Si rivers; some Chinese chroniclers date the Hong Gou to the Wu the Great, the legendary founder of the Xia dynasty, five thousand years ago. The Sui Dynasty (581-618 C.E.) extended this into a Grand Canal stretching almost twelve hundred miles from Beijing in the north to Hangzhou (near Shanghai), connecting China's two great waterways, the Yellow and Yangtze Rivers. It is both the oldest and the longest man-made waterway in the world.

Infrastructure is China's backbone. The great riparian projects that begin in legendary prehistory with Wu the Great, five thousand years ago, and transformed central and Western China under China's founding Qin Dynasty in the 3rd century B.C.E., provided flood control, irrigation, commercial transport and imperial communications, including the rapid movement of soldiers and supplies. As I explained in chapter one ("An Empire of Emperors"), China's imperial system regenerated itself no matter how many dynasties fell, despite long periods of foreign invasion and civil chaos, because the strong bones of the imperial system remained intact. No matter how often the Chinese empire fell, the Chinese had no choice but to re-create it. Together, the Yellow and Yangtze Rivers stretch for more than nine thousand miles, not including their major tributaries, and nothing but a unified state can turn their often-destructive power into life-giving irrigation. The strong centralized state levied taxes and conscripted labor, but in return tamed rivers and brought water to dry plains, and made life possible for the world's largest farming population.

Nature has had a great deal to do with the tragic cycle of Chinese history. China's riparian plains supported the largest population of any political entity in the history of the world, thanks to flood control and irrigation. But the best efforts of Chinese hydraulic engineers were not sufficient to prevent devastating floods at frequent but irregular intervals, as well as famines due to drought. As I noted, a major famine occurred in some part of China on average of once a year during the past two millennia. The consequences of flood and famine were horrendous; the large populations supported by improved land declined sharply, whole provinces became depopulated, and local warlords as well as barbarian invaders exploited the resulting weakness wrest control of the empire. The Mongols under Kublai Khan did so in 1271, and the Manchus did so four centuries later. China's rulers presided over an empire where loss of life on a catastrophic scale was commonplace, and regarded as a mere overhead cost of management. As I observed in chapter one, this was true of Chiang Kai-Shek as well as Mao Zedong. The cruelty of Chinese governance astonishes and disgusts Westerners who do not know Chinese history.

There's a world of difference, though, between a real empire, where the central government can give orders and make sure they are followed, and a virtual empire, in which China depends on less-than-stable, and often less-than-honest, governments to see infrastructure projects through. While China's infrastructure at home has mostly proven successful, its track record in the Belt and Road Initiative is less impressive. For one thing, China mixes strategic and foreign policy objectives with economic goals, often to the detriment of the latter. For another, China's diplomats and business leaders have little experience in overseas investment, and stumble over local political obstacles.

Meanwhile, US officials have denounced the Belt and Road Initiative as a gigantic debt trap. Secretary of State Mike Pompeo inveighed against China, in a March 2019 address:

> By blocking development in the South China Sea through coercive means, China prevents ASEAN members from accessing more than $2.5 trillion in recoverable energy reserves. To contrast, the United States Government promotes energy security for those Southeast Asian nations. We want countries in the region to have access to their own energy. We want to help them. We want to create partnerships. We want transparent transactions, not debt traps. We explore responsibly.
>
> China doesn't play by that same set of rules. Its values are simply different. You see that in places as diverse as Africa, where they often ship in their own labor, creating jobs for Chinese workers rather than for those in the local economy. It's using the debt trap which I referred to just a moment ago to put these countries in a place where it isn't a commercial trans-

> action, it's a political transaction designed to bring harm and political influence in the country in which they're operating.
>
> Many of you may not know this: China's largest creditor today—excuse me, Latin America's largest creditor today is China.[74]

After Italy became the first Group of Eight nation to sign on to the BRI Initiative in March 2019, Secretary Pompeo said, "It's disappointing any time any country begins to engage in behavior and commercial interactions with China that aren't straight up. We're saddened because we think the people of those countries ultimately lose."[75]

China botches the Belt and Road in many cases.

China's economic diplomacy has been clumsy. Thailand is a case in point. In 2014, an adviser to Thailand's then Prime Minister Yingluck Shinawatra approached Reorient Group, my employer at the time, with a plan to transform Thailand's economy into a truck farm for the Chinese market. I visited Bangkok with colleagues to work out some of the commercial implications. Yingluck had succeeded her brother Thaksin as head of the farm-based Pheu Thai Party. Thailand's farmers depended on a government rice subsidy which strained the country's finances. The construction of a high-speed rail line over the eight hundred miles from Bangkok to the southern Chinese city of Kunming in Yunnan province would make it possible to ship fresh produce directly to the Chinese market, where demand for high-quality fruits and vegetables is insatiable—and Thailand's offerings are among the best in the world. Pheu Thai hoped to raise the living standards of Thai farmers without repeating the wrenching experience of mass urbanization, which the Thais feared would erode their culture. Thailand has been an American ally since the Vietnam War, the adviser noted, but business is business.

The benefits for China seemed obvious. Southeast Asia has the world's richest agriculture, with three growing seasons, and produces high-quality products that upwardly mobile Chinese want to buy. "The Chinese think their food is poison!" Yingluck's adviser laughed. "The rice is full of cadmium, so they will pay double to buy Thai rice for their little princeling."

Politically, China stood to peel off a longstanding American ally and make it dependent on the Chinese market. China's Premier Li Keqiang had visited Thailand in 2013, and offered a loan package that could be repaid with agricultural products, and Yungling's government tried to push financing through the legislature.

Thailand and China just might sign an agreement to build section of the railway linking Bangkok with its northern border, in early 2020. Thailand and China have been dickering over terms for the past five years, and Thai political parties have been fighting over how to finance it. The military removed Yungling from office in May 2014, and the project languished. Thai sources claim that the Chinese made rapacious demands, including extensive land use rights along the route. That rankled the Thais, for whom real estate is the main currency of political patronage. Greedy Chinese jousted with greedy Thais, and the project was left to languish for five years.

Ultimately, China will build a high-speed rail all the way from Kunming City to Singapore, linking Vietnam, Myanmar, Thailand, Malaysia, and Laos. That will bring about two hundred fifty million Southeast Asians into China's economic sphere. As I noted in chapter three ("World Domination, One Country At a Time"), China's labor force stopped growing in the late 2010s. Chinese manufacturers have moved production to countries where labor is still plentiful and cheaper than at home, and will continue to do so as China's labor force declines.

Pakistan, the largest single destination for Belt and Road investment, has become an economic quagmire for Beijing. Only 39 percent of Pakistani primary school students go on to secondary school, according to the World Bank, compared to 75 percent to 85 percent in Southeast Asia, and 62 percent in India. Pakistan reports a literary rate of only 58 percent, one of the world's lowest. China prefers to keep it that way. Over drinks at a Beijing Hotel, I asked a senior adviser to China's Foreign Ministry whether China worried about Pakistan's nuclear weapons.

"Pakistan doesn't have nuclear weapons," said my Chinese interlocutor, whose business card identified him as a South Asia expert at a foreign ministry think tank.

"Everybody knows that Pakistan has nuclear weapons," I protested.

"Pakistan doesn't have nuclear weapons. The Pakistani Army has nuclear weapons. And we have the Pakistani Army," the Chinese expert said, triumphantly. "Pakistan is simple," he continued. "Do not modernize! Keep them barefoot! Keep them illiterate! Make sure the Army Chief of Staff is the biggest landlord."

Pakistan is a perpetual enemy of India, and India is China's only prospective strategic rival in Asia. Pakistan first tested a group of nuclear devices in 1998. US Intelligence was caught flat-footed. Classified State Department reports to Congress subsequently released under the Freedom of Information Act had certified that China was abiding by its commitments under the Nuclear Non-Proliferation Treaty.[76]

Pakistan's nuclear weapons as well as its conventional forces command the undivided attention of India's military. That keeps India cautious about military collaboration with other prospective adversaries of China. India and Japan are set to become "quasi-allies" as they bolster security ties in the face of China's rising military capabilities. China fears an Indian-Japanese alliance. Japan has formidable technological capacity, and could probably produce a deliverable nuclear weapon in less than a year if it so chose. In November 2019, Japan and India began to negotiate a military exchange that would make them "quasi-allies," according to Nikkei Asian Review. "The new move will extend existing Japanese policy—in coordination with the U.S.—of checking China's military expansion, specifically calling for a 'free and open Indo-Pacific,' as well as maintaining maritime order based on the rule of law."[77]

The unretouched cynicism with which China regards its principle Asian ally is jarring to Western ears. But China and Pakistan have been collaborating on nuclear weapons for decades. Chinese support for Pakistan's nuclear weapons program began in the 1970s. In 1982, then Pakistan President Zia al-Haq "sent his military aide, Lieutenant-General Syed Ali Zamin Naqvi, to request weapons grade fissile material and the bomb design from China, in an effort to speed Pakistan's efforts along. Deng Xiaoping agreed," according to a book by Andrew

Small.[78] Chinese bomb designs made their way from Pakistan to any number of aspiring nuclear states. When Libya turned over the plans for a nuclear weapons program to American and British disarmament experts in 1982, the package included a sheaf of documents in Chinese.

In September 2018, Pakistan's Commerce Minister Abdul Razak Dawood suggested a one-year moratorium on new projects in the Pakistani leg of the Economic Belt, the China-Pakistan Economic Corridor. The head of Pakistan's army, General Qamar Javed Bajwa, repaired to Beijing, and top Chinese officials assured him that military cooperation was the "backbone" of China-Pakistan relations.[79]

Belt and Road has been a disappointment for Pakistan. In April 2019, Saeed Shah reported, for *The Wall Street Journal*:

> The Pakistani effort to revamp what is known as the China Pakistan Economic Corridor, a showcase for China's seventy-nation world-wide infrastructure building spree, isn't the success story Chinese leaders would like heading into its big Belt and Road Forum this month in Beijing. The program helped China largely displace the U.S. as a key partner for Pakistan.
>
> Pakistan isn't the only country that has failed to turn massive lending and construction by Chinese state companies into self-sustaining economic momentum—or that is pushing back against China. While the Chinese leadership got a big boost recently when Italy became the first European to officially sign on to Belt and Road, new governments have come to power in Malaysia, Sri Lanka, and the Maldives complaining about debt levels and secrecy surrounding Chinese deals.
>
> In Pakistan, where the powerful army has overseen the decades-long strategic relationship with China, public criticism from the government has been muted. But new Prime Minister Imran Khan was critical of many of the projects his predecessor Nawaz Sharif initiated with China in the four-year-old program.
>
> Mr. Khan's government has quietly put on hold many of the remaining $62 billion of CPEC proj-

> ects—so far, $19 billion of roads, power plants and port development were started or completed, Beijing said.[80]

Pakistan will have to pay China some $40 billion over the next twenty years for projects already in progress, Mr. Shah reported. China and Pakistan targeted a total of $62 billion in investments for the China-Pakistan Economic Corridor, of which $19 billion has been committed. Pakistan's government has quietly postponed the rest of the projects.

Military concerns also motivate China's Belt and Road diplomacy in Central Asia. Late in 2019, James Dorsey of the Begin-Sadat Center at Bar-Illan University wrote that there are security issues with China's takeover of state assets in neighboring Tajikistan and its construction of a road along the Chinese border in adjacent Afghanistan. China wants to be able to move soldiers to the border of Xinjiang province, home to twelve million Muslim Uyghurs. Dorsey wrote:

> The pending Chinese acquisition of a stake in Tajikistan's aluminum smelter, coupled with earlier tax concessions to Chinese companies that would substantially reduce the trickle-down effect of investments for the troubled Tajik economy, suggest that China has yet to fully take into account frequent criticism of its commercial approach to Belt and Road-related projects. Desperate for cash, Tajikistan is about to sell yet another vital asset to China at a time when countries like Sri Lanka and the Maldives are demanding renegotiation of debt settlements that either forced them to surrender control of critical infrastructure, or left them with unsustainable repayments...progress on the construction of a road in Afghanistan's Wakhan Corridor, a narrow strip in the east of the country that touches the Chinese border and separates Tajikistan from Pakistan and Pakistan-controlled Kashmir, may explain China's seeming insensitivity to the concerns of beneficiaries of the People's Republic's largesse.

> The road would link the corridor to Central Asia in the north and Pakistan's Chinese-built Arabian Sea port of Gwadar in the south, a crown jewel in China's infrastructure and energy-driven Belt and Road Initiative. For China, the stakes are geopolitical and economic. The road would not only facilitate commerce with Central Asia as well as traffic from Gwadar, but also construction of shorter pipelines as well as a fiber optic cable.
>
> Perhaps more importantly, it would, together with a military base in Tajikistan and Chinese cross-border operations in the corridor itself, facilitate the movement of troops in China's gradual projection of military power beyond its borders, particularly in regions adjacent to its troubled northwestern province of Xinjiang.[81]

Malaysia, Sri Lanka, and the Maldives, major beneficiaries of BRI financing, are pushing back aggressively against China's seizure of national assets in response to non-payment of loans. In June 2019, Malaysia obtained a one-third reduction in the price of a 640-kilometer rail line along its East Coast, to be constructed by China Communications Construction Co. Prime Minister Mahathir Mohammed, who returned to office in a surprise 2018 election victory, and had campaigned against "unfair" terms for BRI projects negotiated by his predecessor.[82]

Meanwhile, in December 2019, Sri Lanka demanded that China return ownership of its Hambantota Port, forfeited to China two years ago after the country fell behind in debt payments. "The port, located at the heart of a busy shipping route in southern Sri Lanka, has been held up by critics as a symbol of the worst aspects of China's 'debt trap diplomacy,' with many locals regarding it as a sign of subordination to Beijing," the *South China Morning Post* reported.[83]

Twenty-three countries receiving Belt and Road financing are at risk of financial distress, according to a 2018 report by a Washington think tank, and eight are at acute risk. According to the Center for Global Development's study, "Some public reporting has expressed alarm about the implications of BRI for debt sustainability. The primary concern is that an $8 trillion-dollar initiative will leave countries with debt "overhangs" that will impede sound public investment and economic growth more generally. There is also concern that debt problems will create an unfavorable degree of dependency on China as a creditor.[84]

Belt and Road is Still the Only Game in Town

There is a great deal to deplore in China's Belt and Road Initiative. The trouble is that it is the only game in town. In a 2017 article for the Journal of American Affairs, I argued:

> ...the United States should compete head to head with China for predominance in the communications and information revolution now underway in the developing world, especially with countries that look with dismay at the growth of Chinese power—for example, India, now the world's most populous country. China's One Belt, One Road program does not guarantee its success in high-tech trade. There are some sectors in which it may be in our interest to cooperate with China, but many others in which competing institutions, for example the Asian Development Bank, can offer effective competition to Chinese influence. The United States and Japan are natural partners for this kind of enterprise. With a rapidly aging population and net foreign assets of $3.12 trillion as of the end of 2016, Japan needs high-return investment opportunities.[85]

With $350 billion in net foreign assets and extensive investments in Southeast Asia, South Korea could also play a major role in building regional infrastructure.

The United States and its allies have cobbled together some financing vehicles out of existing institutions as an alternative to BRI, but their efforts to date are miniscule compared to the Chinese design. In 2019, the US proposed to create a "robust alternative" to BRI through its Overseas Private Investment Corporation (OPIC). But as Jason Thomas noted, in The Asean Post, "OPIC's US $20 billion portfolio is dwarfed by the BRI's with an estimated US $1 trillion in value, the majority coming from China's state-owned Development Bank."[86]

China's advantage extends beyond the size of its purse. It has the experience of transforming a large economy from the grass roots upwards, and turning an impoverished rural population into a prosperous urban population. The tools of transformation—communications, information, and infrastructure—are in the hands of Chinese companies. Huawei dominates the construction of broadband networks in the developing world, and China's rail construction companies are the best and most cost-efficient in the world as well. Despite China's many missteps and distractions, it has a leading position in global infrastructure construction that is hard to challenge—hard, but not impossible. For the time being, China can get away with a lot of mistakes, because the United States and its allies offer no real competition.

CHAPTER FOUR

AMERICA'S LOSING TECH WAR WITH CHINA: THE BIGGEST STRATEGIC DISASTER IN US HISTORY

Former House Speaker Newt Gingrich told me late in 2019, that America's failure to take the lead in Fifth Generation (5G) mobile broadband was "the biggest strategic disaster in US history." The Republican elder statesman isn't exaggerating. During 2018 and 2019, the Trump Administration identified China as a long-term threat to American economic leadership. It introduced tariffs on Chinese imports to the United States and blocked exports of high-tech components to Chinese economies. The tariffs barely made a dent in China's economy. And the tech boycott spurred China to develop homegrown substitutes and align its supply chain with other Asian countries. The US cajoled and threatened its allies to stop them from using Huawei's state-of-the-art technology to roll out their own 5G broadband networks. With few exceptions, America's allies ignored the threats. Meanwhile, America's own 5G rollout lags China's by years.

Shortly after he stepped down as National Security Adviser in September 2019, John Bolton told me, "The Chinese were way ahead of us before we figured out what was going on. Now we're trying to catch up." Both parts of Bolton's statement are incorrect. The US government doesn't appear to understand what China is planning, and the US is falling further behind rather than catching up. China's campaign for world technological leadership is so ambitious that we still don't get it. We're playing power checkers and China is playing Go—an ancient board game of slow and inexorable encirclement, whose objective is to choke off the opponent's ability to move.

A year after the United States threw everything it had into a campaign to prevent Huawei from dominating the global market for 5G mobile broadband systems, China has widened its lead in this game-changing technology.

- China is outspending the US on 5G infrastructure three times over, according to Deloitte. Twenty-one European countries have ordered Huawei's 5G equipment, including Britain, France, Germany, Italy, Spain, Switzerland, Ireland, the Netherlands, Finland, Greece, Austria, Romania, Hungary, Turkey, Sweden and Russia.[87] It is still possible that a few of them will back out under American pressure, but the vast majority of the Eurasian continent will work with Huawei.
- Huawei's Chief Technology Officer Paul Scanlan says that his company has signed up fifty major telecom providers around the world to roll out 5G mobile broadband.
- Huawei's top-of-the-line smartphone, the Mate 30, unveiled in September 2019, contains zero US components, according to a breakdown by Union Bank of Switzerland and Japan's Fomalhaut Techno Solutions.[88] Huawei used to buy $11 billion worth of US components a year. After sustained American efforts to shut it down, the Chinese national champion has shifted to home-produced items and foreign components.
- Huawei is also producing 5G base stations, the core building-block of 5G broadband networks, without US components. Huawei will ship six hundred thousand 5G base stations in 2019 and 1.5 million in 2020, according to its founder, Ren Zhengfei.[89]
- Not only has Huawei locked up most of the world's telecom providers as customers, but it has replaced American suppliers with Asian competitors. Nikkei Asian Review reports, "All across Asia, companies in the computer chip industry were receiving similar messages from Huawei: Boost your

production, and we will buy your product. In a slowing global market, Huawei made a commitment that was impossible to resist: The company guaranteed up to 80 percent utilization rates for the next two years to potential and current suppliers."[90]

- Huawei now sells some of the world's fastest chips for smartphones and artificial intelligence processors. That puts it in direct competition with American chipmakers like Nvidia and Qualcomm. The company says it has no plans to do so, but Huawei could launch a price war for high-end computer chips and drive American brands out of the Asian market.

In August 2019, the news site Huawei Central reported:

> Ren Zhengfei, founder and CEO of Huawei, recently sat down in an interview with Sky News and revealed that the company plans to sell more than two million 5G base stations over the next two years, despite US ban.
>
> Back in June, during MWC Shanghai 2019. Huawei announced that it has so far gained fifty 5G commercial contracts and shipped more than 150,000 base stations. Moreover, it's looking to over five hundred thousand bases stations by this year.
>
> "In August and September, we will undergo a run-in period before we can mass produce these new versions. So, we can only produce around five thousand base stations each month during that period. Following that, we will be able to produce six hundred thousand 5G base stations this year and at least 1.5 million next year. That means we don't need to rely on US companies for our survival in this area."

American diplomacy never has suffered such a comprehensive, resounding, and humiliating defeat. Starting in November 2018, the Trump Administration "initiated an extraordinary outreach campaign to foreign allies, trying to persuade wireless and internet providers in these countries to avoid telecommunications equipment from China's Huawei Technologies Co.," as *The Wall Street Journal* reported, at the time. "The international effort extends the battle lines of a U.S. campaign to keep Huawei electronics out of the U.S. Some officials see the initiative as part of a broader technological Cold War between U.S.-led allies and China for control of a world that is increasingly digitally connected—and thus increasingly vulnerable to surveillance and malfeasance. They fear the rise of technological giants that could benefit authoritarian governments, including irritants or outright foes of the U.S. American officials have briefed their government counterparts and telecom executives in friendly countries where Huawei equipment is already in wide use, including Germany, Italy and Japan, about what they see as cybersecurity risks."[91]

At the end of January 2020, the US, in effect, conceded defeat in its long battle to suppress Huawei. The Defense Department reportedly vetoed a proposal from the Commerce Department that would have hindered Huawei's efforts to source components outside the United States, by banning sales to Huawei of any items containing more than 10 percent American content. According to *The Wall Street Journal*, the Pentagon feared that the impact on US technology companies would be severe enough to cut into research and development budgets, and leave the United States at a disadvantage.[92] As I reported in chapter two, Chinese analysts predicted that top US chip producers such as Nvidia and Qualcomm would run out of cash in eighteen to twenty-four months, in a price war with Huawei. Apparently the Pentagon had crunched the same numbers and come to a similar conclusion. On February 4, 2020, presidential economic adviser Larry Kudlow explained the Defense Department's objections to the trade hawks at the Commerce Department. "We don't want to put our great companies out of business; the president is a strong believer in that. But on the other hand, we are very aware that Huawei is a threat to our national security."[93]

In another defeat for American diplomacy, the United Kingdom and the European Union both rebuffed American demands to exclude Huawei from the buildout of their 5G broadband networks, and ignored American threats to withhold intelligence sharing if they failed to comply. The dust has not settled on this dispute, but it seems most likely that the British and the Europeans have called an American bluff. As I explain later in this chapter, the biggest risk to US Intelligence is not that China will steal its secrets, but rather that the embedding of quantum cryptography in the new 5G networks will deny access to electronic communications to America's intelligence agencies.

Huawei and the Chinese-American Intelligence War

America's spy agencies warn that Huawei might steal customer data transmitted through its telecom equipment. On February 14, 2018, the Senate Intelligence Committee heard testimony from the heads of the CIA, National Security Agency, and FBI, as well as the Director of National Intelligence. FBI chief Chris Wray said, "We're deeply concerned about the risks of allowing any company or entity that is beholden to foreign governments that don't share our values to gain positions of power inside our telecommunications networks....That provides the capacity to exert pressure or control over our telecommunications infrastructure. It provides the capacity to maliciously modify or steal information. And it provides the capacity to conduct undetected espionage."[94]

On May 28, 2018, Secretary of State Michael Pompeo told Fox News:

> Huawei is an instrument of the Chinese Government. They are deeply connected. It's something that's hard for Americans to understand. We would—our companies cooperate with the United States Government; that is, they comply with our laws; but no president directs an American private company. That's very different in China. They just simply operate under a different set of rules. That's the most fundamental thing I think people need to try and get their head around. If it's the case that the Chinese Communist Party wanted to get information from technology that was in the possession of Huawei, it is almost certainly the case that Huawei would provide that to them. That deep connectivity exists inside the way their political economy operates. That's very

> different than the United States. That's the threat that President Trump sees from Huawei.[95]

During a May 2010 visit to London, Secretary Pompeo cautioned the United Kingdom to keep Huawei out of its networks—on pain of losing access to sensitive American Intelligence. Pompeo declared, "China steals intellectual property for military purposes. It wants to dominate A.I., space technology, ballistic missiles, and many other areas....Why would anyone grant such power to a regime that has already grossly violated cyberspace? What can Her Majesty's government do to make sure sensitive technologies don't become open doors for Beijing's spymasters? Insufficient security will impede the United States' ability to share certain information within trusted networks. This is just what China wants—to divide western alliances."[96]

U.S. officials have good reason to worry about Chinese government hacking of telecommunications networks provided by Chinese companies. In 2017, Wikileaks[97] revealed that the U.S. National Security Agency had planted hacking tools in communications hardware built by Cisco, then the top provider of internet routers and related equipment.[8] National Security Agency consultant Edward Snowden revealed meanwhile that the NSA had collected hundreds of millions of phone records of US citizens. In June 2019, the American Civil Liberties Union obtained and published documents showing that the NSA continued to improperly collect millions of American phone records,[98] even after it was compelled to destroy earlier records.[99]

---

8 "The Wikileaks documents described how the Central Intelligence Agency had learned more than a year ago how to exploit flaws in Cisco's widely used Internet switches, which direct electronic traffic, to enable eavesdropping.

"Senior Cisco managers immediately reassigned staff from other projects to figure out how the CIA hacking tricks worked, so they could help customers patch their systems and prevent criminal hackers or spies from using the same methods, three employees told Reuters on condition of anonymity.

"The Cisco engineers worked around the clock for days to analyze the means of attack, create fixes, and craft a stopgap warning about a security risk affecting more than 300 different products, said the employees, who had direct knowledge of the effort.

"That a major U.S. company had to rely on WikiLeaks to learn about security problems well-known to U.S. intelligence agencies underscores concerns expressed by dozens of current and former U.S. intelligence and security officials about the government's approach to cybersecurity."

American Intelligence officials had every reason to believe that Huawei would exploit its control of 5G broadband to tap data for China's intelligence agencies. After all, if America's spy agencies ignored the law and collected hundreds of millions of illicit records from American citizens, all the more so would China—which has no legal constraints against spying on foreigners—use whatever advantage it might have to spy on Americans.

In a May 2019 visit to London, Secretary of State Mike Pompeo threatened the United Kingdom—America's oldest and most trusted ally—with a cutoff of intelligence sharing if it used Huawei equipment. "We don't believe you can have those technologies in your systems and still have a trusted network," Pompeo told Britain's Sky News. "The United States, for its part, will only participate in trusted networks. We will only share America's information with those networks that we are confident aren't under the control of China or China's government."[100]

In December 2019, US National Security Adviser Robert O'Brien repeated the threat. "[Huawei is] just going to steal wholesale state secrets, whether they are the UK's nuclear secrets or secrets from MI6 or MI5,' O'Brien said, in a newspaper interview. He added, "It is somewhat shocking to us that folks in the UK would look at Huawei as some sort of a commercial decision. 5G is a national security decision."[101]

How to Hack Microchips

The threat to US Intelligence is graver than American officials are willing to admit. The next generation of mobile broadband will incorporate cybersecurity so foolproof that American cyberspooks won't be able to tap into the world's communications, as they have for decades. America's threats to cut off intelligence sharing ring hollow, because when the dust settles, the United States will have a lot less intelligence to share. As I explain in chapter five, encryption is only part of the problem. Even if data itself is protected by un-hackable cryptography, "backdoors" hidden among the billions of transistors in a computer chip could be used by a bad actor to sabotage critical infrastructure.

The National Security Agency and its British counterpart, the Government Communications Headquarters, haven't found evidence that Huawei systems steal data. Absence of evidence, though, isn't evidence of absence. US researchers have shown that it's possible to build nearly undetectable "backdoors" into chips that allow transmission of data, or the takeover of tainted systems by hostile actors. A team at the University of Michigan built such a booby-trapped device for a security symposium of the Institute of Electrical and Electronics Engineers (IEEE) in 2016. Andy Greenberg explained, in wired.com:

> Security flaws in software can be tough to find. Purposefully planted ones—hidden backdoors created by spies or saboteurs—are often even stealthier. Now imagine a backdoor planted not in an application, or deep in an operating system, but even deeper, in the hardware of the processor that runs a computer. And now imagine that silicon backdoor is invisible not only to the computer's software, but even to the chip's designer, who has no idea that it was added by the chip's manufacturer, likely in some far-flung Chinese factory. And that it's a single component hidden among hundreds of millions or billions. And that each one of those components is less than a thousandth of the width of a human hair.
>
> In fact, researchers at the University of Michigan haven't just imagined that computer security nightmare; they've built and proved it works. In a study that won the Best Paper Award at last week's IEEE Symposium on Privacy and Security, they detailed the creation of an insidious, microscopic hardware backdoor proof-of-concept. And they showed that by running a series of seemingly innocuous commands on their minutely sabotaged processor, a hacker could reliably trigger a feature of the chip that gives them full access to the operating system. Most disturbingly, they write, that microscopic hardware backdoor wouldn't be caught by practically any modern method of hardware security analysis, and could be planted by a single employee of a chip factory.[102]

The head of chip engineering for a large South Korean foundry told me, "I could put a backdoor anywhere in a chip with billions of transistors, and no one would ever find it." It wouldn't be like looking for a needle in a haystack. Think of looking for a needle in all the haystacks in the world.

The University of Michigan demonstration has two big implications for American policy. First, a hostile actor—for example, China—could put minute and practically undetectable "backdoors" into hardware sold to the West, including America's military, which uses foreign-made computer chips. Second, excluding Huawei from Western 5G networks in favor of competitors like Ericsson and Nokia won't ensure secure networks, *because Ericsson and Nokia buy the same components from Chinese manufacturers.*

The security threat isn't hypothetical. In 2017, Dan Nidess reported, in *The Wall Street Journal*:

> In 2011, microchips headed for U.S. Navy helicopters were found to carry defects that would have prevented them from firing missiles. Given that the chips came from China, there was a strong suspicion that the defect was the result of deliberate tampering. Sabotaging an adversary's military equipment has a long and colorful history, and it would fit squarely in China's strategy of asymmetrically undermining America's conventional military superiority.
>
> After an investigation, the Navy concluded the defect was an unintentional flaw. This only raised additional concerns about the quality of critical electronics produced in China. Counterfeit Chinese chips have become a rampant problem affecting America's military, the Intelligence Community, and the Missile Defense Agency. Long and obscure supply chains make it almost impossible to verify the reliability and source for weapons-grade microchips.[103]

The Pentagon buys computer chips from foreign suppliers not because it is stupid, but because most chip production left the United States long ago. America has only a few fabrication plants left onshore, and ships only about 10 percent of the world's semiconductors, down from 25 percent in 2014. Massive investments in chip fabrication plans would be required to reverse the decline. Duplicating chip fabricators in the United States to supply a small fraction of total chip demand, namely military use, will be expensive. The price tag would run into the scores of billions. Taiwan Semiconductor's latest chip foundry will cost upwards of $20 billion, and the United States would need several foundries to free itself from dependence on Asian suppliers. But there isn't any other way to guarantee the security of American military systems.

All the 5G Hardware Providers, Including Huawei's Competitors, Use Chinese Hardware

For the same reason, dependence on Chinese components makes Ericsson and Nokia just as insecure as Huawei. All three firms use the same manufacturing firms in China, according to industry sources. Whether a 5G base station carries a Huawei or Ericsson label doesn't matter. The University of Michigan researchers showed that the vulnerability is built into the miniscule innards of the chip itself, and could be planted by a single employee at a chip factory, without the knowledge of the chip's designer.

If China's Ministry of State Security wants to hide "backdoors" in components, it can hide them under an Ericsson or Nokia label just as easily as under a Huawei label. Huawei's competitors are no more secure than Huawei. The biggest risk isn't large-scale data theft. If you steal data, you have to transmit it, and transmissions of large amounts of data are detectable. Data itself can be encrypted in ways that defeat any possible code-breaking. But a backdoor hidden inside a chip in a communications system could be exploited to sabotage the system during a crisis.

Not until June 2019, seven months after US officials began a global campaign to blacklist Huawei, did it occur to the Trump Administration that Huawei's competitors used the same Chinese components as Huawei. "US officials are asking telecom-equipment manufacturers whether they can make and develop US-bound hardware, which includes cellular-tower electronics as well as routers and switches, and software outside of China," *The Wall Street Journal* reported, on June 23rd. "The conversations are in early and informal stages."

The Journal added, "The proposals could force the biggest companies that sell equipment to U.S. wireless carriers, Finland's Nokia Corp. and Sweden's Ericsson, to move major operations out of China to service the U.S., which is the biggest market in the $250 billion-a-year global industry for telecom equipment and related services and infrastructure. There is no major U.S. manufacturer of cellular equipment. U.S. officials have long worried that Beijing could order Chinese engineers to insert security holes into technology made in China. They worry those security holes could be exploited for spying, or to remotely control or disable devices." [104]

Meanwhile, Ericsson and Nokia began to consider plans to remove their supply chains from China. In June 2019, Anna Isaac broke the story, in the *Telegraph*:

> Nokia and Ericsson, two of Europe's biggest technology titans, are weighing drastic changes to their corporate structures, including setting up separate units in the Eastern and Western Hemispheres, in a bid to protect themselves against the escalating global trade war. Both companies, which make equipment used to run 5G networks, have started drawing up emergency plans to move some of their most sensitive operations out of China and split up their supply chains to counter increasing national security concerns, sources have told The Sunday Telegraph.
>
> European firms are concerned that it will become increasingly difficult to sell Chinese-made parts and software in the EU and the US, according to industry and government sources. Likewise, components made in the US or Europe could face more barriers from Beijing. The companies are currently discussing different options. Nokia is considering setting up an EU-only operation for its 5G supply chain so that there can be no question of interference or security breaches resulting from its Chinese activities.[105]

Nokia and Ericsson haven't said how long it might take to move their supply chain out of China or how much it might cost. Huawei generally sells equipment at 40 percent less than Ericsson and Nokia, who use the same Chinese-made specialized chips but charge more for the overall package. Building secure fabrication plants outside of China would take several years and raise the overall cost of the networks drastically.

The trouble is that the Scandinavian companies have increased their dependence on Chinese components during the last several years. Ericsson is in no hurry to leave China. In September 2019, three months after the US government raised questions about the Swedish firm's dependence on Chinese hardware, Ericsson boasted of an upgrade in its main Chinese factory. A company press release declared, "September 2019 marks a major milestone in Ericsson's smart manufacturing capabilities as a SEK 500 million transformation of the company's existing factory in Nanjing, China, reaches its conclusion. The resulting automated factory stands among the most advanced manufacturing facilities in the industry. Ericsson produces 5G and 4G radio technology products at the factory, most of which support communication service providers in the Chinese market to increase network capacity, rollout 5G, and make Industry 4.0 a reality. The eighteen-month upgrade has seen Ericsson modernize every step of the production process in Nanjing, in preparation for the introduction and rapid deployments of 5G in China. This includes the first modular-designed automatic assembly line for 5G radios, which will enable Ericsson to produce the latest 5G radios in the capacity needed for the Chinese market."[106]

Washington hasn't told its allies whether it will cut off intelligence sharing if they install Nokia or Ericsson broadband equipment that contains Chinese components—as all network equipment does at present. The Trump Administration hasn't yet said what it wants, but the logic of its position is to require the West to wait several years to launch 5G broadband and to pay twice as much, by which time China will have an insuperable lead both in the communications technology and in new applications made possible by 5G.

Europe can't afford to wait that long. That is why the threats and remonstrations of America's top diplomats and national security officials got a collective raspberry from America's allies. Not only has the

United States fallen behind China, but our efforts to stop China from dominating broadband technology have pushed large parts of the world into China's camp. Most of the world now looks to China rather than America for technological leadership in critical areas.

Europe Looks to China for Technological Leadership

At stake for Europe is the future of its industrial competitiveness. France rejected Washington's demand to exclude Huawei in no uncertain terms. In November 2019, a French economics ministry official, Agnes Pannier-Runacher, announced, "We do not target one equipment maker. There is no exclusion. The government will not exclude anyone. We are not following the position of the United States."[107]

Industry sources told me that the French automaker Peugeot persuaded the government of President Emmanuel Macron to work with Huawei. In 2017, Peugeot and Huawei announced a global alliance. Peugeot's "Connected Vehicle Modular Platform" will be "deployed globally on top of Huawei's Cloud Family public cloud," Huawei announced.[108]

According to an industry source, "Peugeot went to the president [of France] and said, 'We make the engine, the drive train, and the chassis. Anyone can do that today. We don't have any special advantage. What will give us a competitive edge is electronics and connectivity, and for that, we need Huawei.'"

Huawei's advantage isn't just price and speed of construction of 5G networks for mobile broadband. We are well past that. Huawei's 2019 Shanghai Connect conference (as I report in chapter two) was a showcase for a whole range of disruptive new technologies, ranging from manufacturing to mining and medicine. This isn't the first time that the United States has faced competition that had the jump on us several times in game-changing technologies. In 1939, Japan still flew the world's best fighter plane, the Mitsubishi Zero. Nazi Germany invented the cruise missile (the V-1 "buzzbomb"), the long-range guided missile (the V-2), and the first operation jet warplane (the Messerschmidt Me 262, credited with nearly six hundred kills of Allied aircraft). Russia sent the first satellite into space with its 1957 Sputnik launch. Fortunately,

Hitler wasn't able to deploy the new weapons until 1944, when he already had lost the war. And fortunately for the United States, American forces sequestered the German rocket science team at Peenemunde and put their talents at the disposal of the United States. America's economy was so much larger than any of our adversaries that we could overwhelm the competition. We also had some of the competition's best scientists and engineers working for us. And we reacted to the competition quickly enough to claw back the top spot.

This time it's different. The US is at least two years behind China in developing and deploying 5G broadband technology. That's long enough for China's national champion, Huawei, to lock up the market across the whole of the Eurasian continent, despite America's best efforts to stop it. China's economy is bigger than ours, adjusting for actual prices of goods and services, and it is adding six times as many scientists and engineers as we do each year.

Trade War Versus Tech War

China and the United States are fighting a trade war and a tech war, with distinct agendas. President Trump wants more American exports and manufacturing jobs, and imposed tariffs on Chinese imports starting in July 2018, to force China to buy more US goods and to protect US manufacturers against Chinese competition. The tech war began after the US intelligence community claimed that China's market leader Huawei would use its telecommunications hardware to steal the world's data, and perhaps even sabotage critical economic functions. But the intelligence community has a bigger worry than the *possibility* that Huawei might use yet unspecified "backdoors" to siphon America or allied data out of broadband networks. It faces the *certainty* that Chinese domination of the next generation of global broadband will destroy the global eavesdropping capabilities that US signals intelligence (SIGINT) has built over decades at an annual cost of scores of billions of dollars (see chapter five). Whether China can steal the world's data is uncertain. But China is offering the world a revolutionary approach to data secrecy in the form of quantum cryptography, which will deny America's spooks access to the world's data.

A Trump Administration official who stepped down from a senior position at the National Security Council in 2019, told me that the Intelligence Community had hijacked President Trump's trade agenda in a desperate—and unsuccessful—effort to defend its turf against encroaching Chinese technology. The spooks persuaded Secretary of State Mike Pompeo, former National Security Advisor John Bolton and his successor Robert O'Brien to threaten America's allies with a suspension of intelligence sharing if they bought mobile broadband equipment from the Chinese company. With few exceptions, the allies pushed back. As we will see, the threat is less credible than it might have been in the past, because the United States will have a great deal less intelligence to share as the new 5G networks come on line.

President Trump campaigned on a promise to restore American jobs lost to foreign manufacturers, and to stop China from stealing American intellectual property. Eighteen months into his administration he made good on his threats. On July 6, 2018, the US placed a 25 percent tariff on 818 Chinese products for which Americans had paid $34 billion the previous year. Four days later, the US added a 10 percent tariff on a list of six thousand Chinese products with a 2017 import bill of $200 billion. China retaliated on August 3, 2018, with a 25 percent tariff on $16 billion of US imports, and announced additional tariffs on $60 billion worth of US goods in September.

Negotiations between the US and China began almost as soon as the trade war opened. President Trump's objective was to extract concessions from China, not to crush the Chinese economy. Nor did the president worry much about the technology issue. On the contrary, he intervened personally to work out a way to keep China's ZTE in business. Talks began at sub-ministerial level between the US and China in August 2018, and on September 12, 2018, presidential economic adviser Larry Kudlow told the press that the US had invited China to come to the negotiating table before the next round of tariffs of $200 billion of Chinese goods would take effect. In fact, talks were planned for late September, but China cancelled them on September 22, 2018.[109] US Treasury Secretary Steve Mnuchin and Chinese Vice Premier Liu He revived negotiations in a November 9, 2018, phone call.

When Presidents Trump and Xi sat down to dinner on December 2, 2018, at the Group of Twenty Summit in Buenos Aires, the stage was set for a resolution of the trade issues. The US and China agreed to a ninety-day truce in which neither side would impose new tariffs. China agreed to buy more US energy and agricultural products, and let it be known that it would pay for the construction of new liquefied natural gas terminals on the West Coast of the United States, with a $50 billion per year target for LNG imports. Two weeks later, China announced that it would rescind the 25 percent retaliatory tariff it had previously imposed on US auto imports, and would also resume imports of US soybeans.

But while Trump, Xi, and their principal trade negotiators talked in Buenos Aires, the Canadian government arrested Huawei's chief financial officer Meng Wanzhou, the daughter of Huawei's founder and chairman Ren Zhengfei. Economic advisor Larry Kudlow told the press the following week that Trump hadn't been informed of the impending arrest. A US official told Reuters that "it was a Justice Department matter and not orchestrated in advance by the White House."[110] The Justice Department had asked the Canadian government to detain the Chinese executive on charges that she abetted violations of sanctions against Iran. This was the first time in history that the United States asked for an extraterritorial arrest in a matter of sanctions violations. Although Trump was not informed, then National Security Advisor John Bolton told the press, "I knew in advance."[111]

As this book goes to press at the beginning of 2020, the trade war looks like a draw, and the tech war looks like an unambiguous Chinese victory.

Where trade is concerned, the United States was ten years too late. *China is no longer an export-dependent economy.* In 2008, China exported one-third of its gross domestic product, flooding the United States with cheap consumer goods. If Wal-Mart were a country, its $50 billion of purchases from China would have placed it sixth on the list of China's largest trading partners in 2013, just below Germany. By 2018, though, China exported only one-sixth of its GDP. More important, in 2008, its trade surplus totaled an enormous 8 percent of GDP. By 2019, that had fallen to just 1.3 percent. After the 2008 crisis, China decided to reduce its dependence on the US consumer market, and shifted economic growth toward domestic consumption. China still has a large bilateral trade surplus with the United States, but total exports to the US amount to just 5 percent of GDP. Most economists who crunched the numbers estimated that China would lose about half a percentage point of GDP growth after the US imposed tariffs on its goods, and that's more or less what happened.

The Trump Administration's tariffs on Chinese imports resulted in a global manufacturing recession, including in the United States. The Markit Purchasing Managers' Index for US industrial production stood at fifty-six in July 2018, when the US imposed its first round of tariffs on Chinese imports. By August 2019, it had fallen to fifty, indicating zero growth, while the Federal Reserve's Index of Industrial Production registered declines during each of the first three quarters of 2019. A similar gauge for Chinese industrial production also indicated contraction during the first half of 2019, before recovering during the third quarter. Steeper declines occurred in Western Europe, Japan, South Korea, and Taiwan. Because industrial supply chains are distributed globally, the trade war prompted businesses to postpone investment decisions until the dust settled. Declining business fixed investment reduced US GDP growth during the second third and fourth quarters of 2019.

The data show clearly that the trade war hurt the United States as well as China, which nonetheless continues to grow at round 6 percent per annum, versus growth of about 2 percent in the United States. The Trump Administration wisely negotiated a truce in mid-December 2019.

China Achieves Silicon Self-Sufficiency

One of history's big shifts in geopolitical power took place in December 2018, but the American media barely noticed—although Asian news outlets such as *Asia Times*, Nikkei Asian Review, and the *South China Morning Post* covered the story extensively. China, for the first time, became self-sufficient in computer chip technology, and out of the reach of American sanctions or boycotts.

In April 2018, the US banned exports of American components to the Chinese telecom equipment firm ZTE after ZTE was found in violation of Iran sanctions. That effectively shut the company down until the US allowed sales under stringent conditions. The United States fired the first shot of the tech war on April 16, 2018, banning US companies from selling components to China's number two telecom equipment maker ZTE. Earlier, US authorities caught ZTE in violation of sanctions against Iran, and later determined that the Chinese firm broke its promise to demote the executives responsible for the violation. In response, the US took the unprecedented measure of imposing a boycott. Dependent on Qualcomm for chips to power its handsets, ZTE ceased most of its business operations. The Shanghai and Hong Kong stock markets suspended its shares from trading, and the firm's future hung in the balance. China's President Xi Jinping personally asked President Trump to reconsider, and on May 13, Trump tweeted an offer of leniency for ZTE. On June 7, 2018, ZTE agreed to pay a $1.4 billion fine and to submit to US government monitoring of its operations. "ZTE will also be required by the new agreement to retain a team of special compliance coordinators selected by and answerable to [the Commerce Department's Bureau of Industry and Security] for a period of 10 years. Their function will be to monitor on a real-time basis ZTE's compliance with U.S. export control laws," the US Commerce Department announced.[112]

Within six months, Huawei introduced its own high-end handset chip to compete with Qualcomm's top-of-the-line Snapdragon series. Huawei's Kirin 980, introduced in December 2018, was the first to seven nanometer chipset for mobile phones, packing 6.9 billion transistors into an area less than a square centimeter, matching the best that Qualcomm could offer.[113] The Kirin series of chipsets were designed by Huawei's subsidiary Hsilicon and fabricated by the Taiwan Semiconductor Manufacturing Corporation, the world's most advanced production firm. In August 2019, Huawei released its Ascend chipset for servers, claiming that it is the world's most powerful artificial intelligence chip.

Within less than a year, China had shed its status as America's technologically poor cousin dependent on American components, to an industry leader competing for the top position in the world's highest-tech hardware products.[114] The US Commerce Department placed Huawei on its "entity list" in May 2019, effectively shutting off US exports of components, but the horse was long out of the barn. The American ban also applied to products manufactured outside the United States, with "controlled US content" of more than 25 percent of the product's value. In late 2019, the US reportedly asked the government of Taiwan to urge Taiwan Semiconductor to stop doing business with Huawei, its number two customer. The Taiwanese government denied the reports.[115] Huawei accounts for more than one-tenth of Taiwan Semiconductor's total revenue.

Barely a year after the export ban on ZTE, Huawei is able to produce handsets, mobile base stations, and other equipment, without any US components. Huawei has shifted its sourcing to Taiwan and Japan. Huawei claims that it will ship two million 5G base stations by 2020, and claims to have signed contracts with fifty telecom providers to sell 5G equipment. Except for Japan, the whole of the Eurasian continent is buying equipment from Huawei, despite urgent remonstrations from the U.S. government and threats of suspension of intelligence sharing. Meanwhile, Japan and Taiwan are selling components to China that the United States has banned, and thousands of Taiwanese engineers are staffing China's aggressive plans to dominate world chip production. Rather than constrain China's dominance of telecommunications equipment, American export controls elicited a successful drive for Chinese self-sufficiency. In short, America's relative position has deteriorated drastically during the past year. Without an American national champion to contend with Huawei, America's efforts to suppress Huawei's dominant position have failed.

Washington continues to play whack-a-mole with China at this writing. In addition to placing Huawei and other Chinese firms on the Commerce Department's "entity list," requiring a special license for exports, the United States has tried to extend its reach overseas, banning foreign companies from selling components to Chinese companies if the "American content" of the technology exceeds 75 percent. More recently, the Commerce Department mooted extending the "American content" rule to 90 percent. China and its suppliers have worked around the boycotts and the American content rule.

US policymakers thought that the United States could pull the plug on China's emerging technology sector. Instead, China brought to the surface long-prepared plans for technological autonomy. Not only can China pursue its goal of dominating mobile broadband without interruption, but high-end Chinese chips for telephone handsets and computer servers will compete with American giants like Intel, Qualcomm, and Nvidia.

A little over a month after the Commerce Department put Huawei on hold, President Trump announced that he would allow American companies to sell to Huawei once again, provided that the items in question had low priority for national security. In a June 29, 2019, press conference, the president said, "US companies can sell their equipment to Huawei. We're talking about equipment where there's no great national security problem with it. I said that's OK, that we will keep selling that product. These are American companies that make these products. That's very complex, by the way. I've agreed to allow them to continue to sell that product so that American companies will continue."

After Trump's statement, the Commerce Department received over one hundred thirty applications from US companies asking for exemptions from the Huawei ban. The status of the applications remains unclear.

The American Semiconductor Association declared, "We encourage prompt action to issue approvals for sale that do not implicate national security concerns, particularly where there is foreign availability for competing products."[116]

Administration policy baffled the tech industry as well as political observers, who wondered whether Trump was using the Huawei export ban to pressure China about trade issues, or whether the Intelligence bureaucracy had nullified the president's June 2019 announcement by refusing to approve export licenses. China was not waiting to find out what Washington really had in mind, and shifted its purchases of high-tech components out of the United States, to friendlier Asian suppliers as well as its burgeoning domestic tech industry.

America's attempt to deny technology to China is risky. If China can develop its own products, alone or in combination with other Asian countries, the result might be the end of some de facto American monopolies. With good reason, American high-tech companies fear that China will start a price war in high-end chips and other products to push them out of world markets. Huawei became a dominant player in telecom equipment by offering its products 40 percent below its competitors' prices. Huawei's return on equity is just over 8 percent as of the third quarter of 2019. Cisco, American company that might have been the world leader in 5G broadband, reported a return on equity of 35 percent. With patient shareholders (its employees) and privileged access to Chinese bank credit, Huawei can afford to be patient, cutting its profit margin to gain market share. Huawei's chief technology officer Paul Scanlan told me that the Kirin handset chip is not intended to displace Qualcomm's products, and the Ascend server chip is not aimed at American companies like Nvidia. That's for now. If the tech war gets dirty, it isn't clear who the last man standing will be.

Another risk of blowback arises from America's threat to deny Huawei access to updates of Google's Android operating system, used by Huawei's mobile handsets. Updates to Google's Android system as well as popular software preloaded into smartphones falls under the "entity list" ban. Despite the possibility that Google Play Store might not be available to new Huawei handsets, Huawei's smartphone sales continued to grow in 2019, tipping the 200 million mark at the end of September, sixty-four days earlier than it took in 2018. As of late November 2019, Huawei had 21 percent of the global smartphone market, up from 18 percent in 2018.

In response, Huawei will introduce its own Harmony Mobile operating system to compete with Android, available sometime in mid-2020. Long under development, the decision to launch an alternative to Android was accelerated by the prospect of an export ban. Google lobbied energetically with the Trump Administration to rescind the ban on Huawei's use of its operating system, fearing, with good reason, that Huawei would eventually cut into its market share. China buys four hundred million handsets a year, and its market is big enough to persuade developers to rewrite most of the 1.7 million native Android apps for its own operating system. At that point, consumers around the world will be able to choose between Google's system and Huawei's, with no loss of functionality. There are enough governments in the world, including in

Europe, with a grudge against Google to give Huawei a critical advantage in important markets.

At the end of December 2019, Huawei announced that it has enlisted a team of Indian developers to create alternatives to Google's most popular applications, including maps. The Hindustan Times reported:

> Huawei is turning to India to build an ecosystem of applications which will be an alternative to Google's popular applications. The company is said to be actively working with the Indian developers for the new solution. Huawei is confident of developing alternatives to Google's key apps such as Maps, payments, and messaging by December end.
>
> Huawei and its sub-brand Honor currently face an uncertainty over the usage of Google Media Service (GMS) after the US restrictions earlier this year. The company recently launched a premium Mate 30 smartphone without Google applications. Huawei, however, is betting on its home-grown Huawei Media Services (HMS).
>
> "We have our own HMS and are trying to build a mobile ecosystem. Most of the key apps such as navigation, payments, gaming and messaging will be ready by December end," Charles Peng, CEO Huawei and Honor India, Consumer Business Group told Economic Times.
>
> Peng is confident that the HMS applications will be as good as Google's applications. Huawei plans to offer one hundred to 150 applications under its suite.[117]

America's semiconductor companies make the majority of their sales in Asia, and also lobbied the Trump Administration to let them continue to do business with Huawei. Instead of shutting Huawei down, the Trump Administration may have created a monster, namely a Chinese chip designer determined to wrest global market share away from America's top firms.

Huawei's handset business is a high-volume but low-margin affair, and ancillary to its main strategic objectives. The Chinese company would not have taken the trouble to compete with Google if its access to Android were not compromised. American technology companies have done their best to explain to President Trump that the Huawei ban may hurt them more than it hurts the Chinese.

Meanwhile, Bloomberg News reported, in November 2019: "Several of the largest U.S. corporations, like Intel Corp. and Micron Technology Inc., have resumed some business with the Chinese firm. After a closer look at the rules, they determined they could continue supplying some products based on an export control law. The rule doesn't subject a product or service to the entity listing's constraints if a company can prove that a piece of technology owes less than 25 percent of its origins to U.S.-based activities."

At the end of 2019, rumors floated out of Washington that the US would forbid sales of foreign-made products to Huawei if they contained more than 10 percent of American content. Taiwan Semiconductor leaked internal documents to the tech industry press arguing that its most advanced seven nanometer chips used less than 10 percent of US content, and therefore would be exempt from event more stringent American rules.[118] Huawei also shifted business away from the United States to Japan. Huawei's purchases of Japanese components will reach $10 billion in 2019, twice the 2017 level, making Japan Huawei's biggest national supplier. In 2018, American companies sold $11 billion worth of components to Huawei.[119]

Another possible stumbling block for Huawei's chip designs was removed in late 2019, when the UK chip design firm ARM announced that its technology had British rather than American content. ARM is the world's leading provider of chip design software, and Huawei's Hsilicon subsidiary used ARM technology to create the Kirin chipset. In 2019, ARM, owned by Japan's Softbank, suspended business dealings with Huawei after the Commerce Department put Huawei on the "entity list." But in October, Reuters reported that ARM's lawyers decided that its chip-design architecture is British rather than American content, and resumed operations with Huawei.[120]

ARM's belated discovery that its technology doesn't have much American content came after China's Alibaba group unveiled a competing chip design architecture based on open sources. The homegrown

Chinese alternative may not offer quite as much functionality as the industry-standard ARM chip design architecture, but the British firm knows which way the wind is blowing.

In October 2019, Japan's Nikkei news reported:

> China is stepping up its efforts to break its dependence on chips based on proprietary technology from SoftBank Group-owned processor designer ARM, employing open-source alternatives to bolster its self-sufficiency and resilience against U.S. trade war retaliation….Building up China's ability to develop and manufacture its own semiconductors is a key goal of the government's "Made in China 2025" strategy issued in 2015. The plan seeks to catapult China to the forefront of the world's modern economies, but the trade war with the U.S. that has seen bans on chip exports to major Chinese companies has added new urgency to the effort. Made in China 2025 sets self-sufficiency goals for semiconductors at 40 percent for 2020 and 70 percent for 2025.

The president of China's semiconductor industry association, Lung Chu, told Nikkei, "While U.S. pressure may affect the operations of companies such as Huawei Technologies in the short run, on a medium to long-term basis, Chinese manufacturers will increase procurement from within China, and it will result in the growth of domestic equipment and materials makers."[121]

China is poaching some of the best engineers in semiconductor fabrication from Taiwan. "China is ramping up recruitment of Taiwanese talent in semiconductors, attracting top executives and engineers alike to bolster an industry that the U.S. trade war has shown to be a Chinese Achilles' heel," Kensaku Ihara wrote, in Nikkei Asian Review, late 2019. "More than three thousand semiconductor engineers have departed Taiwan for positions at mainland companies, the island's Business Weekly reports. Analysts at the Taiwan Institute of Economic Research say this figure appears to be accurate. That amounts to nearly one-tenth of Taiwan's roughly forty thousand engineers involved in semiconductor research and development. The aggressive campaign has sparked concerns about a brain drain within Taiwan's chip industry, which is struggling to compete with generous offers by cash-rich mainland companies."[122]

China Outspends the US on 5G Three Times Over

The global consulting and accounting firm Deloitte reckons that China is investing three times as much as the US, adjusting for land mass and population:

> The United States, Japan, and South Korea have all made significant strides toward 5G readiness, but none to the same extent as China. Infrastructure spending and tower density distinguish China's leap forward and highlight the degree to which China outpaces the United States during these early stages of 5G deployment. 5G's speed and coverage capabilities rely on network densification, which requires the addition of towers and small cells to the network. 5G standards provide for less spectral efficiency gains than previous generations of network technology. Instead, improved speed and capacity stem from the ability to utilize large blocks of contiguous spectrum and higher frequencies. This requires carriers to add three to ten times the number of existing sites to their networks.
>
> Most of this additional infrastructure will likely be built with small cells that use lamp posts, utility phones, or other structures of similar size able to host smaller, less obtrusive radios required to build a densified network. China is building network site density at an unprecedented rate. China Tower is the leading provider of sites and owns approximately 96 percent of macro towers, small cells, and distributed antenna system sites that serve China's wireless carriers. China Tower has invested $17.7 billion in capital and added more than 350,000 sites since 2015. China Tower has a total of approximately 1.9 million wireless sites, compared to approximately two hundred thousand

> in the United States. This means the United States has 0.4 sites compared to China's 5.3 sites for every ten square miles. *Comparing tower density on a per capita basis is marginally more equitable, where the United States lags China by approximately three times.* [Emphasis added].[123]

Regulatory barriers also impede the rollout of 5G in the United States. In a 2019 book, former House Speaker Newt Gingrich argues that the US government and telecom providers failed to advance a competent plan for 5G rollout. "The dominant voices on 5G have been the old bureaucracy and the old corporations who reject change and cling to outdated perspectives," Gingrich argues. "And even 11 years after Huawei began its investments to dominate the internet and all global communications, the United States is still without a global strategy." The US military reserves most of the communications spectrum for its own use, leaving only the "higher millimeter wave spectrum for 5G deployment."[124]

Gingrich also notes that "there are only four nationwide carriers in the US, and two of them—T-Mobile and Sprint—are trying to merge. If this merger is successful, it would leave only three nationwide American wireless network operators. This limited competition creates an oligopoly rather than an intensely competitive system."[125] In consequence, US and Canadian mobile broadband prices are six times higher than the median for OECD countries, and ten times higher than the European Union median.

At the inception of the Fourth Industrial Revolution, the United States has three strikes against it.

- The US is dependent on imported chips, whose security it can't guarantee.
- The US lacks a national champion in the critical sector of telecommunications hardware.
- The US has a regulatory system that impedes rather than encourages 5G rollout.

It's no wonder the United States lost the first round of the tech war. Without an aggressive and comprehensive change in US policy, there may not be a second round to contest.

A Belated and Inadequate American Response

"Virtual networks" popped up in February 2020, as the Trump Administration's proposed alternative to Huawei's 5G technology. All broadband networks run on computer switches, and some of the American software giants now propose to locate the switches in the "Cloud," namely on remote computers, rather than in smart switches embedded in the network itself. The technology might work, but if it does, it would come online at enormous cost and years too late to stop Huawei. And it has the same vulnerability I reported earlier: American software running on Asian chips remains exposed to undetectable hacks inserted at the point of production.

"Seeking to blunt the dominance of China's Huawei Technologies Co., the White House is working with U.S. technology companies to create advanced software for next-generation 5G telecommunications networks," *The Wall Street Journal* reported, on February 5, 2020. "The plan would build on efforts by some U.S. telecom and technology companies to agree on common engineering standards that would allow 5G software developers to run code on machines that come from nearly any hardware manufacturer. That would reduce, if not eliminate, reliance on Huawei equipment."[126] The Defense Advanced Research Projects Agency explained what the Administration envisions, namely a "four-year program organized into three phases: two eighteen-month phases followed by a twelve-month phase. Although DARPA anticipates multiple awards for each technical area, funding levels have not been determined and will depend on the quality of the proposals received and the availability of funds."[127]

Microsoft, Dell, and other big US tech companies are promoting the project. With luck, the "virtual systems" approach might come on in four to five years. Meanwhile, China's 5G network will be completed in the next two to three years, and Europe's not long afterwards. The United States will still need base stations and other hardware, and presently manufactures none of it. By the time that the "virtual network" is available, China and its Russian, Southeast Asian, and European partners will have had several years to develop the spinoff technologies that make 5G important in the first place.

The proposed program amounts to a federal boondoggle for America's software giants. It isn't so much rearranging the deck chairs on the Titanic as stealing silver spoons from the Titanic's dining room.

CHAPTER FIVE

THE TWILIGHT OF THE SPOOKS: QUANTUM CRYPTOGRAPHY AND THE END OF AMERICAN SIGINT HEGEMONY

America's Intelligence Community spends nearly $80 billion a year, including $57 billion for the National Intelligence Program[128] and $20 billion for the Military Intelligence Program. Some 70 percent of this is paid to private contractors, according to investigative journalist Tim Shorrock.[129] Signals intelligence (SIGINT), mainly electronic eavesdropping, takes up the lion's share of the budget; one-fifth of the Intelligence budget is devoted to codebreaking alone.[130]

Among other things, the National Security Agency recorded more than half a billion calls and text messages of Americans in 2017. In response to a Freedom of Information Act lawsuit by the American Civil Liberties Union, the National Security Agency admitted—for the second time—that it improperly eavesdropped on Americans. The spooks' ability to tap the conversations of prospective terrorists, foreign leaders like Germany's Angela Merkel, and pretty well anyone it wants is a source of enormous power as well as justification for continued funding.

All of that is about to come to an end. That has a great deal to do with the tech war between China and the United States.

The US intelligence services argue that if China's national champion, Huawei, dominates the installation of 5G mobile broadband, it can build "backdoors" into its hardware to steal information, and perhaps even sabotage communication and industrial control networks in case of conflict. The US has threatened its allies with a cutback on intelligence sharing if they use Huawei equipment. So far, no country but Japan has acceded to American demands. Huawei denies that it has the capacity or intention to steal data, but charges of this sort are hard to disprove.

"The issue comes down to whether we get everyone's data or China gets everyone's data," a former director of the Central Intelligence Agency told me, recently. That isn't quite accurate. Technology now exists that will make large-scale data theft from broadband networks impossible—not just difficult or expensive, but outside the realm of physical possibility. That does not mitigate the risk that foreign components might contain malicious backdoors that enable a foreign power to tap certain information, or—more ominously—sabotage the system via remote instructions. As noted, all three major telecommunications equipment manufacturers—Huawei, Ericsson, and Nokia—manufacture key hardware in China. Theoretically, virtually all the broadband hardware sold over the world is vulnerable to Chinese hardware hacks. But the vast surveillance capability of the US National Security Agency and its partners in the Five Eyes group will come to an end in the age of quantum cryptography.

China Gets to the Holy Grail of Cryptography First

The Holy Grail of data security is quantum communications, an application of physics that China has pioneered. In June 2017, China created the first quantum communications link between a satellite and a ground station twelve hundred kilometers away. This got the scientific world's undivided attention. Gabriel Popkin reported, in Science Magazine:

> Quantum entanglement—physics at its strangest—has moved out of this world and into space. In a study that shows China's growing mastery of both the quantum world and space science, a team of physicists reports that it sent eerily intertwined quantum particles from a satellite to ground stations separated by 1,200 kilometers, smashing the previous

> world record. The result is a stepping-stone to ultra-secure communication networks, and eventually, a space-based quantum internet.
>
> "It's a huge, major achievement," says Thomas Jennewein, a physicist at the University of Waterloo in Canada. "They started with this bold idea and managed to do it."
>
> Entanglement involves putting objects in the peculiar limbo of quantum superposition, in which an object's quantum properties occupy multiple states at once: like Schrödinger's cat, dead and alive at the same time. Then those quantum states are shared among multiple objects. Physicists have entangled particles such as electrons and photons, as well as larger objects such as superconducting electric circuits.[131]

China named its groundbreaking satellite *Micius*, or *Mozi*, after an ancient Chinese philosopher. In 2018, Micius allowed a joint Chinese-Austrian team to distribute quantum keys for a secure video call between the satellite and ground stations in China and Austria. Physics.org reported:

> A joint China-Austria team has performed quantum key distribution between the quantum-science satellite Micius and multiple ground stations located in Xinglong (near Beijing), Nanshan (near Urumqi), and Graz (near Vienna). Such experiments demonstrate the secure satellite-to-ground exchange of cryptographic keys during the passage of the satellite Micius over a ground station. Using Micius as a trusted relay, a secret key was created between China and Europe at locations separated up to 7,600 km on the Earth.

The system that makes the communication possible cannot be hacked, because any outside intervention disrupts the signal itself and alerts the participants to eavesdropping. Commercial applications of this technology will be available soon. In 2018, Huawei conducted field trials for data security in optical networks with the Spanish telephone company Telefónica. As the Chinese company reported, in a June 2018 press release:

> Telefónica, Huawei, and UPM (Universidad Politécnica de Madrid) have performed a groundbreaking field trial, the first one worldwide, demonstrating the application of quantum cryptography on commercial optical networks, and their operational integration by means of Software Defined Networking (SDN) technologies.
>
> It is an advanced research pilot of secure communication services based on quantum technologies that Telefonica could provide to its customers in future. As Juan-Ignacio Cirac, distinguished physicist specialized in quantum computing and member of the Telefónica Board, says: "We can make a random bit sequence to appear at one place and simultaneously at another one, without making it pass in between. It is sort of magic, but something that Quantum Physics predicts. It is a way of exchanging secure keys that we have to make the most of, since it cannot be hacked."
>
> All secure communications are based on the use of cryptography, so data are encrypted using a secure key in a way that only those knowing that key can decrypt the messages exchanged among them. Current cryptographic techniques for key generation are based on highly complex mathematical problems that require long calculations to be resolved. As computational capacity grows, the time required to solve these problems becomes shorter, reducing the security of the keys.
>
> The continuous growth in computational capacity has required a steady increase in key sizes and the complexity of key generation algorithms. And these techniques can become completely futile with the advent of quantum computers, able to apply the principles of Quantum Mechanics to resolve problems considered unsolvable so far, including breaking the

> keys used by current methods, thus rendering most of our security infrastructure useless....
>
> Quantum technologies themselves provide a solution to this vulnerability of current cryptographic key generation methods. Quantum principles can be applied to exchange a key between the two ends of a communications link so that this key remains secure with respect to any attack, and any attack attempt becomes detectable. This technique, known as Quantum Key Distribution (QKD), not only provides protection against the threat posed by quantum computation to current cryptographic algorithms, but it can also provide a much higher security level for any exchange of data. However, QKD requires a high-quality optical fiber physical infrastructure, and Telefónica is very well positioned to provide services based on this technology.[132]

SK Telecom, South Korea's largest wireless carrier, conducted its own field trials of quantum key distribution to its 5G and 4G LTE mobile networks, in April 2019.[133] Industry experts predict that quantum cryptography will become the standard for data protection. Dr. Andrew Shields of Toshiba Research's Cambridge Research Laboratory writes:

> With the potential to become the cornerstone technology in the future of data security, it won't be long before we see corporations and government agencies adopting quantum cryptography to greatly advance their capabilities and day-to-day operations. However, it remains essential that quantum-resistant public-key cryptography becomes available within the near future in order for us to maintain existing levels of information security within the age of quantum computing. Unlike other existing security solutions, quantum cryptography is secure from all future advances in mathematics and computing, including from the number-crunching abilities of a quantum computer.[134]

In plain English, this meant that the US Intelligence Community knew by the middle of 2018 that Chinese technology would drive them out of the eavesdropping business. That is strategic setback for the United States of grave proportions. Like the Russians at Port Arthur or the Americans at Pearl Harbor or the British at Singapore, the West once again underestimated an Asian challenger.

It's Not Only That China Might Steal US Data— It Will Blind US Signals Intelligence

US officials charge that Huawei plans to steal data from the broadband networks it sells to the West. Even more damaging for US Intelligence is that China will sell the world technology which makes it impossible for the United States to steal data from the next generation of mobile broadband networks.

That constitutes a far more insidious attack on American SIGINT. America's National Security Agency and its British, Canadian, Australian, and New Zealand partners—the Five Eyes group—has operated a massive surveillance system codenamed ECHELON that came to light almost twenty years ago. Sixty Minutes ran a feature on ECHELON in 2000; Mike Frost, a former official of Canada's Signals Intelligence Unit, told the CBS program, "Echelon covers everything that's radiated worldwide at any given instant." The European Parliament conducted a high-profile investigation in 2000–2001. That is old news, but documents made public in 2013, by the American whistleblower and defector Edward Snowden show that the program expanded despite the earlier exposure.

Snowden's documents first appeared in the UK newspaper *The Guardian*, which revealed:

> ...the National Security Agency is currently collecting the telephone records of millions of US customers of Verizon, one of America's largest telecoms providers, under a top-secret court order issued in April. The order, a copy of which has been obtained by *The Guardian*, requires Verizon on an "ongoing, daily basis" to give the NSA information on all telephone calls in its systems, both within the US and between the US and other countries. The document shows for

> the first time that under the Obama administration the communication records of millions of US citizens are being collected indiscriminately and in bulk—regardless of whether they are suspected of any wrongdoing.
>
> The secret Foreign Intelligence Surveillance Court (Fisa) granted the order to the FBI on April 25, 2013, giving the government unlimited authority to obtain the data for a specified three-month period ending on July 19, 2013. Under the terms of the blanket order, the numbers of both parties on a call are handed over, as is location data, call duration, unique identifiers, and the time and duration of all calls. The contents of the conversation itself are not covered.
>
> Under the Bush administration, officials in security agencies disclosed to reporters the large-scale collection of call records data by the NSA, but this is the first time significant and top-secret documents have revealed the continuation of the practice on a massive scale under President Obama.
>
> The court order expressly bars Verizon from disclosing to the public either the existence of the FBI's request for its customers' records, or the court order itself.[135]

The Snowden documents also showed that a top-secret NSA program codenamed Prism gave the NSA directed access to the servers of Google, Apple, Facebook, Yahoo, and other major US internet firms. *The Guardian* reported:

> The National Security Agency has obtained direct access to the systems of Google, Facebook, Apple and other US internet giants, according to a top-secret document obtained by *The Guardian*. The NSA access is part of a previously undisclosed program called Prism, which allows officials to collect material including search history, the content of emails, file transfers and live chats, the document says. *The Guardian* has

> verified the authenticity of the document, a forty-one-slide PowerPoint presentation—classified as top secret with no distribution to foreign allies—which was apparently used to train intelligence operatives on the capabilities of the program. The document claims "collection directly from the servers" of major US service providers.[136]

According to Wikipedia's summary:

> Reports also revealed details of Tempora, a British black-ops surveillance program run by the NSA's British partner, GCHQ. The initial reports included details about NSA call database, Boundless Informant, and of a secret court order requiring Verizon to hand the NSA millions of Americans' phone records daily, the surveillance of French citizens' phone and internet records, and those of "high-profile individuals from the world of business or politics." XKeyscore, an analytical tool that allows for collection of "almost anything done on the internet," was described by *The Guardian* as a program that shed light on one of Snowden's most controversial statements: "I, sitting at my desk [could] wiretap anyone, from you or your accountant, to a federal judge or even the president, if I had a personal email."[137]

As Lucas Matney reported, in Techcrunch, the system "reportedly utilized massive ground-based radio antennas to intercept satellite transmissions containing the digital communications of millions. It then relied on its content-sensitive dictionaries of keywords and phrases to scour the communications for relevant information."[138]

One can debate whether it is a good or bad thing for the intelligence services of the Anglophone world to listen to the world's satellite communications. Some of the eavesdropping targets very bad actors. As National Public Radio reported in September 2019, hacked satellite communications helped the US military suppress ISIS.[139]

Other NSA activities are harder to explain to friendly governments. Edward Snowden revealed that the NSA had tapped the mobile phone of German Chancellor Angela Merkel to the chagrin of the German government. In 2016, WikiLeaks revealed a much more extensive US surveillance program targeting the German government. As a German news site reported:

> The secret files seen by the Süddeutsche Zeitung (SZ) show that the NSA listened in as Merkel had private conversations with other European heads of government and with the Secretary General of the United Nations, Ban Ki Moon. One of the stolen documents seen by the SZ contains details of a meeting between Merkel and then French president Nikolas Sarkozy with the ex-Italian Prime Minister Silvio Berlusconi in 2011. The document describes how at the meeting the French and German leaders put pressure on Berlusconi to enact financial reform. Information from this meeting seems to have been lifted from Berlusconi's advisor Valentino Valentini, who was quoted directly in the report, describing the mood as "very unfriendly."
>
> In a conversation with Ban Ki Moon in 2008, Merkel discussed climate change and expressed hope that the EU could make progress on common environmental goals at a summit in Poland. It is unclear how the NSA obtained the details of this conversation. But another document obtained by Wikileaks relating to the same time period shows that senior UN officials were seen as potential eavesdropping targets by the American spooks.[140]

According to a senior German government official, Secretary of State Pompeo urged Germany's Ambassador to the United States not to buy equipment from Huawei because the Chinese would use it to eavesdrop on German communications. "Mr. Secretary," the German diplomat replied, "we haven't noticed that the Chinese are listening to Mrs. Merkel's phone calls."

The National Security Agency and its Five Eyes counterparts have had the capacity to tap into every satellite transmission in the world, eavesdropping on friends as well as foes. That is the foundation of the

US Intelligence Community's enormous influence in policy-making, as well as the rationale for an $80 billion intelligence budget, of which $56 billion is spent on private contractors. SIGINT is one of the world's biggest businesses. Thanks to China's aggressive development of quantum cryptography and Huawei's rollout of mobile broadband, all of that is about to go the way of the crossbow and the flintlock. The screens soon will go dark at the National Security Agency, and an entire generation of tech spooks and codebreakers will become obsolete. Hundreds of private firms operated by former intelligence officials and employed by the intelligence establishment will go out of business.

That helps explain American officials' sense of urgency in their efforts to derail Huawei's rollout of 5G broadband—and also why the rest of the world has ignored American pleas to shun the Chinese company. Washington isn't fooling anybody. Quantum cryptography will prevent the United States from eavesdropping on the conversations of its allies. It will also ensure that the US has a great deal less intelligence to share.

CHAPTER SIX

THUCYDIDES CLAPTRAP: HOW CHINA PLANS TO WIN WITHOUT FIRING A SHOT[9]

America and China are in "the foothills of a Cold War," Henry Kissinger told a Bloomberg News conference in Beijing, in November 2019. "So a discussion of our mutual purposes and an attempt to limit the impact of conflict seems to me essential. If conflict is permitted to run unconstrained, the outcome could be even worse than it was in Europe. World War I broke out because a relatively minor crisis could not be mastered," the former US Secretary of State added. Dr. Kissinger's warning elicited widespread mention of the so-called "Thucydides Trap," a reference to the supposed causes of the twenty-nine-year war between ancient Sparta and Athens that began in 431 B.C.E. An established power, the argument goes, won't allow the ascension of a rising power without a fight. Professor Graham Allison of Harvard coined the phrase in an influential 2017 book that claimed to have discovered a universal strategic principle applicable across all of history, and especially relevant today. [141]

There are three problems with Professor Allison's Thucydides Trap thesis.

First, it didn't apply in 431 B.C.

Second, it doesn't apply to most of the great conflicts of the past.

9 Parts of this chapter were first published in Claremont Review of Books (Fall 2017) and are used with permission.

And third, it has nothing to do with the present tensions between the US and China.

US-China relations are frosty and may well freeze further, but the likelihood of hot war between the world's two most powerful countries is small. Some American analysts warn that China's impressive military buildup of the past ten years makes war more likely. On the contrary: the old Roman adage applies, "If you want peace, prepare for war." China has created a formidable set of capabilities to control its coast and the seas a couple of hundred miles from its coast. These capabilities include surface-to-ship missiles that can swamp the anti-missile defenses of American aircraft carriers and other surface ships; at least fifty diesel-electric attack submarines that run almost silently on battery power; missiles that can blind or destroy American military satellites; and Russian-built air defense systems that can sweep the skies of fourth-generation military aircraft up to 250 kilometers from its coast.

Chinese Missiles Can Destroy American Assets in the Western Pacific

China's long-range missiles could destroy all of America's military assets in the Western Pacific in the first few hours of a conflict, according to an August 2019 study by the University of Sydney's United States Studies Center. The report elicited consternation from press and think-tank commentators. It stated:

> This growing arsenal of accurate long-range missiles poses a major threat to almost all American, allied and partner bases, airstrips, ports and military installations in the Western Pacific. As these facilities could be rendered useless by precision strikes in the opening hours of a conflict, the PLA missile threat challenges America's ability to freely operate its forces from forward locations throughout the region. Alongside China's broader A2/AD capabilities—including large numbers of fourth-generation fighter jets, advanced C4ISR systems, modern attack submarines, electronic warfare capabilities and dense arrays of

> sophisticated surface-to-air missiles—it permits the PLA to hold US and allied expeditionary forces at risk, preventing them from operating effectively at sea or in the air within combat range of Chinese targets. Following Beijing's construction of a network of military outposts in the South China Sea that can support sophisticated radars, missile batteries and forward-based aircraft, the A2/AD [Anti-Access/Area Denial] threat is further intensifying in this critical waterway.[142]

The Australian report adds:

> Having studied the American way of war—premised on power projection and all-domain military dominance—China has deployed a formidable array of precision missiles and other counter-intervention systems to undercut America's military primacy. By making it difficult for US forces to operate within range of these weapons, Beijing could quickly use limited force to achieve a fait accompli victory—particularly around Taiwan, the Japanese archipelago or maritime Southeast Asia—before America can respond, sowing doubt about Washington's security guarantees in the process. This has obliged the Pentagon to focus on rebuilding the conventional military capabilities required to deny Chinese aggression in the first place, placing a premium on sophisticated air and maritime assets, survivable logistics and communications, new stocks of munitions and other costly changes.

The most formidable addition to China's nuclear arsenal are hyper-velocity glide missiles that China has tested during the past several years, and deployed during 2019. These missiles travel at several times the speed of sound. The United States presently has no defense against them. Defense Undersecretary for Research and Engineering Michael Griffin warned, in 2018:

> When the Chinese can deploy [a] tactical or regional hypersonic system, they hold at risk our carrier battle groups. They hold our entire surface fleet at risk. They hold at risk our forward-deployed forces and land-based forces. Without our ability to defend and without at least an equal response capability on the offensive side, then what we have done is we have allowed a situation to exist where our deployed forces are held at risk and we cannot do the same for them. And so our only response is either to let them have their way or to go nuclear. And that should be an unacceptable situation for the United States.[143]

The United States won't launch a nuclear attack on China because China can launch a nuclear counterstrike against the United States. Its hypervelocity missiles can reach targets in the continental United States. The Defense Department is scrambling to respond, but the United States still lacks the manufacturing capacity to build hypervelocity missiles in large numbers. Undersecretary Griffin explained, "It is an effort to get these systems into the field in the thousands...we are going to have to create a new industrial base for these systems."[144] China also has at least four ballistic missile submarines that each carry twelve JL-2 submarine-launched ballistic missiles with nuclear warheads. The United States and China, that is, both possess the capacity to destroy each other. Neither has any incentive to use it.

The world has changed since 1996, when the Clinton Administration responded to Beijing's saber-rattling against Taiwan by sending two aircraft carrier battle groups into the region. The group centered on the USS Nimitz sailed directly into the Taiwan Straits which separate the Republic of China from the mainland by just eighty miles. A carrier group headed by the USS Independence stood in readiness. The result was a humiliating backdown for Beijing, which had no ability to stop American forces from coming to Taiwan's assistance. China since has invested massively in weapons systems that dominate its coasts.

There may be any number of other unpleasant surprises in store.

In 2015, I called on Dr. Liu Ruopeng, president of the Shenzhen-based startup Kuang-Chi Science. Reorient Group, my employer, had taken Kuang-Chi public (Hong Kong Stock Exchange ticker 0439). Its stock price since did poorly due to expensive, ill-considered acquisitions. I had stopped by Dr. Liu's office to discuss a technology his group had developed to use light impulses to transmit electronic payment and other signals from smartphones. He took out his smartphone and said, "I want to show you a new app." On the small screen there appeared a map of the South China Sea with hundreds of tiny dots." Dr. Liu said, proudly, "Each of these dots shows the location of a ship in the South China Sea as well as its heading and the condition of its motor."

"Where do you get the data?" I asked.

"From balloons!" Dr. Liu exclaimed. "There are hundreds of observation balloons tethered to merchant and fishing vessels in the South China Sea that cover the whole of the Chinese coast out to two hundred miles."

One of Kuang-Chi's signature products was an ultra-light, strong synthetic material that allowed observation balloons to operate at extremely high altitudes. The company tried without success to market its balloons as a cheaper alternative to telecommunication satellites. Apparently, Kuang-Chi found a customer in the Chinese military. The strategic implications of this casual revelation were dire: China first tested a satellite-killer missile in 2007,[145] and it is widely believed that China could blind the satellites on which the American military relies for communications as well as its Global Positioning System. The United States could do the same to Chinese satellites. If Liu Ruopeng gave me a straight story, though, China has already built massive redundancy into its observation systems around its coasts, with far too many observation balloons for the American military to destroy. In the event of war, the US military would be blinded in the South China Sea while China would maintain full communication and reconnaissance in and around its own territory. Dr. Liu might have been feeding me misinformation; it was no secret that I had occasionally consulted for the Defense Department's Office of Net Assessment, and he might have handed me a red herring to pass on to my Pentagon contacts. But there is nothing stopping China from deploying a balloon array of this sort. The US has been using high-altitude reconnaissance balloons since the

1950s,[146] and is presently testing solar-powered surveillance balloons that fly at sixty-five thousand feet as an aid to border security.[147]

New Chinese Electronic Warfare Weapons

American analysts are alarmed at China's progress in electronic warfare. Mark Harris reported, in MIT Technology Review in 2019, that China has the capacity to "spoof" the Global Positioning System of ships around China's cost—that is, give false information to the thirty GPS satellites that the US military as well as civilians use to determine geographical position. Merchant ships report failing GPS systems as well as the appearance and disappearance of "ghost ships" reported by GPS. According to the MIT journal, ships "are falling victim to a mysterious new weapon that is able to spoof GPS systems in a way never seen before." Ships have "been spoofed—their true position and speed replaced by false coordinates broadcast from the ground. This is serious, as 50 percent of all casualties at sea are linked to navigational mistakes that cause collisions or groundings. When mariners simply lose a GPS signal, they can fall back on paper charts, radar, and visual navigation. But if a ship's GPS signal is spoofed, its captain—and any nearby vessels tracking it via AIS—will be told that the ship is somewhere else entirely."

Russia has employed GPS spoofing on its coasts, and the Center for Advanced Defense Studies in Washington reported that GPS signals have been spoofed during President Vladimir Putin's public appearances, by Russian electronic warfare specialists. But the manipulation of GPS on China's coasts is of an entirely different order. Todd Humphreys, the director of the Radionavigation Laboratory at the University of Texas at Austin, told the MIT reporter that "to be able to spoof multiple ships simultaneously...looks like magic." Humphreys added, "I don't think it's some rogue actor. It may be connected with some experimental capability that [the Chinese authorities] are trying to test. But I'm genuinely puzzled how this is being done."[148]

A Chinese Breakthrough in Quantum Radar?

In September 2016, the *South China Morning Post* reported:

> China Electronics Technology Group Corporation (CETC), one of the "Top 10" military industry groups controlled directly by the central government, said on Sunday that the new radar system's entangled photons had detected targets 100km away in a recent field test. That's five times the "potential range" of a laboratory prototype jointly developed by researchers from Canada, Germany, Britain and the United States last year.
>
> America's Defense Advanced Research Projects Agency has reportedly funded similar research and military suppliers such as Lockheed Martin, and are also developing quantum radar systems for combat purposes, according to media reports, but the progress of those military projects remains unknown.
>
> In a statement posted on its website on Sunday, CETC said China's first "single-photon quantum radar system" had "important military application values" because it used entangled photons to identify objects "invisible" to conventional radar systems.[149]

The National Interest's defense correspondent Dave Majumdar commented, "While theoretically, if such a radar existed, it would be able to detect and track stealth aircraft with impunity, but it is unclear if China truly mastered such technology. The Chinese defense industry has claimed a breakthrough in mastering quantum radar technology, but Western defense industry officials said that such a system is not likely to exist outside a laboratory. Even then, the quantum radars would be difficult to build and test reliably even in a lab environment. Indeed, it is likely that networked low-frequency radars—which can also detect and track fighter-sized stealth aircraft—are more likely to be a more pragmatic development. Last year, China Electronics Technology Group Corporation (CETC) announced it had tested such a radar at ranges of roughly sixty miles. While sixty miles is not a particularly huge feat, the fact that such a radar would be able to provide a weapons quality track on a stealth aircraft at those distances is impressive."[150]

We don't know how much progress has made in detecting stealth aircraft, but the combination of superior radars and drone swarms is likely to work to China's advantage, neutralizing America's edge in stealth aircraft. The capacity of the US to project power in Western Asia will shrink even further.

As matters stand, the United States couldn't fight a war with China if it wanted to. Its forces in the region would be devastated by Chinese missiles in the first hours of combat, along with its communications and surveillance capability. The US could blockade oil shipments to China from the Persian Gulf, and severely damage the Chinese economy. But according to the World Bank, China produces 85 percent of its energy use from domestic hydrocarbon, nuclear, and alternative sources, and its economy could survive an oil blockade. An increasing share of China's energy imports, moreover, comes from Russia via pipeline, and China's dependence on Persian Gulf oil has been shrinking.[151] China might retaliate by blockading oil shipments to America's allies Japan (which imports 93 percent of its energy) and Taiwan (which imports 99 percent of its energy).

The only remaining option, as Undersecretary of Defense Griffin noted, is "to go nuclear," which we won't, because China can go nuclear, too.

Massive Deterrence on China's Coasts, But No Capacity to Project Power Globally

The dog that doesn't bark in this particular night is China's land army. China has about thirty-thousand marines and an additional sixty-thousand seaborne mechanized infantry poised to invade Taiwan.[152] Otherwise, its ground forces are poorly equipped and poorly trained. China spends about $1,500 to arm an infantryman, as compared to $17,500 for his American counterpart.

In 2014, *The Wall Street Journal* reported:

> China's military has splashed the cash in recent years even as the U.S. reined in defense spending, but

> are Chinese soldiers kitted for war as well as their American counterparts? Apparently not, a Chinese newspaper says, after adding up the average costs of equipping Chinese and U.S. infantrymen. From rifle to raincoat, helmet to haversack, the Chinese soldier's kit list costs just under 9,400 Chinese yuan ($1,523), or roughly the value of two entry-level iPhone 6s in China, according to Southern Weekly, a Guangzhou-based newspaper.
>
> U.S. soldiers, meanwhile, typically carry around $17,500 worth of gear, according to Associated Press. Nearly half of the equipment value comes from the soldier's most-important tool: The standard-issue Type ninety-five automatic rifle, a Chinese-made weapon valued at 4,300 yuan. Helmets come a distant second, at 1,580 yuan each, the newspaper said.
>
> In contrast, the average U.S. soldier's combat gear costs the equivalent of nearly twenty high-end iPhone 6s, the newspaper estimated, without stating its sources. According to an Associated Press report in 2007, which cited Pentagon officials, the average U.S. soldier costs about $17,500 to equip.

China's main battle tank is inferior to Russian and American armor. National interest writer Charlie Gao asked, in 2019, "Is China's ZTZ-96 main battle bank any good? Russia and America don't think so."[153] China owns no ground-attack aircraft like the American A-10 or the Russian SU-25. It retired the Shenyang J-6, its 1958-vintage knock-off of the Russian MIG-19, about twenty years ago. A country that doesn't own ground attack aircraft probably isn't giving priority to ground warfare.

Unlike the United States, China hasn't equipped its forces for any foreign expeditions, excepting of course the threat against Taiwan. It doesn't have the air- or sealift capability to place substantial forces in conflict zones outside its borders. Its special forces number between seven thousand and fourteen thousand soldiers, including the small Sea Dragon commando force featured in the 2018 action film *Operation Red Sea*, based on the 2015 evacuation of Chinese nationals from Yemen. By contrast, US Special Operations Command's 2020 budget request calls for 66,553 military personnel.[154]

With few exceptions, its military priority is control of its own coastline. In my view, that is why a shooting war is not likely. America cannot win a war on China's coast, and China has scant interest in fighting anywhere else.

For all these reasons, Kissinger's analogy to the outbreak of World War I seems overwrought. For several reasons, a Sarajevo-style trigger for conflict between the US and China is improbable. The European powers in 1914, had large standing armies ready to invade each other; if one power mobilized, its adversaries had no choice but to do so. The military capabilities of each of the great powers threatened the home territory of the others. Meanwhile, Germany's naval buildup challenged Britain's ability to defend its empire, and therefore the soundness of the British economy. As the Australian historian Christopher Clark demonstrated in his 2012 book *The Sleepwalkers*, Russia's decision to mobilize irrevocably set the Great War in motion. China's military buildup threatens America's ability to project power in the Western Pacific, but it presents little threat to American territory or to the territory of America's allies. America faces a challenge to its preeminent position in the world, but not an existential threat to its national existence.[10]

---

10 In an essay commemorating the anniversary of the First World War, I summarized the causes of the conflict as dissected by historians over the past century:

"The objective causes of war all are well known and endlessly analyzed. Germany had the fastest-growing economy and population, and its rivals countered its influence by encircling her.

"With a stagnant population, France could not hope to win back the provinces of Alsace and Lorraine it had lost to Germany in 1870—or to win any future war-unless it fought soon. From parity in the middle of the 19th century, the German population had become half again as large as France's by 1914.

Germany could not concentrate its army on a crushing blow against France if it waited for Russia to build out its internal railway network.

"Austria could not keep its fractious ethnicities within the empire if it did not castigate Serbia. It could not grant equal rights to Serbs without provoking the Hungarians, who held a privileged position in the empire, so it could only suppress them.

"Russia could not maintain control over the industrialized western part of its empire - Poland, Ukraine, the Baltic States and Finland—if Austria humiliated its Serbian ally, and Russia depended on these provinces for the bulk of its tax revenues.

"England could not maintain the balance of power in Europe if Germany

If the analogy to August 1914 in Europe seems strained, the popular Thucydides Trap argument comparing America and China to Sparta and Athens on the eve of the Peloponnesian War is even less appropriate. Athens and Sparta were unstable societies dependent on slaves and tribute, and had the capacity to destroy each other's economic foundation in short order. Each side therefore had an incentive to initiate war. Game theory dictated a high probability of war. No such vulnerability exists in Sino-American relations.

Neoconservatives, progressives, and assorted foreign-policy utopians believe that the United States can replay the 1980s, when—in their view—democracy movements in Eastern Europe brought down the Soviet Empire. Then, as now, the neoconservatives make the mistake of thinking that they matter. Poland's Solidarity movement, the church-centered protests in East Germany, and other protests among Russia's satellites, were a sideshow. The main event was military technology.

The "Thucydides Trap" Argument Is Wrong, Even About Thucydides

Graham Allison's 2017 book warned that China's challenge to American strategic dominance sets us on a path to war. He dubbed this peril the "Thucydides Trap," a term that has since become ubiquitous in public dialogue about China. Allison claims that the Sino-American rivalry is similar to other great power conflicts in history, above all Athens' challenge to Sparta before the Peloponnesian War in 431–404 B.C. Expanding on a 2015 Atlantic essay admonishing American planners to avert a looming war with China, *Destined for War* urges Americans to accept China as a great power. *The Thucydides*

---

crushed France.

None of the powers could go on without facing existential risk: in the case of France, a hopelessly weakened position against Germany; in the case of Germany, an eventual threat from an industrialized Russia; in the case of Austria, breakup of the Empire due to Slavophile agitation; in the case of Russia, loss of its Western provinces to the Teutonic orbit; and in the case of England, irrelevance on the continent and an inevitable challenge to its sea power.

https://pjmedia.com/spengler/2014/6/30/the-inevitable-first-world-war-musil-and-meta-musil/

Trap demarcated a crucial turn in the thinking of America's foreign policy establishment. Through most of the George W. Bush and Obama Administrations, conventional thinking held that America would promulgate the liberal international order in the Middle East and elsewhere, while China would struggle with the internal weaknesses inherent in a dictatorial regime. Allison's book offers a different and darker vision: he argues—correctly, in my view—that China's economy will continue to grow in breadth and depth to challenge America, and concludes—wrongly, in my view—that America can do nothing except to accommodate the rising Asian superpower.

Why call on the authority of Thucydides to make the case for American strategic decline? Victor Davis Hanson, the classicist and military historian, observes: "When statesmen pontificate about idealism or noble intentions, Thucydides is ready to differentiate *prophasis* (pretext) from ulterior or real motive (*aitia*)."

Fairly, may we inquire about Allison's *aitia.* Conservative writers cast America in the role of Athens and saw a precedent for President Bush's 2006 Freedom Agenda. In his 2006 history book, *A War Like No Other,* Hanson wrote:

> Contemporary America is often now seen through the lens of ancient Athens, both as a center of culture and as an unpredictable imperial power that can arbitrarily impose democracy on friends and enemies alike. Thomas Paine long ago spelled this natural affinity out: "What Athens was in miniature, America will be in magnitude...." Americans...in a very Athenian mood, have sought to remove oligarchs and impose democracy—in Grenada, Panama, Serbia, Afghanistan, and Iraq—enemies, allies, and neutrals alike are not so impressed. They understandably fear American power and intentions while our successive governments, in the manner of confident and proud Athenians, assure them of our morality and selflessness.[155]

Athens' defeat, Hanson added, "has been troubling us supporters of democracies these past 2,400 years." Historians still replay the tape in hope of isolating the arbitrary error that ruined Athens, hoping to show that Athens really should have won (Hanson blames the daring and ambitious Alcibiades, while Yale classicist Donald Kagan blames the blunders of the Athenian general Nicias). In my view, the interests of imperial Athens were radically different from ours. Moreover, Athens' democracy was not our democracy. It was the sort of democracy that Alexis de Tocqueville warned that a corrupted America might become, the kind of state the might have emerged if the Confederacy had won the Civil War and extended its slave empire deep into Central and South America.

Much less were the Athenians like today's Chinese, whom Allison casts in the role of the "Athenian" challenger to the United States; today's Sparta, by analogy. By reversing the historical roles, Allison wants to nullify the notion that America is the heir to Athenian democracy as well as to its foreign ambitions. If America-as-Athens was a Shibboleth for Wilsonian idealism and neoconservative nation-building, America-as-Sparta encapsulates Allison's realism. That is a clever move, but enormously overdone.

The nub of the so-called Thucydides Trap is the assertion that an established power, happy with the international status quo, is "destined for war" against a rising challenger. In Allison's account, this becomes a Procrustean bed in which the history of warfare is stretched or lopped off to fit his thesis. Allison derives from Thucydides the axiom that "the fundamental explanation" for conflicts up to and including war "lies in the depth of the structural stress between a rising and a ruling power.... As this rivalry led Athens and Sparta into successive standoffs, the most passionate voices in each political system grew louder, their sense of pride stronger, their claims about threats posed by the adversary more pointed, and their challenge to leaders who sought to keep the peace more severe. Thucydides identifies three primary drivers fueling this dynamic that lead to war: interests, fear, and honor."

Among these he is most impressed by the last: Thucydides' concept of honor "encompasses what we now think of as a state's sense of itself, its convictions about the recognition and respect it is due, and its pride." Allison has little to tell us of the interests that lurked behind the pride. That is unsatisfactory, because the devil in strategy always is in the details.

"Self-interest" is indeed a powerful geopolitical motive, but imperial Athens' interests were radically different from ours, so different that Athens offers a misleading example. Athens and Sparta were nothing like modern nation-states. They were, rather, fragile and ultimately unsustainable slave economies at constant risk of catastrophic disruption. Neither interest, fear, nor honor fully explains why Athens fought to demographic exhaustion. Men do not bleed their nation dry for honor. They do so in the face of existential threats. To identify such threats, we must consider economics and demographics, subjects which classical historians too often disregard.

Dependent on foreign trade for half its food supply and to replenish the ranks of perhaps one hundred fifteen thousand slaves, Athens could not restrict its empire without a wrenching disruption in its way of life. Its lifeline of grain imports as well as its source of new slaves stretched to the Black Sea. Athens had long ceased to be a city of small-holding farmers, its celebrated leisure supported by imported grain, timber, and slaves, in a maritime empire at constant peril of disintegration. Empire transformed Athenian society and underwrote a burgeoning class of state dependents. Tribute exacted from the two hundred member states of the Delian League funded Pericles' ship-building program and built the Parthenon. Athens asserted its authority by means as cruel as any empire in history, notoriously the massacre of the inhabitants of Melos in 416.

Against the forty thousand citizens of Athens stood thirty-two Spartans ruling perhaps one hundred seventy thousand helots, at perpetual risk of mutiny. The war was a clash between two inverted pyramids, inherently unstable and threatened by ruin through an interruption of the maritime lifeline and a rebellion of the helots. Moreover, Sparta suffered from a long demographic decline noted by Aristotle in *Politics*. Sparta parried the threat from Athens, only to find its fears realized a generation later by Epaminondas, the Theban general who defeated Sparta and liberated the helots. As Paul Rahe observes, in *The Spartan Regime* (2016), "...[t]he Spartans were acutely aware that they were interlopers in the Peloponnesus, that they had invaded and seized Laconia by force, and that their servants—the 'old helots' of the provinces—were descended from the original Achaean stock, which had ruled Lacedaemon in the epoch described by Homer."

An external power supporting a helot rebellion could have ruined Sparta. Sparta planned to invade Athens in response to the latter's attack on the island of Thasos in 470, forty years before what we call the Peloponnesian War began, but demurred after a severe earthquake led to a helot rebellion. In 465, Athens sent troops to support Sparta, still its nominal ally, but the Spartans sent them home. Thucydides comments that the Spartans feared the Athenians would back the helots instead, adding, "It was because of this expedition that the Spartans and Athenians first came to an open quarrel." Athens and Sparta warred from 460 to 445 B.C., before signing the Thirty Years' Peace. The rebellion of Athens' dependency on Samos in 440, with Persian assistance, showed how easily the Delian League might collapse. Sparta might have finished Athens then, but elected not to go to war. It was not the established power responding to an emerging challenger that undid the Thirty Years' Peace, but Pericles' decision to starve out Sparta's ally Megara, thirty-three kilometers west of Athens.

Thucydides was a partisan of Pericles, and blames not the hubristic "first citizen" of Athens, but rather the fearful Spartans for the war. Allison takes Thucydides at his word:

> The Spartan king Archidamus II and Pericles were personal friends. Archidamus could see the situation from the Athenian point of view, and he recognized that his people were moved more by emotion than reason. Appealing to the Spartan virtue of moderation, Archidamus urged the Spartan Assembly not to demonize the Athenians....But Sparta's hawks disagreed. They argued that Athens had become so arrogant that it posed an unacceptable danger to Spartan security.[156]

Allison does not inform the reader how controversial this reading was and remains. Donald Kagan observes that Athenian opinion in 430, blamed Pericles for starting the war. Thucydides was the revisionist, a member of Pericles' party anxious to shift the blame to an amorphous Spartan fear of Athenian predominance. In several surviving comedies, we have the testimony of Aristophanes—a traditionalist who despised Pericles and his popular support, bought with the Delian League's tribute—that Pericles was responsible for the ultimate ruin of his polis. That was also the view of Plato's Socrates as well as Aristotle.

We are so beguiled by Thucydides, however, that we readily blame the nasty Spartans, and absolve democratic Athens. Not the fearful major power, but the upstart challenger started the war—an anomaly repeated in numerous of Allison's examples of his thesis: Japan in 1905, Germany in 1939, and Japan in 1941. The economics of empire helps explain why the Athenians, who gave logic to the West, acted illogically in war. Allison writes:

> Athens [during the Thirty Years' Peace] continued to use its powerful navy to dominate—and extract gold from—its own subjects throughout the Aegean. It amassed a strategic reserve amounting to the previously unheard-of sum of six thousand talents of gold, and was adding one thousand talents per year in revenue.[157]

Athenian democracy had fallen into what one might call the Tocqueville Trap: the Athenians voted themselves rich—in this case, at the expense of the Delian League. Aristophanes' play *The Wasps* bemoaned the deterioration of civic mores: "We have now a thousand towns that pay us tribute; let them command each of these to feed twenty Athenians; then twenty thousand of our citizens would be eating nothing but hare, would drink nothing but the purest of milk, and always crowned with garlands." Thucydides later blamed the mob for some of Athens' worst decisions. For example, the catastrophic Sicilian campaign of 413–415. The polis voted to attack Syracuse "on a slight pretext, which looked reasonable, [but] was in fact aiming at conquering the whole of Sicily….The general masses and the average soldier himself saw the prospect of getting pay for the time being and of adding to the empire so as to secure permanent paid employment in the future."[158]

Without its empire, Athens' economy would have collapsed. This dependency led to the willingness to take risks and make sacrifices unfathomable today. Sixty percent of Athens' military-age male population died in the Peloponnesian War, historian Barry S. Strauss estimates. By contrast, the Napoleonic Wars, the American Civil War, and the Second World War ended after the defeated side lost 30 percent of its military-age male population.[159]

There are few modern parallels to the circumstances of 430 B.C. One not cited by Allison was the American Confederacy on the eve of the Civil War, nearly 50 percent of whose wealth was in the persons of slaves.[160] Cotton planting destroyed the soil, and thus required a never-ending supply of new territories; Abraham Lincoln's election in 1860, pledged to prevent the further spread of slavery, threatened to suffocate the cotton monoculture of the South. The South understood from the outset that its livelihood was at risk. In this case, an emerging power started a war with an established one, the opposite of the Thucydides model, which Allison treats as paradigmatic.

Allison offers an erroneous reading of the causes of the Peloponnesian War and then attempts to extrapolate this to a recurring pattern in which established powers go to war to prevent the rise of challengers. His other examples are wrong, too. For example, a common explanation of the outbreak of the First World War points to Germany's emergence as a naval power and a potential challenger to Britain's superiority on the seas. Thanks to Cristopher Clark's brilliant 2012 book *The Sleepwalkers*, we now have archival evidence that Russia started the war with French instigation, not Germany. Clark was the first historian to gain access to Russian military archives after the fall of the Soviet Union, and shows that Russia's mobilization forced war upon German and Austrian governments that still expected a localized conflict.[161] The French and Russians had been waiting for a pretext to start a war: "It was not just that [French Prime Minister Raymond] Poincaré and [French Ambassador to Moscow Maurice] Paléologue had pressed so hard for Russian firmness on the Serbian question, it was that a crisis of this kind conformed exactly to the Balkan inception scenario that the alliance, over many discussions and summit meetings, had come to define in recent years as the optimal *casus belli*."[162] That doesn't fit the Thucydides Trap pattern at all; France was a declining power whose population had barely changed since it was beaten by Prussia in 1870, while Germany's population had grown by 80 percent. France saw its last chance for revenge on the Germans and the return of the forfeited provinces of Alsace and Lorraine, and pushed a reluctant Czar Nicholas II into war.

Of all the actual and potential conflicts we can invoke, however, the current Sino-American strategic relationship bears the least resemblance to a collision two-and-a-half millennia ago between fractious little slave-states. China and the United States need not pose a threat to each other's existential interests. Moreover, among the world's great powers, China and America stand out for their lack of interest in colonialism. After expanding to its natural borders in the 8th century under the Tang Dynasty, China has shown little interest in adding territory. Their trading relationship has elements of mutual benefit as well as tension, particularly as China gains industrial market share at America's expense. Internally, China is more stable than at any time in its long history. Household consumption rose sixteenfold in the quarter century from 1986 to 2011. In the past generation, 550 million people have moved from countryside to city. For the Chinese, sinologist Francesco Sisci observes, this is a Golden Age, the first time in Chinese history when no one need fear hunger or war. Athens exacted by tribute and lavishly spent the savings of its subjects in the Delian League; China, by contrast, is the world's greatest saver, and next to Japan, the world's largest exporter of savings, including $1 trillion lent to the U.S. Treasury.

It is not clear how any of this might lead to war. America has strategic commitments to China's neighbors—Japan, Korea, and Taiwan—that might, in theory, become a source of conflict. Allison spins some scenarios in which frictions between China and American allies might lead to war. In practice, though, Korea and Taiwan have already taken Chinese high-tech dominance as a feature of the future landscape. The biggest foreign investors in China's burgeoning semiconductor industry are Samsung—a Korean firm that is now the world's largest semiconductor manufacturer—and Taiwan Semiconductor. Having no prospect of beating China, some of our allies have decided to throw in with China's high-tech ambitions.

Japan is a sleeping dog that China would rather let lie. Under duress, Japan could assemble nuclear weapons and intercontinental ballistic missiles in a matter of a year or less.[11] Its capacity for deterrence is buried but nonetheless formidable. Chinese planners remember well the deaths of twenty-five million citizens at the hands of the Japanese Imperial Army during World War II. The Chinese strategist General Luo Yuan, frequently cited as an exponent of nationalist and anti-American views, told me that the United States had done the Chinese a favor by keeping Japan away from them. India will remain China's competitor, but there isn't much for China and India to have a war about except for disputed territory in the Himalayas.

America does not present an existential threat to China's regime, although with some effort it could try to create one. "Could [Washington] openly call into question the legitimacy of the Chinese Communist Party, the way Ronald Reagan bluntly called the Soviet Union the Evil Empire in 1983?" Allison says. "If democracy is the best form of government for all nations, why not for China?" However, the Chinese people have shown little interest in changing the character of their government. The Hong Kong democracy protests had no resonance on the mainland. Moreover, the revolution in mobile communications has given the Chinese authorities unprecedented power to control public debate, and there is not much America can do about it.

---

11 Mark Fitzpatrick, "How Japan Could Go Nuclear," *Foreign Affairs*, October 3, 2019: "As the only country to experience a nuclear bombing, Japan is a leading proponent of nonproliferation. Quietly, however, it pursues a strategy of "nuclear hedging," preserving the capacity to develop nuclear weapons without intending to do so. Officials occasionally reveal the existence of this policy. In the wake of the Fukushima nuclear disaster in 2011, for example, former Defense Minister Shigeru Ishiba, a prominent Liberal Democratic Party politician, explained that Japan couldn't shut down its nuclear power plants because the nuclear fuel cycle—the industrial processes that turn uranium into electricity and recycle the waste—was necessary in order to maintain "technical deterrence." Japan is the only nation that has the ability to enrich uranium and reprocess plutonium but has no nuclear weapons.

"In theory, Japan could develop a small atomic arsenal in as little as a year or two. It would need to produce weapons-grade plutonium, a process that would most likely require repurposing civil reactors. It would also need to reengineer its advanced space launch rockets to deliver nuclear warheads. Japanese scientists are technically capable of both tasks and could accomplish them on a tight timetable if the government felt compelled to minimize concerns about safety, secrecy, reliability, and accuracy (and shirk its international obligations)."

https://www.foreignaffairs.com/articles/asia/2019-10-03/how-japan-could-go-nuclear.

China's insistence on a dominant position in the South China Sea stems from this deep-seated anxiety. Per the proverb, China is killing the chicken for the instruction of the monkey. The monkey, in this case, being Taiwan. If China is willing to take risks for uninhabited reefs, it will a fortiori go to war over Taiwan. It invests enormous resources in high-tech coastal defense, but spends about $1,500 to equip an infantryman, roughly one percent of the American expenditure.

That contrast sums up China's strategic priorities. If the United States abandons the One-China policy and takes a stand for Taiwanese independence, we will have war with China. It would be the most foolish of wars: China is willing to let Taiwan conduct its internal affairs as it sees fit, so long as the principle remains intact that Taiwan remains a Chinese province. Washington, Beijing, and Taipei can tolerate this arrangement indefinitely, and it would require a paroxysm of folly on the part of an American government to attempt to change the status quo.

How a War with China Won't Start

In peacetime, military planners devise scenarios for possible wars, and America's planners have lots of scenarios for how war might start with China. It's their job, and they have to do it, but the rest of us don't have to regard them as high probability events. The dean of American military reporters, Bill Gertz, recounted some of the more creative scenarios floated by the Pentagon, in a 2019 book.[163] According to Gertz, "The PLA, as a Party army and not a national army like the US military, is fundamentally different. The PLA is ideologically driven, and its leaders have been trained, as a core belief, with the idea that the United States is an imperialist enemy that engaged in a conspiracy to defeat the People's Republic of China and therefore must be defeated by all means necessary."[164] That's the sort of assertion that seems reasonable until you ask what it actually means.

China has already "defeated" the American military in the Western Pacific by assembling a formidable complex of missile, submarine, and other access-denial weapons that control its coast and a couple hundred miles beyond. America is not going to attack with F-35's launched from aircraft carriers, which China, in turn, could sink with long-range surface-to-ship missiles.

In a chapter entitled "The Coming Space War with China," Gertz offers a fictional scenario: "The year is 2025. China has covertly declared war on the United States of America...The war started with a solar flare on the surface of the sun....[A Chinese general] saw the coming solar storm as the perfect opportunity for a surprise anti-satellite attack on critical satellites used by the Americans for intelligence, navigation, and communications—the backbone of the high-technology US military forces....The ultimate target of the planned Chinese satellite attacks was not the United States. It was Taiwan, the vibrant democratic state two miles off the coast of southern China that has been a thorn in the side of the Communist rulers for decades....China waited patiently for decades to take back the island state that is the main obstacle preventing Chinese Communist leaders from achieving their dream of total regional hegemony."[165]

Gertz allows, "This scenario is fictional. But the description is a very real danger posed by China's secret program of anti-missile weaponry." Although the Chinese do not openly discuss their capability, anti-satellite weapons are about as secret as fireworks on the Lunar New Year. A Google search for the terms "China anti-satellite missile" turns up 4,700,000 hits. There isn't much the United States could do to defend Taiwan, even it if wanted to. If it sent in aircraft carriers, the Chinese could sink them. China's Russian-built S-400 air defense system can sweep the skies of fourth-generation aircraft over Taiwan. With control of air and sea, China's standing invasion force of about one hundred thousand could take over the island in a matter of days.

The question is why China would want to do this. If the United States placed nuclear weapons in Taiwan, for example, or stationed US troops there, or sold Taiwan a squadron of F-35's, China might consider this a *casus belli*. Barring a drastic change in US policy, China has no reason to invade Taiwan. It is getting everything it wants from Taiwan. As I reported in chapter four, about 10 percent of Taiwan's semiconductor engineers are working on the Mainland. America's May 2019 ban on US sales to Huawei turned into a bonanza for Taiwanese companies. Taiwan Semiconductor Manufacturing Corporation, the world's most advanced chip fabricator, is building plants in China.[166] And TSMC is fabricating Huawei's new high-end chips.

One hears an occasional dark hint from American officers about doomsday scenarios—for example, an F-35 attack on China's enormous Three Gorges Dam that would produce a catastrophic flood along the twelve hundred kilometers that separate the dam from the mouth of the Yangtze River. The F-35 has a combat radius of just eleven hundred kilometers; even if its range were extended to reach the Three Gorges Dam, it is unlikely to carry enough ordinance to destroy a dam that Chinese planners claim is capable of withstanding a nuclear attack.[167] If the US succeeded in destroying the dam and inflicting catastrophic loss of life throughout the Yangtze Valley, it would invite nuclear retaliation from China.

The soldiers are paid to fight wars, but the war that China has in mind lies outside their field of vision. China's goal of technological supremacy in the game-changing technologies makes Taiwan a critical player, a source of talent and expertise for the Mainland. Nothing benefits China more than the status quo.

Contending With China Isn't Like Fighting Russia in the 1980s—It's More Like Fighting America in the 1980s

The great, glaring difference between America's confrontation with the Soviet Union in the 1980s and its rivalry with China in the 21st century is this: Russia's civilian economy was stagnant, inefficient, and corrupt, and unable to muster the range of technologies that America brought to bear on warfighting, despite the occasional excellence of Russian science and engineering. China's civilian economy, despite important inefficiencies, remains the stupor mundi, the wonder of the world, fifty times larger in US dollar terms (and eighty times larger in purchasing power parity) than it was in 1979, when Deng Xiaoping introduced his market reforms.

Russia starved its consumer economy to feed its military, while China has produced both guns and butter. Unlike Russia, which devoted enormous military resources to keeping and equipping a vast land army, China has minimized its expenses on soldiery while spending lavishly on missiles, satellites, artificial intelligence, and other advanced technology that also has benefits for the civilian economy—just as America's military and space expenditures did from Eisenhower through Reagan.

By 1982, when the US-built Israeli Air Force shot down Syria's Russian-built Air Force over the Bekaa Valley, Russia knew its massive investment in conventional weapons had gone wrong. During the Syrian collapse in June 1982, Israel deployed a combination of American and locally developed weapons systems and technologies, many in their first combat use, including F-15s and F-16s, AWACs, lookdown radar, and remotely piloted vehicles. Decoy drones drew fire from the Soviet-made SAM batteries while Israeli fighters destroyed seventeen out of the Syrians' nineteen batteries. Superior command and control through faster computation and lookdown radar allowed Israeli F-4s, F-15s, and F-16s to destroy nearly one hundred Syrian planes over the Bekaa Valley while losing just one Israeli fighter.

Such a victory would have been impossible without the new fast and light microchips that enabled the American-made fighters to carry sufficient onboard computing capacity for the new radar systems. The CMOS chips that powered the F-15's lookdown radar (beginning in 1978) were manufactured for the first time only ten years earlier, and for entirely different reasons. Originally the Defense Advanced Research Projects Agency (DARPA) commissioned RCA researchers to manufacture fast and light chips for weather analysis. In fact, the definitive inventions of late twentieth century technology—laser-powered optical networks, fast and light integrated circuits, and the internet—all came out of Defense Department projects whose originators could not have foreseen the impact of the new discoveries.[168]

The "Bekaa Valley Turkey Shoot" of 1982, as it came to be called, marked a decisive shift in the Cold War. During the 1973 Israel-Arab war, Russian surface-to-air missiles (SAMs) shot down almost one hundred Israeli aircraft, mostly American F-4 Phantoms and A-4 Skyhawk fighters. The Soviet Union had good reason to believe that it would control the skies in any conventional war in Europe and easily roll over NATO resistance. This perception encouraged Soviet aggression, including the 1979 invasion of Afghanistan.

I discuss this in more detail in chapter eight.

By 1984, Russia knew that it economy could not keep up with America's stupendous rate of technological advancement. A report—still classified—commissioned by the leading Russian plasma physicist, Evgeny Velikhov, and prepared at the Siberian branch of the Academy of Sciences at Novosibirsk early in 1984, informed the Russian military that US president Ronald Reagan's Strategic Defense Initiative would push the envelope of defense technology to a dimension that Russia could not emulate. This should not be confused with the 1983 "Novosibirsk Report" on the backwardness of Russian agriculture, whose contents long have been public. Moreover, by 1984, the United States had succeeded in frog-marching its European allies into deploying the Pershing II medium-range missiles in Germany and Italy, fundamentally altering the strategic balance to Russia's disadvantage. That is why Russia opted for reforms, and ultimately lost its nerve in 1989. A strong and confident Russia would have asked how many divisions the pope had and simply killed the dissidents en masse, as it did in Hungary in 1956 and Czechoslovakia in 1968. The neoconservatives watched Russia fall and imagined that the magic of democracy had defeated the wicked sorcerer-kings of Moscow, and looked forward to the end of history as liberal capitalism inexorably spread throughout the world. This illusion was responsible for America's plunge from the status of sole world superpower in 1989, to a prospective number two power in the second half of the 21st century.

China has learned from America's experience with state-directed investment in dual-use technologies, and taken it a step further. The Defense Department's 2019 report to Congress on Chinese military developments states:

> China continues to implement long-term state-directed planning, such as "Made in China 2025" and other industrial development plans, which stress the need to replace imported technology with domestically produced technology. These plans present an economic challenge to nations that export high-tech products. These plans also directly support military modernization goals by stressing proprietary mastery of advanced dual-use technologies. China's

> leaders seek to align civil and defense technology development to achieve greater efficiency, innovation, and growth. In recent years, China's leaders elevated this initiative, known as Civil Military Integration (CMI), to a national strategy that incentivizes the civilian sector to enter the defense market. The national CMI strategy focuses on hardware modernization, education, personnel, investment, infrastructure, and logistics.
>
> China has increasingly funded basic research and made comprehensive efforts to grow the country's inventive capabilities over the last decade. The 2017 National Artificial Intelligence Plan describes steps for China to become the "world's major AI innovation center" by 2030, and calls for the country to accelerate the integration of AI with the economy, society, and national defense. The plan foresees a great expansion in the "breadth and depth of AI applications in...national defense construction." Other plans address the development of various sectors of China's robust Internet ecosystem to include cloud computing, the big data industry, e-commerce, and next generation broadband wireless communications networks, including fifth generation (5G) wireless networks. Due to information-sharing requirements with Chinese security services as stipulated in Chinese laws, worldwide expansion of Chinese-made equipment in 5G networks will challenge the security and resiliency of other countries' networks.[169]

Artificial intelligence threatens to transform the nature of warfare. The People's Liberation Army may not spend much on equipping conventional foot soldiers. Soon, it won't have to, as AI-guided drones do the killing on the battlefield. In May 2019, China's *Global Times* reported:

> China's domestically developed helicopter drones carrying proximity explosive mortar shells, grenade launchers and machine guns can now form swarms and engage in coordinated strikes. The intelligent

> swarming attack technology enables as many as ten unmanned helicopter drones to autonomously form up into a swarm....With a single push of a button, the drones can autonomously take off, avoiding colliding in the air and finding their way to their designated target. Once they receive an order to attack, they will engage the target autonomously in a coordinated manner. Upon finishing a mission, the system will lead the drones back to base and land automatically. The operator does not need to expose himself or herself in a dangerous frontline as the drones can easily be controlled remotely....The ten drones can be a combination of different types, including those that can drop proximity explosive mortar shells, while others can carry grenade launchers, or make suicide attacks.[170]

The United States and China are in a race to build aerial drone swarms that will fly alongside fighter planes, and possibly replace manned fighters altogether one day. The US Air Force began testing fighter-directed drone swarms in 2019.[171] Ominously, China appears to have gained an edge in frontier radar technology that is capable of detecting and targeting US stealth aircraft.

China's Global Role Will Grow, But Cautiously

China's global military presence will grow, and it will overlap with regions in which the US has had a deep interest. But that won't lead to a US-Chinese war, either.

In 2013, I conjectured that a "Pax Sinica" might emerge in the Middle East—a "Chinese peace," like the 19th century Pax Britannica and the 20th century Pax Americana. China is the largest buyer of Middle East oil and gas (Japan is the second). The United States is now a net exporter of hydrocarbons. America's appetite to spill blood and spend treasure in the region is disappearing. China has deep interests in the region. How long will it be before China replaces the United States as the geopolitical arbiter in the Middle East, I asked:

> Iran sits between two Sunni powers—Turkey and Pakistan—that depend to a great extent on Saudi financing, and that also have excellent relations with China.…Turkey is the logical terminus for the "New Silk Road" of road, rail, pipelines and broadband that China has proposed to build in Central Asia.
>
> China, it might be added, also has excellent relations with Israel, whose premier technical university just was offered a $130 million grant from Hong Kong magnate Li Ka-shing to fund part of the costs of building a branch in China. Chinese provincial and local governments will contribute another $147 million. Without attributing any geopolitical intention to Beijing, the visible facts make clear that China has the capacity to exercise strategic influence in the Middle East, and it has an unambiguous interest in maintaining stability. What China might choose to do, Washington will learn after the fact, if ever. If China wished to influence Iran, for example, it has considerable means to do so, and a great deal else besides.[172]

The problem, as Afshin Molavi wrote in 2019, on the website of the Hoover Institution, is that "China remains a free-rider on the American security umbrella over the Persian Gulf. The United States has, contrary to headlines, hardly been addicted to Middle East oil over the past decade (only two or three Middle East countries consistently make the top ten of import sources), and yet it still remains the paramount policeman of the Gulf. In the usual litany of US Middle East interests, Persian Gulf security always stands alongside support for Israel and protection against terrorism."[173] US taxpayers bear the cost of a blue-water navy that protects the sea lanes, and China is the major beneficiary of that protection. Molavi added, "This poses three key questions for U.S policy makers: Is the US willing or interested in burden sharing on Persian Gulf security with China? Is China interested? More importantly, are Gulf Arab leaders interested? On the latter, thus far, most Gulf Arab leaders have been content with the existing arrangement: The United States underwrites their security, while Asia underwrites their prosperity. This arrangement is unlikely to change soon, but is the carrier ship shifting ever so slightly?"

More recently the Georgian political scientist Emil Avdaliani wrote, on the website of Bar-Illan University's Begin-Sadat Center, that "China will find it increasingly difficult to stay above the fray in the Middle East. It will have to become more responsive to rising challenges to its businesses and sea and land trade routes. This will inevitably lead to greater insecurity between the US and China. Top US officials have already warned about China's efforts to gain influence in the Middle East, which could undermine defense cooperation between the US and its traditional regional allies in the region. The Middle East is thus transforming into yet another arena of competition between the US and China."[174]

It would appear that China has more to lose from prospective instability in the Persian Gulf than the United States. In the event of a Saudi-Iranian war, for example, disruption of energy supplies would inflict heavy damage on China's economy. Professor Advliani speculates that China, nonetheless, may encourage Iran to misbehave. "Iran's strategic location and human resources, as well as its intention to serve as a civilizational center of gravity for neighboring states, could divert American military and economic capabilities away from the South China Sea, which would work in Beijing's favor," he observes.

All of this is conjecture. I doubt that Beijing has the will or the self-confidence to calibrate a crisis in the Persian Gulf, and balance its energy security requirements against its desire to distract the United States from the South China Sea.

Indicative of Beijing's caution about projecting its power outside its borders is a November 2019 report that China has canceled plans for two nuclear-powered super aircraft carriers. The *South China Morning Post* reported:

> The Chinese navy is moving ahead with plans to build another aircraft carrier, but plans for a fifth have been put on hold for now, according to military insiders. They said that technical challenges and high costs had put the brakes on the program and the recent merger of the country's two major shipbuilders was unlikely

> to have a significant short-term impact. The country currently has just one active carrier, the Liaoning—a refitted Soviet-era vessel—but the first homebuilt carrier, the Type 001, is undergoing sea trials and may soon be ready for service. Work on the more modern Type 002 carrier started two years ago, and a naval source said construction on the second Type 002 could start as early as 2021....China will end up with four carriers under the current plans. But plans for a next-generation carrier appear to be on hold for now as engineers struggle to overcome technical problems. "There is no plan to build more aircraft carriers," said one military source.[175]

Ultimately, the United States and China have the same basic interest in the Middle East, namely stability. They may disagree about how to get it, and wrangle about responsibilities for it, but they are not going to go to war over something they agree about.

The Myth of Chinese "Unrestricted Warfare"

Steve Bannon sat across from me in his West Wing office, in July 2017, a week before President Trump fired him as chief strategist. Television viewers have a distorted view of that exclusive piece of political real estate. The actual West Wing is tiny, providing modest office space for a few top officials. Most of the staff works across the way in the Executive Office Building. Bannon's office had the size and décor of a dorm room, dominated by whiteboards with to-do lists. I had met Steve years before—we had discussed but never completed a transaction in Asia—and we had worked together on the Ted Cruz presidential campaign before Steve shifted to Trump, where he contributed mightily to the 2016 victory.

China, Steve insisted, was engaged in "unrestricted warfare" against the United States. We were discussing plans to rebuild America's defense industrial base, a conversation that ended when Steve left the White House. As he told the *South China Morning Post* a few weeks later, a twenty-year-old essay by two Chinese military officers persuaded him that "China was engaging in economic warfare against us."[176] The offending document, translated into English as "Unrestricted Warfare," was written by Qiao Liang and Wang Xiangsui, in 1999. Qiao is now retired; Wang teaches at Beihang University. Bannon explained that since it would take time for China to catch up with the United States militarily, Beijing had been focusing for the past decades on using information and economic means to weaken the US. "The whole [Chinese] strategy is to avoid kinetic warfare and focus on information and economic [warfare]," he told the Hong Kong newspaper.

Michael Pillsbury, the author of *The Hundred Year Marathon: China's Secret Strategy to Replace America as the Global Superpower*,[177] makes Liao and Wang his prime exhibits for the prosecution. "China's nationalists called themselves *ying pai*, meaning *hawks* or *eagles*. Many of these *ying pai* are generals and admirals and government hardliners. Few Americans have ever met them. They are the Chinese officials and authors I know the best, because since 1973, the U.S. government has instructed me to work with them. Some of my colleagues wrongly dismiss the *ying pai* as nuts. To me, they represent the real voice of China…the hawks appear to be supportive of the narrative of the decline of the United States and the rise of a strong China," Pillsbury wrote. "Unrestricted Warfare: War and Strategy in the Globalization Era, [is] a work of military analysts in which two Chinese colonels recommend that Beijing 'use asymmetrical warfare, including terrorism, to attack the United States.'"

What Michael Pillsbury calls "the real voice of China" turns out to be a quirky, oddball minority opinion that the People's Liberation Army rejected. Its authors were put out to pasture rather than promoted. In fact, China did precisely the opposite of what the authors of "Unrestricted Warfare" proposed. Pillsbury's argument is nonsense in the dictionary sense of the word.

Liao and Wang inveighed vociferously against the strategy that the People's Liberation Army actually embraced during the past twenty years—to invest in advanced military technology to achieve regional superiority in high-tech weapons. Chinese military strategy during the past two decades has focused almost exclusively on technological superiority, in particular the use of missiles to neutralize American satellites and naval power. As I detailed earlier in this chapter, China has spent massively on military technology, with the goal of controlling a perimeter of two hundred miles or so around its coasts, but it has invested little in force projection far from its borders.

"Unrestricted Warfare," by contrast, argues that technological superiority in armaments is a mug's game. Here is what the authors wrote twenty years ago:

> Compared to new-concept weapons, nearly all the weapons that we have known so far may be termed old-concept weapons. The reason they are called old is because the basic functions of these weapons were their mobility and lethal power. Even things like precision-guided bombs and other such high-tech weapons really involve nothing more than the addition of the two elements of intelligence and structural capabilities. From the perspective of practical applications, no change in appearance can alter their nature as traditional weapons, that is, their control throughout by professional soldiers and their use on certain battlefields. All these weapons and weapons platforms that have been produced in line with traditional thinking have without exception come to a dead end in their efforts to adapt to modern warfare and future warfare.
>
> *Those desires of using the magic of high-technology to work some alchemy on traditional weapons so that they are completely remade have ultimately fallen into the high-tech trap involving the endless waste of limited funds and an arms race.* [Emphasis added] This is the paradox that must inevitably be faced in the process of the development of traditional weapons: To ensure that the weapons are in the lead, one must continue to up the ante in development costs; the result of this continued raising of the stakes is that no one has enough money to maintain the lead. Its ultimate result is that the weapons to defend the country actually become a cause of national bankruptcy.

Russia's efforts to achieve technological superiority, Liao and Wang added, brought about the downfall of the Soviet Union:

Perhaps the most recent examples are the most convincing. Marshal Orgakov, the former chief of the Soviet general staff, was acutely aware of the trend of weapons development in the "nuclear age," and when, at an opportune time, he proposed the brand-new concept of the "revolution in military technology," his thinking was clearly ahead of those of his generation. But being ahead of time in his thinking hardly brought his country happiness, and actually brought about disastrous results. As soon as this concept—which against the backdrop of the Cold War was seen by his colleagues as setting the pace for the time—was proposed, it further intensified the arms race which had been going on for some time between the United States and the Soviet Union. It was just that, at that time no one could predict that it would actually result in the breakup of the Soviet Union and its complete elimination from the superpower contest. A powerful empire collapsed without a single shot being fired, vividly corroborating the lines of the famous poem by Kipling, "When empires perish, it is not with a rumble, but a snicker."

Not only was this true for the former Soviet Union, today the Americans seem to be following in the footsteps of their old adversary, providing fresh proof of the paradox of weapons development that we have proposed. As the outlines of the age of technology integration become increasingly clear, they are investing more and more in the development of new weapons, and the cost of the weapons is getting higher and higher. The development of the F-14 and F-15 in the '60s and '70s cost one billion dollars, while the development of the B-2 in the '80s cost over $10 billion, and the 24 development of the F-22 in the '90s has exceeded $13 billion. Based on weight, the B-2, which runs $13–$15 billion each, is some three times more expensive than an equivalent weight of gold. Expensive weapons like that abound in the U.S. arsenal, such as the F-117A bomber, the F-22

> main combat aircraft, and the Comanche helicopter gunship. The cost of each of these weapons exceeds or approaches $100 million, and this massive amount of weapons with unreasonable cost-effectiveness has covered the U.S. military with increasingly heavy armor, pushing them step by step toward the high-tech weapons trap where the cost stakes continue to be raised. If this is still true for the rich and brash United States, then how far can the other countries, who are short of money, continue down this path? Obviously, it will be difficult for anyone to keep going. Naturally, the way to extricate oneself from this predicament is to develop a different approach.[178]

Unfortunately for the United States, China's strategists ignored Liao and Wang's dire predictions about the unsustainable costs of high-tech weapons, and invested massively in anti-satellite missiles, surface-to-ship missiles, hypervelocity glide missiles, ultra-silent submarines, stealth aircraft, electronic warfare, quantum radar, and—most devastating for America's intelligence gathering—quantum cryptography. Liao and Wang thoroughly misunderstood the American model, in which defense R & D created new technologies that transformed the civilian economy.

Pillsbury claims that the Chinese plan an asymmetrical war with the U.S. But that is *not* what Liao and Wang wrote in "Unrestricted Warfare." They note that "weak countries, poor countries and non-state actors" have used asymmetrical warfare in the form of terrorism effectively.[12] The most prescient observation in their 1999 treatise is that

---

12 Liao and Wang wrote: "No matter whether it serves as a line of thought or as a principle guiding combat operations, asymmetry manifests itself to some extent in every aspect of warfare. Understanding and employing the principle of asymmetry correctly allows us always to find and exploit an enemy's soft spots. The main fighting elements of some poor countries, weak countries, and non-state entities have all used "mouse toying with the cat"-type asymmetrical combat methods against much more powerful adversaries. In cases such as Chechniya vs. Russia, Somalia vs. the United States, Northern Ireland guerrillas vs. Britain, and Islamic Jihad vs. the entire West, without exception we see the consistent, wise refusal to confront the armed forces of the strong country head-to-head. Instead, the weaker side has contended with its adversary by using guerrilla war (mainly urban guerrilla war) [9], terrorist

the American military of twenty years ago made poor preparations against terrorism:

> Even though the United States bears the brunt of being faced with the threat of this type of nonmilitary war and has been the injured party time after time, yet what is surprising is that such a large nation unexpectedly does not have a unified strategy and command structure to deal with the threat. What makes one even more so wonder whether to laugh or cry is that unexpectedly they have forty-nine departments and offices responsible for anti-terrorist activities, but there is very little coordination and cooperation among them. Other nations are not that much better than the United States in this area. The allocations and basic investment directions of various nations for security needs are still only limited to the military and intelligence and political departments, but there are few and pitiful investments in other directions. Again using the United States as an example, it uses seven billion dollars in funds for anti-terrorism which is only 1/25 of the $250 billion military expenditure.[179]

It was unfair of Liao and Wang to blame the Pentagon for America's intelligence failure on 9/11. The principle failure lay in poor coordination between the Central Intelligence Agency and the Federal Bureau of

---

war, holy war, protracted war, network war, and other forms of combat. Mostly the weaker side selects as its main axis of battle those areas or battle lines where its adversary does not expect to be hit. The center of mass of the assault is always a place which will result in a huge psychological shock to the adversary. This use of asymmetrical measures which create power for oneself and make the situation develop as you want it to, is often hugely effective. It often makes an adversary which uses conventional forces and conventional measures as its main combat strength look like a big elephant charging into a china shop. It is at a loss as to what to do, and unable to make use of the power it has. Apart from the effectiveness it displays when used, asymmetry in itself is a rule of action suggested by the golden rule. Of all rules, this is the only one which encourages people to break rules so as to use rules. Also, it is an effective prescription for methodical and well-balanced medical treatment for a chronic illness of thought."

Investigation.[180] Contrary to Liao and Wang's predictions, terrorism did *not* present an existential threat to the United States. The United States was entirely capable of suppressing the terrorist threat. Since 9/11, no large-scale terror attacks have occurred on American soil, Bin Laden is dead, and ISIS is broken, if not extinct.

Despite the sensational title of Pillsbury's book—*China's Secret Strategy to Replace America as the World's Superpower*—there is nothing secret about China's military plans. China displays its missile force proudly in military parades and makes sure that the West is aware of its capabilities—as the University of Sydney report on Chinese military capacity makes clear. The most important military innovation China has introduced, namely quantum cryptography, was introduced in public and rushed into commercial applications. China tested its anti-satellite missiles in a way that made sure the world took notice. It flies its prototype fighters at public air shows. China may have a few nasty surprises lurking in the shadows, such as the mysterious spoofing of GPS signals, but the foundation of its strategy is massive deterrence against any possible American attack along its coasts. Deterrence depends on the other side knowing what you can do.

Liao and Wang's treatise is an unsurprising survey of the ways in which finance, politics, and civil unrest affect geopolitics. Military thinking, Qiao and Wang argued, must take all of these elements into account:

> He who wants to win today's wars, or those of tomorrow, to have victory firmly in his grasp, must "combine" all of the resources of war which he has at his disposal and use them as means to prosecute the war. And even this will not be enough. He must combine them according to the demands of the rules of victory. Even this will still not be enough, because the rules of victory cannot guarantee that victory will drop like ripe fruit into a basket. It still needs a skilled hand to pluck it. That hand is the concept of "going beyond limits," surpassing all boundaries and conforming with the laws of victory when conducting warfare with combinations. Thus, we obtain a complete concept, a completely new method

> of warfare called "modified combined war that goes beyond limits."[181]

It's not surprising that the People's Liberation Army put "Unrestricted Warfare" in the circular file. Some of Liao and Wang's arguments are downright kooky. They spend ten pages extolling a form of Pythagorean number mysticism under the subhead, "Secretly Conforming to the Rule of the Golden Section," a characteristic ratio of self-similar growth. This "secret" explains not only the success of Mongol cavalry during the Middle Ages, Liao and Wang contend, but also Duke Li's victory in the Battle of Yanling in 575 B.C.E., Alexander's victory over Darius in the Battle of Arabela in 331 B.C.E., and the prowess of Gustavus Adolphus of Sweden during the Thirty Years' War.[182] This sort of argument in any respectable army would peg the authors as Section Eight cases, and the PLA is no exception.

Although Qiao and Wang write about so-called asymmetric warfare (guerilla operations, terrorism, and so forth), China, with few exceptions, has stayed clear of activities of this kind—in marked contrast to the Soviet Union, which backed subversive organizations around the world, from the PLO to the Sandinistas. Beijing isn't squeamish about trucking with terrorists. It blocked a United Nations Security Council resolution in March 2019, that would have designated a terrorist Masood Azhar, the head of the Pakistani jihadist group Jaish-e-Mohammed. As Michael Kugelman observed in *Foreign Policy*, the veto shows "how far Beijing is willing to go to defend its 'iron brother'" Pakistan.[183]

This sort of dalliance with terrorists follows China's diplomatic interests, rather than a military objective. China is far more worried about Western efforts to destabilize China through "asymmetric warfare." Contrary to Michael Pillsbury's assertion that Westerners don't talk to China hawks, the hawks, such as they are, are happy to talk to Westerners. One of the hawks mentioned by Pillsbury is Real Admiral Luo Yuan, a theorist at the People's Liberation Army's Academy of Military Science. His views of the United States are just as distorted as Pillbury's views about China.

China's Paranoia About the United States

Over dinner, in 2015, Admiral Luo told me that "General Petraeus created ISIS in order to destabilize China."

"That's ridiculous," I said.

"It is not ridiculous in the least," Luo continued, in the benevolent tone in which one instructs especially slow students. "There are ISIS leaders whom we have identified and tracked, who were trained by Petraeus during the 'Surge,'" the counter-insurgency campaign that Petraeus conducted in 2008–2009 to contain a Sunni rebellion against the majority Shi'ite government that the United States had helped bring to power in 2007.

I took a deep breath and explained: "This was a comedy of errors. The neo-conservatives in the Bush administration believed in majority rule as a matter of dogma, so the US held elections in 2007 and the Shi'ite minority won. Then the Sunnis who used to run Iraq under Saddam Hussein resisted with guerilla war and terrorist attacks. Petraeus was just a careerist looking for another star, and he told the Bush Administration that he could fix the Sunni problem by paying off the Sunni tribal leaders. He handed out hundreds of millions of dollars to the Sunnis and gave them weapons and training through the 'Sons of Iraq' and the 'Sunni Awakening.'" When Obama took US forces out of Iraq, a lot of the same Sunnis who took money from Petraeus faced the same Shi'ite state, and became non-state actors, that is ISIS. And the CIA's support for Sunni jihadist opponents of the Assad government in Syria made matters worse, as the Defense Intelligence Agency warned in a notorious 2012 report."[184]

Of course, I wasn't quite that coherent, but that was the gist of my reply.

My Chinese interlocutor was not impressed. "You're trying to tell me that the people who run the world's great superpower are complete idiots who don't think about the consequences of their actions?"

That was exactly what I was trying to say, and it's not an easy position to defend in China. It doesn't help that the American Establishment continues to lionize Petraeus, by way of distracting attention from the collective blunder that helped Donald Trump kick them out of power. In June 2019, I heard Petraeus address an adoring Economic Club of

New York lunch hosted by Mrs. Henry Kravis. The roomful of Wall Street swells cooed as Petraeus hailed the "great ideas" of his generation… "Jack Ma…Jeff Bezos…the Surge." If that's what the American elite thinks, who can blame the Chinese for taking all of this at face value?

I suggested that the Chinese general read Lt. Gen. Daniel P. Bolger's 2014 memoir, *Why We Lost*,[185] for an inside account of the disaster that Petraeus set in motion. It didn't wash. My Chinese interlocutor said, "America deliberated created ISIS. I refuse to believe that America did all of this by accident."

Of course, it wasn't an accident; Americans suffer from a chronic narcissism that assumes that the rest of the world longs to be like the U.S., from Baghdad to Beijing and Fallujah to Fujian Province. It isn't that we like ourselves that much, but rather that we can't imagine anything different. This leads us to do stupid things, for example, conquer a country ruled by the Saddam Hussein's Sunni mafia, and in the name of majority rule, turn it order to Shi'ite sectarian parties allied with Iran, which is a bigger threat to the United States than Iraq ever was.

China well remembers that the United States armed the Afghan Mujahidin against Russian occupiers during the 1980s, with shoulder-fired anti-aircraft missiles and other sophisticated weapons, and contributed to Russia's humiliating withdrawal from Afghanistan. Uyghur terrorism is an urgent security concern for Beijing. In March 2014, a group of eight Uyghurs drew long-bladed knives and attacked passengers at Kunming Railway Station in Yunnan province, killing thirty-one and injuring one hundred forty.[186] A senior Chinese officer at the People's Liberation Army's Academy of Military Science in Beijing explained China's concerns as follows during a closed-door conference in 2015:

> Twelve million Uyghurs in Xinjiang province present a problem. There are another ten million Hui Muslims scattered through China. But to our South, Islam is a sleeping serpent. The three hundred million Muslims of Indonesia have long kept their own ways, but there are radical Muslims there now who demand a Sharia state. In 1998, they instigated riots and murdered hundreds of ethnic Chinese. They are agitating

> for Sharia law in Indonesia. They might make common cause with the Muslim rebels of the Philippines in Mindanao, and the three million Muslims in the South of Thailand. The Thais have contained Muslim rebels so far, but they are fighting on the border of Malaysia. The Malays control the politics of the country and overseas Chinese control the economy, and it is a delicate balance. What if the war on Malaysia's frontier with Thailand became the cause of radical Muslims in Malaysia? What if the Muslim rebels in Mindanao demanded a separation from the Catholic Philippines and a union with Malaysia? What if Muslim radicals in Indonesia held the Chinese community hostage to support them? China would have a series of wars on its southern border, rather than a stable and prosperous set of trading partners.[187]

That helps explain why China herded between one and two million of its Uyghur Muslims into "re-education camps" during 2019. If China has built up assets among restive Muslim populations that might threaten the West, Western intelligence services have yet to detect them. But Beijing's security services have good reason to fear asymmetric warfare directed against China. The Chinese authorities claim to have arrested thirteen thousand terrorists in Xinjiang Province between 2013 and 2019. A government white paper released in March 2019, claims that the authorities "destroyed 1,588 violent and terrorist gangs, arrested 12,995 terrorists, seized 2,052 explosive devices, punished 30,645 people for 4,858 illegal religious activities, and confiscated 345,229 copies of illegal religious materials."[188] One reads such reports with a high degree of skepticism. But the fact remains that China's view of "asymmetric warfare" is defense rather than offensive. The Chinese Empire has a lot more to lose than to gain by loosing these particular dogs of war.

As the United States Institute of Peace, a US government-sponsored think tank, wrote in a 2017 evaluation:[189]

> China's interests are driven by a desire to ensure domestic stability in Xinjiang and throughout China,

> to promote regional stability (especially in Central Asia, South Asia, the Middle East, and Africa), and to protect Chinese citizens and businesses abroad.
>
> Especially since the outbreak of riots and violence in Xinjiang in 2009, the Arab Awakening in 2011, and a string of high-profile terrorist attacks within China's borders (including a suicide bombing under Mao's portrait in Tiananmen Square, a mass knife attack in a Kunming train station, and a number of violent incidents in Xinjiang), China's sensitivity to the potential impact of international terrorism on domestic stability in China has escalated. In particular, Beijing is concerned that Uighurs will join transnational terrorist organizations such as IS and al-Qaeda and return to China radicalized and ready to disturb the social order. They also worry that external funding will be funneled to Islamic insurgency groups within China by sympathetic outside groups. Although China's fears of domestic terrorism, insurgency, and potential international links are often exaggerated and its treatment of Uighurs strongly contributes to unrest and violent incidents, Beijing is genuinely concerned that it is vulnerable to terrorism and fears perceived insurgency activity in Xinjiang that could threaten China's territorial integrity.

In summary, there is no arcane Oriental secret plan, no Fu Manchu pulling strings behind the scenes to subvert the West, no recondite Communist conspiracy. There is nothing but the fact that China copied the best of American practice and put vast government resources into advanced military technology with the objective of denying the United States military access to its coastlines. All of this happened in the clear light of day, and with the knowledge of top American officials. In 2014, the late Andrew Marshall, then head of the Pentagon's Office of Net Assessment—for which I sporadically consulted—told me that China's surface-to-ship missiles could sink American aircraft carriers. We knew what the Chinese were doing and couldn't rouse ourselves to take decisive action to in response.

As Newt Gingrich wrote in a 2019 book, "It is not China's fault that the Department of Defense bureaucracy is cumbersome and convoluted. The slow pace blocks small entrepreneurs from competing. It guarantees that most major procurement will take so long that it will be a decade or more behind the available technology by the time it is adopted. This also raises the cost of new equipment unnecessarily. Our current system favors old systems and old habits over the needed breakthroughs to new technologies and new strategies."[190]

CHAPTER SEVEN

CHINA'S SOVEREIGNTY TRIPWIRE IN HONG KONG[13]

Hong Kong is a British city that happens to have an ethnic Chinese majority. It never wanted to be Chinese, still does not want to be Chinese, and never should have been Chinese. For reasons that remain obscure, Britain in 1997, abandoned its perpetual rights to Hong Kong and the Kowloon peninsula, at a time when China wasn't sure it wanted the British colony. Once Hong Kong became Chinese sovereign territory by treaty, however, it fell under the iron law of Chinese imperial governance: China will tolerate no infringement on its sovereignty anywhere, because loss of sovereignty anywhere poses a threat to all Chinese sovereignty everywhere. The majority of Hong Kong's people wanted to remain under British rule but with stronger democratic institutions. Instead, Hong Kong got the worst of both worlds. It continues to be ruled by a colonial-style executive, and remains under Beijing's shadow as an "autonomous zone" of the People's Republic of China.

For the seven million inhabitants of Hong Kong, that is a tragic outcome, compounded by the spillover of China's corruption into Hong Kong's economy. The likeliest outcome is a perpetuation of an uncomfortable status quo, with cosmetic political reforms to vitiate the protests, and economic reforms to mitigate the underlying causes of discontent. President Trump signed the Hong Kong Human Rights

[13] Portions of this chapter were first published on the website of *First Things* magazine on Dec. 2, 2019. They are used by permission.

and Democracy Act in November 2019, after both Houses of Congress passed nearly unanimously. The world braced itself for a Sino-American confrontation over Hong Kong's future. Beijing has denounced the legislation as interference in its internal affairs, and warned of dire consequences if the U.S. implements any of the act's punitive measures.

The initiative for the Hong Kong legislation came from Senator Marco Rubio and other neoconservatives, not from the White House. The same wing of the Washington foreign policy establishment that promised us democracy in Iraq and Afghanistan has undertaken a crusade for democracy in China. This whim has no more chance of succeeding than the Iraq and Afghanistan adventures, but there is a difference—China is not Iraq. It now has the capacity to neutralize every American asset in East Asia within hours of the outbreak of conflict. Iraq could only wear us down; China can blow us up. That should set a limit to our experimentation in regime change.

A prominent Chinese political observer told me after the Hong Kong act passed Congress that in China's view, none of this is accidental: "I think none of the actors involved in this game—Beijing, the government of Hong Kong, the oppositions, the US—has made any mistakes. In the past months, all parties are collectively doing one job—transforming HK's local unrest into grand geo-political confrontation between China and the US. So, any possible future outcomes of HK issue would be directed by other bigger events from now on."

I think this is overwrought, but in the wrong circumstances, perceptions can be self-fulfilling.

After the dust settled, then nothing happened. The op-ed pages of American newspapers and the pages of opinion-setting journals swelled with support for the brave democracy protesters of Hong Kong, and then the issue fizzled away. The sad fact is that nothing could have happened, except a confrontation that neither Beijing nor Washington wanted.

In the worst case, Beijing might have simply terminated Hong Kong's status as an Autonomous Region under its "one country, two systems" rubric, and incorporated it into the mainland. Perhaps two million of Hong Kong's best educated and most productive citizens would have emigrated, first of all to Great Britain and then to Taiwan,

Singapore, and other Asian destinations. But that is the last thing Beijing wants. Hong Kong offers enormous advantages to China, whose own currency is inconvertible and whose capital markets operate under a legal system that inspires scant confidence among foreign investors.

Hong Kong's Blessing is Also its Curse

Hong Kong's strong financial markets are its blessing and its curse. It has the world's fourth largest single stock market, with more than twenty-three hundred listed companies and a market capitalization of about US $4 trillion, a US $1.4 trillion local currency bond market, a convertible currency that has been pegged to the US dollar at a fixed exchange rate since 1983, and a strong financial services sector operating under British law. Half of Hong Kong's listed companies are Mainland Chinese, and Mainland companies raised about $38 billion through initial public offerings during 2019, the largest volume in ten years. That compares to just $9 billion raised by Chinese companies in the United States through initial public offerings in 2018, before the US-China trade war effectively closed the market to Chinese issuers. The advantages of British law and a convertible currency prompted Citic, one of China's largest state-owned conglomerates, to shift its assets to Hong Kong in 2014. Local-currency assets in China are subject to exchange controls, but stocks and bonds of Chinese companies traded in Hong Kong are fully convertible into foreign currencies.

High-paying financial services jobs help left Hong Kong's per capita gross domestic product to more than US $46,000, about four times that of Mainland China's. But recent graduates starting out in financial services will need to save for twenty years or more to make a down payment on a home large enough to a small family. China's RMB is convertible into Hong Kong dollars, and the island's real estate has absorbed vast amounts of Chinese cash generated by corrupt or dodgy enterprises. Relative to income Hong Kong has the highest prices in the world, and the biggest losers are Hong Kong's young people.

That is the background to the mass demonstrations for democracy that rocked Hong Kong during 2019, including a peaceful march in August, of two million people—a majority of Hong Kong's adult population. A frisson of hope passed through the West that Hong Kong's resistance to Beijing might portend the fall of the Communist regime on the Mainland itself. Most Americans nodded in agreement with Jimmy Lai, publisher of Hong Kong's anti-Beijing *Apple Daily*, when he declared in *The Wall Street Journal* that "there's hope for freedom, even in China."

> Mao Zedong proclaimed the founding of the People's Republic of China from a podium overlooking Tiananmen Square seventy years ago. This year's celebrations, including in Hong Kong, were meant to pay tribute to Mao's successor Xi Jinping.
>
> But the people of Hong Kong have stood up. Millions have marched in protest of Beijing's undemocratic control.... We are fighting for what was promised us. Universal suffrage is a right to which we're entitled in our Basic Law, the mini constitution that took effect when the U.K. handed over the territory in 1997. Mr. Xi abrogated it in 2014 by imposing limits on elections for Hong Kong's chief executive and members of the Legislative Council, and our rights have been denied to us.
>
> Some find it inconceivable that Beijing would ever give us universal suffrage, but we must persist. We're prepared to make short-term sacrifice to pursue long-term freedom. We believe that if we persist, we may win. China is not as strong as it pretends. What the Communist Party calls its "socialist market economy with Chinese characteristics" has run its course.[191]

In the fall of 2019, a fraction of Hong Kong's democracy demonstrators turned to urban guerilla warfare. Reports like Almen Chui's October 14, 2019, dispatch in the *Asia Times* became Hong Kong's daily fare:

> The anti-government protests continued in multiple locations around Hong Kong on Sunday with one

of the most volatile happening in Kowloon's Mong Kok area.

Starting from late afternoon, relatively small-scale flash-mob protests took place across the city. There was vandalism and arson targeting government offices, subway stations and shops which were claimed to be backed by local gangsters or pro-Beijing supporters.

A number of fistfights also broke out after disputes between groups with different political stances.

In Mong Kok, one of the busiest districts in Hong Kong, protesters blocked the roads with barricades, damaged traffic lights and painted anti-government graffiti on shops and on the road. At 8pm, there was a loud explosion from a flower box on the sidewalk on Nathan Road near Fife Street, close to where a police vehicle was parked.

People found a plastic bag and a blue-colored object like a battery half-hidden under soil in the flower box, the Ming Pao Daily reported. A battery, circuit board, mobile phone, one phone SIM card and cables were later dug out from the soil. The police's Explosive Ordnance Disposal Bureau then arrived and cordoned off the area, but it was not clear if some kind of explosive device was found. At almost the same time, twenty Molotov cocktails were thrown at the huge water barriers placed outside the Mong Kok police station, starting a fire. Riot police aided by firefighters distinguished the blaze.

A woman who protesters accused of taking close-up photos of them was surrounded after refusing to give up her phone. Someone sprayed black paint on her face and others hit her head with a water bottle. Police later led her to safety. At about midnight, a large group of unmasked protesters surrounded a man wearing a red T-shirt near the intersection of Nathan Road and Argyle Street. The man was kicked, punched and beaten up. The man's shirt was ripped off and he fell to the ground repeatedly, but protesters kept stomping on him. A woman shouted: "Stop it! Enough. He will die." The attack finally stopped before riot police arrived on the scene.

Meanwhile, the news department of local broadcaster NowTV issued a statement condemning the excessive force police used on one of their news crew members, leaving a member of the news team requiring surgery and a stay in hospital after he was subdued by police.[192]

Chile and Hong Kong Riots Have a Common Cause

Notably, only one Hong Kong resident died as a direct result of the protests—a seventy-year-old man reportedly hit in the head by a brick thrown by a black-clad protestor.[193] By contrast, twenty-seven people died during the 2019 protests in Santiago, Chile, a country with a democratically-elected government. The Chile protests focused on economic issues such as mass transit fares, healthcare, and pensions.[194] No deaths are attributed to the Hong Kong police. The numbers suggest that Beijing's strategy is to pursue a war of attrition against the protestors, 6,105 of whom have been arrested as of mid-December 2019. Fears of a repeat of the 1989 Tiananmen Square massacre, when the Chinese government sent tanks against student protesters in Beijing's main open square, were exaggerated. China does not want a bloodbath in front of the world's television cameras.

Despite the hopes of Mr. Lai and many American political observers, the Hong Kong protests elicited scant interest on China's Mainland. Hong Kong, as noted, is a British city, and has always been viewed as a foreign entity by Mainlanders, who make much less money than Hong Kongers, and who tend to regard the Hong Kongers as spoiled and lazy. Every Mainlander with whom I spoke during several visits to China in the course of 2019, insisted that the protesters were paid by the Central Intelligence Agency to destabilize China.

A journalist for Germany's government news organization Deutsche Welle reported from Shanghai that "there's little sympathy in Shanghai for the protesters there."

> "What are they doing? Why are they acting up like this?" a thirty-year-old office worker asks. Speaking to German public broadcaster ARD, he commented that the people of Hong Kong should "just get on with their work and peacefully get on with their lives." His opinion was that the whole protest was pointless—and it's a view the majority of mainland Chinese people probably share.
>
> That's certainly the impression gained by the journalist Jose Qian. He estimates that 90 percent of mainland Chinese are critical of the protests in Hong Kong. Qian lives in Shanghai, where he works for various international media outlets and has his finger on the pulse of the city. He says the people of Shanghai are well aware that something's going on in Hong Kong.
>
> "They probably don't know exactly why it's happening, how long it's been going on, or what the phases have been," Qian told DW. "They probably don't really know what the Hong Kong demonstrators' demands are, either." Consequently, he says, public opinion in Shanghai is being shaped by resentment and fears of possible violence in Hong Kong.[195]

Beijing is now trying to back away from years of mismanagement in Hong Kong, blundered by instructing—or allowing—Hong Kong chief executive Carrie Lam—a former British subject and U.K. civil servant—to challenge Hong Kong's administrative independence with an extradition law that the people of Hong Kong rightly viewed with suspicion.

Beijing also helped create the conditions for mass protests by allowing the Hong Kong government to run the land market in the interests of real-estate oligarchs who want to limit the supply of new land for construction to prop up the island's impossibly high home prices. Hong Kong is the only place in the world where Chinese can exchange the otherwise inconvertible national currency, the Renminbi, for a convertible currency, namely the Hong Kong dollar. For years, Hong Kong laundered vast amounts of cash from the Chinese mainland. The Apple Store in Hong Kong Central used to have cash-counting machines for mainland customers who came in with suitcases of cash and left with a hundred iPhones. A great deal of Hong Kong's luxury housing was purchased the same way. Many of the island's luxury buildings are dark at night because they are owned entirely by absentee mainlanders.

Limited land use and laundered money left Hong Kong with a home-price-to-income ratio of nearly 50:1 (versus about 10:1 in most of Europe, 9:1 in China, and less than 4:1 in the United States). A young Hong Konger graduating from university today cannot hope to start a family before saving for twenty years or more. That contributes to the exasperation of Hong Kong's young people, just as it does in Santiago, Chile, and other cities that have witnessed urban upheaval in the past year.

Around the world, housing prices have risen much faster than incomes. Hong Kong and Santiago are among the most egregious cases. The problem isn't the housing market as such, but the market for al income-earning assets. After the 2008 financial crisis, central banks around the world kept interest rates extraordinary low. Nearly $20 trillion of government bonds now trade at negative interest rates, something rarely seen before in financial history, and never for such an extended period and on such a scale.

That forces investors to shift money from government bonds to other income-earning assets, notably real estate, as well as equities. Loose monetary policy, though, hasn't produced a corresponding boom in productivity-enhancing capital assets. Labor productivity has lagged through the past ten years of monetary laxity. That explains why asset prices have outstripped wages. Real estate is simply another asset class, a bubble on the wave of monetary easing.

The people of Hong Kong had legitimate grievances on rights and economic policy. The protest movement drew an estimated two million people, more than one-quarter of Hong Kong's total population, to an August demonstration. Afterward, a small core of protesters terrorized the city, causing hundreds of millions of dollars in property damage. This culminated in the November occupation of the Hong Kong Polytechnic University in Kowloon. Carrie Lam formally withdrew the hated extradition bill on September 4, 2019, though the government still has to address the housing crisis. China believes it acted responsibly against widespread violence.

It is instructive to contrast China's patience in Hong Kong with the extreme measures it employed to crush the threat of Uyghur separatism in its western Xinjiang Province, where between one and two million Uyghurs have been incarcerated in "re-education camps." The Chinese mainland is indifferent to events in Hong Kong, which mainlanders view as a foreign entity. Beijing saw no threat of the Hong Kong protests spilling over into the mainland, and played its cards patiently. But it acted swiftly and with shocking indifference to Western sensibilities when it perceived a security threat in Xinjiang. Western observers who imagine that events in Hong Kong might destabilize the mainland are out of touch.

As I explained in chapter one, China is a polyglot, multiethnic empire, not a nation-state. Infringement of its control over any part of its territory threatens the whole. Foreign intervention and regional divisions is the stuff of China's historical nightmares. Any loss of sovereignty, in China's experience, begins a slippery slope toward imperial crackup. Foreign invasion is still a living memory in China, and Beijing reads the worst into American intervention over Hong Kong.

That explains why Beijing is willing to go to war over the South China Sea. It is an a fortiori demonstration in line with the Chinese proverb, *Kill the chicken while the monkey watches.* If we are prepared for war over a few islands to which our historical claim is arguable, Beijing is saying, think of what we will do in the case of Taiwan. When Xi Jinping met President Obama at the December 2014 APAC summit in Beijing, he said that China is two things—a people, and a territory. The population may grow by 10 percent or shrink by 10 percent, but there will always be a lot of Chinese. The territory of China, though, is sacred and inviolable, and China never will give up the South China Sea.

The West is not guiltless in Hong Kong's present problems, either. It was an unconscionable mistake for Britain to cede the territory to China when it had perpetual claim to Hong Kong and Kowloon, for once any territory passes formally into the Chinese empire, it becomes "sacred and inviolable" by Chinese criteria. The Thatcher government betrayed the people of Hong Kong who wished to remain a British colony rather than become a Chinese province. That is tragic for the people of Hong Kong, although China has respected the "two systems" part of the bargain.

Jimmy Lai's *Apple Daily* continues to publish fiery denunciations of the Beijing regime in Hong Kong. As noted, Mr. Lai believes that Hong Kong's travails and the US-China trade war may bring democracy to China, and argued his case in the American press. I think this scenario far-fetched, but the relevant point is that Mr. Lai is free to preach the overthrow of the Chinese system from his perch in Hong Kong.

How Britain Sold-Out Hong Kong

Britain's sellout of Hong Kong was especially onerous because China in 1997 was not eager to take over the island. This has been reported in major media for years, and confirmed by declassified documents from the Thatcher archives. On May 15, 1997, Peter Stein reported in *The Wall Street Journal*, on the theory that "China's leaders didn't really plan to take back Hong Kong on July 1, 1997; the British made them do it." Stein cited "the latest supporter of this argument, Wong Man-fong, is a former senior Chinese official. An ex-deputy secretary general of China's Xinhua news agency in Hong Kong, Mr. Wong also served on a Chinese task force aimed at formulating Beijing's Hong Kong policy in the early 1980s."

> No historian disputes that in 1979 Britain had a problem. Bankers and investors were growing nervous about Hong Kong's future after 1997. An important lease which Britain had signed with China after the Anglo-Chinese war in 1898 would expire that year. The lease covered large chunks of Hong Kong's suburban hinterland. Businesspeople needed to know: If they signed leases of their own for Hong Kong property that extended beyond 1997, would China support them?
>
> "In the early stages, Beijing hadn't really considered taking back Hong Kong," Mr. Wong said. "Beijing was more inclined to the idea of leaving the situation as it was." China would simply label Hong

> Kong "a historic problem" which the Chinese and British governments "would discuss at an appropriate time." That done, July 1, 1997, could come to pass, and nothing would have to happen. "The status quo," said Mr. Wong, "would continue."
>
> Britain, though, made trouble by insisting on formal talks "to allow the British to continue ruling for another thirty or fifty years," Mr. Wong said. He himself advised the British to take a more "abstract" approach, he says. But the British wouldn't budge. "The British strategy in fact didn't give China any way to step down."[196]

In October 2014, Gywnn Guilford reported in *The Atlantic,* on the implications of newly released materials from Baroness Thatcher's papers:

> When Mao founded the People's Republic of China in 1949, he and Zhou Enlai decided not to seize Hong Kong—which the British at the time expected—because the capitalist territory was their lone source of foreign exchange and a strategic portal for manufacturing trade that would eventually drive China's double-digit growth. As the newly declassified documents reveal, China's leaders explicitly wanted to "preserve the colonial status of Hong Kong" so that the People's Republic could "trade and contact people of other countries and obtain materials" it badly needed. Both the British and the Chinese governments benefited from the nearly 50-year deadlock of Hong Kongers seeing neither democracy nor an invasion.[197]

After the fact, Beijing cannot allow Hong Kong to move towards independence without compromising the sovereignty principle that has governed the Chinese empire since inception. There are no backsies in China. If the West pushes too hard, Beijing will simply discard the "two systems" and integrate Hong Kong into the mainland, despite the inconvenience of losing access to a convertible currency and a financial market governed by Western law. Security always supersedes politics in China.

CHAPTER EIGHT

HOW AMERICA CAN REMAIN THE WORLD'S LEADING SUPERPOWER[14]

The year 2019 ended with a trade deal between the United States and China, under which the US will rescind some but not all the tariffs it previously imposed, and China will buy more US agricultural products, open some parts of its market to US companies, and promise to refrain from technology theft. This is a truce, rather than a peace deal. No one believes that the war is over. The question now is how to pursue it further.

A growing body of opinion—which I share—believes that tariffs won't help, and that the United States instead must take measures to restore its industrial base. For example, Senator Marco Rubio called for an American industrial policy in a December 2019 speech before the National Defense University:

> While it may be true that China is "breaking the rules" or that Chinese companies are engaging in "unfair competition" against the American order, the fundamental challenge will not simply be solved by some future trade agreement....The industries that

[14] Parts of this chapter first appeared in The Journal of American Affairs (Winter 2017) and are used by permission. Additional material first appeared as a response to Senator Marco Rubio's initiative on industrial policy on the website of The American Mind, a publication of the Claremont Institute, and is used with permission.

> China intends to dominate are the very ones that will create the dignified and productive work Americans need for us to remain a strong nation.
>
> The depletion of America's manufacturing sector has left us with a tremendous national security vulnerability. I am not advocating for a government takeover of our means of production. What I am calling for us to do is remember that from World War II to the Space Race and beyond, a capitalist America has always relied on public-private collaboration to further our national security. And from the internet to GPS, many of the innovations that have made America a technological superpower originated from national defense-oriented, public-private partnerships.[198]

Senator Rubio's intervention is a welcomed addition to a growing body of opinion that trade war is not enough, and that the United States requires a concerted national effort to assert technological leadership and rebuild its manufacturing base. Other contributions to the debate have recently come from former House Speaker Newt Gingrich,[199] former NSA Director Admiral Michael Rogers,[200] and Hudson Institute researcher Arthur Herman.[201]

Senator Rubio offers two motivations for industrial policy: First, the need to maintain America's strategic superiority in face of a challenge from China. And second, the damage to the lives of American workers and their communities due to the loss of industrial jobs. It is vital to distinguish between these policy issues. Subsidizing domestic steel production won't prevent China from leapfrogging the US in telecommunications technology, and high-tech R & D to defend against Chinese hypervelocity missiles won't reverse employment losses in the rust belt.

The Chinese model is not new, in principle. America subsidizes sports stadiums, and Asia subsidizes chip fabrication plants. The so-called Asian model of industrial development began with the 1868 Meiji Restoration in Japan, to the postwar Singapore and Korean models, to Deng Xiaoping's 1979 market reforms in China, which in turn emulated Singapore's industrial policy. The Asian model treats capital-intensive industry as infrastructure, and applies subsidies in the same way that the United States subsidizes airports, water treatment plants or sports facilities.

During the 1980s, the United States used tariffs, quotas, and currency policy to stem the loss of American manufacturing jobs to Japan. Japan is an American ally, and its economy and population are much smaller than that of the United States, whereas China has 1.4 billion people, and its economy is roughly the same size as America's and growing three times as fast. As former National Security Agency head Admiral Michael Rogers observed December 3, 2019, "China also represents a significant diplomatic, political and military challenge. But what makes it so different is it combines all of that with this significant economic capability. We have also not had a near-peer economically who is also such a competitor or potential adversary."

No one is more surprised at this outcome than the Chinese themselves. A senior officer of Huawei asked me: "Why didn't the United States just have Cisco buy Ericsson, and create a national champion to compete with us?" Cisco used to dominate the market for internet routers. The answer is that Cisco's return on equity last year was 36 percent, while Ericsson's was -4 percent, as the Swedish telecommunications producer struggled to keep up with its Chinese competition. A merger would bring down Cisco's equity price, and American managers focus on little but returns to shareholders.

Senator Rubio contends that "responding to this challenge will require us to reject the fundamentalism that argues that the greatest virtue in American policy is to maximize 'efficiency.' The market will always reach the most efficient economic outcome, but sometimes the most efficient outcome is at odds with the common good and the national interest." That statement is entirely correct, but it raises some problems:

1. If the US government makes demands on corporations that reduce efficiency, e.g., by forcing a merger between Cisco and Ericsson, why should the costs be borne disproportionately by a specific group of Americans—in this case, Cisco's shareholders?
2. If the United States reduces the efficiency of its economy in the interests of national security, job preservation, or other national goals, how will that affect the creditworthiness of the United States? We currently run a federal deficit of $1 trillion and borrow about $500 billion a year from the rest

of the world. We owe $17 trillion to the public and have an additional $46 billion in unfunded obligations from entitlement programs. Nonetheless, the Federal government is able to borrow at or close to the lowest rates in history because investors have long-term confidence in the efficiency of the US economy. There is a limit past which a reduction in efficiency will undermine confidence.

Why the 1980s Were a Golden Age of Innovation and Employment

In the past, massive public support for basic R & D led to the creation of entirely new industries. The 1980s were a golden age of employment and wage growth, yet employment at Fortune 500 companies declined, and new businesses in nascent industries more than compensated. Data processing was the industry that showed the biggest absolute gain in employment. The greatest employment and wage income gains came from industries made possible by federal R & D support, but whose emergence could not have been predicted in advance.

In 1983, an official of Reagan's National Security Council, Dr. Norman Bailey, asked me to prepare an estimate of the civilian economic gains that might accrue from defense R & D. I offered a positive assessment, but wildly underestimated the actual outcome—the entirety of the digital age came about as a result of the Defense Advanced Research Projects Agency (DARPA) investments. For example, the fast, light, and cheap CMOS chips that powered the digital revolution were supported by a grant to RCA Labs from DARPA. DARPA wanted fighter pilots to have the computational power to perform weather analysis in the cockpit. Only afterward did the Defense Department realize that CMOS chips made lookdown radar possible. The semiconductor laser was also invented through a DARPA grant to RCA Labs, whose original purpose was nocturnal illumination of battlefields. Only later did the industry realize that the technology made possible laser-powered optical networks. From this arose the cable television industry, among many others.

Digital technology is now the key to military strength, but America's capacity to manufacture the major components of digital systems is disappearing. America shipped 25 percent of the world's semiconductors in 2011, but only 10 percent in 2018.

In 2018, Henry Kressel and I wrote, in *The Wall Street Journal*:

> The U.S. pioneered the technology that made today's advanced weapon systems possible. But America's competitive advantage in the digital economy is eroding at an alarming pace, along with its domestic high-tech manufacturing capacity. The majority of electronic systems first invented in the U.S. now are designed and made overseas, mainly in Asia. With few and dwindling exceptions, the U.S. no longer makes things like flat-panel displays, memory devices, light-emitting devices, lasers, imaging chips for digital cameras, and computer system packaging software.

As the manufacturer of these component technologies has migrated offshore, so have many key systems suppliers. Intel is the only remaining U.S. company capable of fabricating high-density, high-performance computer chips in America. International Business Strategies estimates that investors are pouring $50 billion a year into advanced chip production facilities in Asia, more than 10 times the level of domestic spending.[202]

As noted, Huawei certainly stole technology in the past, including computer code from Cisco. In 2004, Huawei settled a suit by Cisco, then America's dominant provider of telecommunications equipment, for alleged technology shift. Today, Huawei spends more on R & D than its competitors combined, and owns 30 percent of the patents relating to 5G internet. Today, America's most urgent concern is not the theft of intellectual property, but the creation of Chinese intellectual property.

Industrial automation, big-data analysis of health information, and so forth are American rather than Chinese concepts. What gives Huawei a decisive advantage over prospective American competitors is its dominance in building the mobile communications networks. Senator Rubio decries China's "use of state-associated firms like Huawei to entice foreign nations into exploitative contracts that give China access to foreign nations' critical national security data." That is the view of the US intelligence services, who, like all intelligence services, exaggerate the importance of secrets because it is their stock-in-trade. Far more threatening to American interests is the likelihood that the whole world will freely give its data to Huawei, in return for the benefits of AI.

We Need an Industrial Policy—But the Right Kind of Industry Policy

What sort of industrial policy should the United States adopt? We cannot protect employment simply because it used to be there. Technology does change. As I reported in chapter two, the chief technology officer of the Swiss-Swedish robotics leader, ABB, told Huawei's September 2019 conference that with 5G broadband and virtual reality, no human being ever need go underground to dig for minerals again. Mining robots controlled by engineers with augmented reality headsets will do the work instead. Employment in some industries will shrivel because of technology rather than trade. I support subsidies for jobs in some cases, but the costs of subsidies in capital-intensive industries such as mining and metallurgy is prohibitive.

But we cannot afford *not* to subsidize key technologies, especially where they bear on national defense. Huawei spends close to $20 billion a year in R & D, more than its competitors combined. Considering the strategic benefits that China derives from Huawei's dominance in broadband technology, that is a trivial sum. I advocate a crash program on the part of the United States and its NATO partners to retake the high ground in telecommunications technology. We have seen that it is not enough to admonish our allies against working with Huawei. We should do whatever it takes to create an alternative, as an emergency measure.

The broader problem of rebuilding American manufacturing requires changing corporate behavior. After the 2000 tech stock crash and recession, American investment shifted out of manufacturing and hardware, and into software. The advantage of software is infinite scalability: the marginal cost of adding a customer is zero, and the great software firms that achieved strong network effects—Google, Facebook, Microsoft, and others—generated an extraordinary level of profitability. Asians were willing to subsidize manufacturing industry to provide cheap hardware for the American market. American software companies were happy to concentrate on high-margin software and leave lower-margin manufacturing to Asia.

Even at the level of seed capital, virtually nothing is left in the high-tech manufacturing pipeline. An insignificant fraction of US venture capital commitments is directed to information technology hardware.

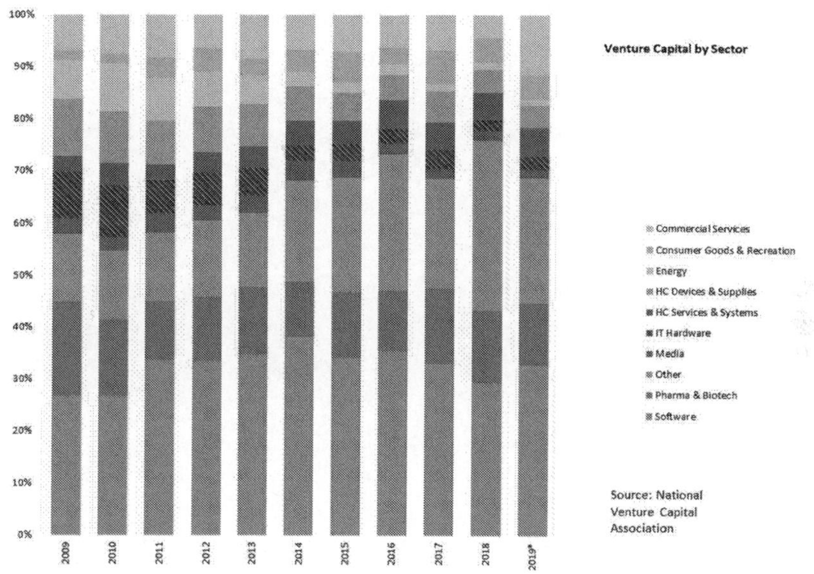

This is an enormous turnaround from the late 1990s, when the telecommunications boom motivated a wave of venture investment in IT hardware. By 2015, hardware investment had all but disappeared.

Cutting off imports from China or other Asian exporters isn't a good option. The American supply chain is so dependent on Asian manufacturing that disruption would be devastating. The Trump Administration was wise to rescind the 25 percent tariffs on $350 billion of Chinese goods originally scheduled for December 15, 2019.

Turning this supertanker around will take ten years and roughly $1 trillion of additional spending. Tax incentives and subsidies will be required, above all for R & D. Much more than money is required. Federal R & D peaked in 1987, as a percentage of GDP at 1.23 percent, or the equivalent of $250 billion in current dollars. In 2017, the United States spent only half that amount, or $127 billion, in federal R & D.

We couldn't spend $250 billion today if we tried to. The corporate laboratories that received the lion's share of DARPA grants—at Bell, General Electric, RCA, IBM, Hughes, and many other firms—have ceased to exist. The national laboratories have shrunk. If the major corporations wanted to revive their laboratories, they couldn't find the engineers; if the universities wanted to train more engineers, they couldn't find the faculty (Edward R. Dougherty, "The Decline of American Science and Engineering," Journal of American Affairs, Spring 2019). We will require educational reforms along the lines of the Eisenhower National Defense Education Act to address the shortfall of skills. Meanwhile, China graduates four times as many STEM bachelor's degrees and twice as many STEM doctorates as the United States, and the gap is widening.

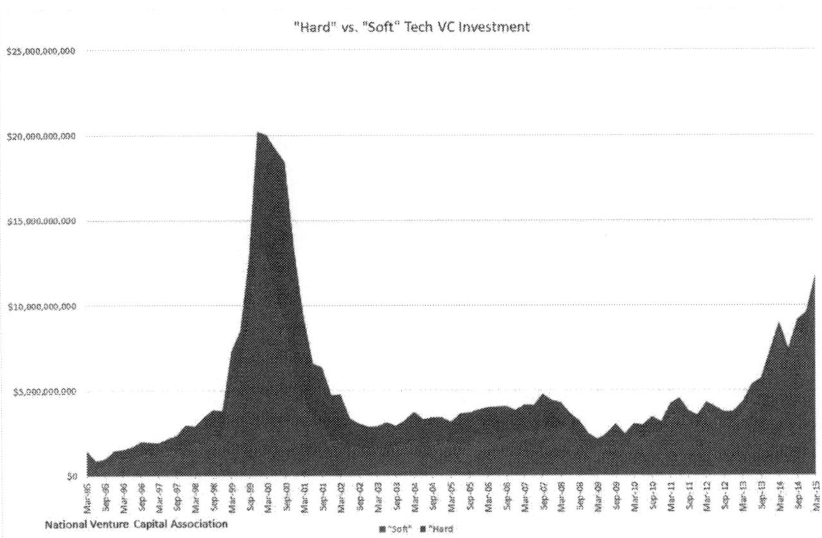

China subsidizes the R & D budgets of its state-owned and private companies. Chuin-Wei Yap estimated in *The Wall Street Journal* that Huawei has received benefits of up to $75 billion in the form of direct grants, tax cuts, property awards, and other indirect subsidies. On December 25, 2019, Mr. Yap wrote:

> Huawei's official grants, disclosed in annual reports, total $1.6 billion since 2008. In the five years to 2018,

> they were seventeen times as large as similar subsidies reported by Nokia Corp., of Finland, the world's second-largest telecom equipment maker. Sweden's Ericsson AB, the third-largest, posted none in the period.
>
> In China's southern city of Dongguan, state records show, Huawei bought more than a dozen state-owned parcels in largely uncontested auctions between 2014 and 2018 for its research campus. The company paid prices that were 10 percent to 50 percent of average rates for similarly zoned land in Dongguan, according to Chinese property-value databases. The discounts saved Huawei some $2 billion, according to a Journal review. Huawei declined to comment on the estimate.
>
> Other savings came from state policies to promote China's tech sector. Tax deductions and exemptions helped Huawei save up to $25 billion in income, value-added and other taxes in at least the past decade, the Journal estimated. Responding to the estimate, a Huawei spokesman said the company is globally tax-compliant.[203]

How that might compare to US DARPA grants, accelerated depreciation for capital gains, local tax breaks, and so forth, is hard to calculate. But it seems clear that China is doing what the United States used to do—namely, whatever it takes to achieve technological superiority.

There are some things that we can and should do immediately. A good place to start is strict enforcement of domestic content for defense technology. We cannot afford to source chips, displays, and other sensitive defense electronics from overseas. An emergency program should be put in place to produce semiconductors, sensors, displays, and other high-tech defense goods. That will require direct subsidies, but these are justifiable on national security as well as economic grounds.

The Unknown Unknowns

The digital age produces binary outcomes. Winners tend to win overwhelmingly—in war as well as in business. The Soviet Union crumbled in the late 1980s, when American technology bested Soviet military spending, then estimated at one-quarter of GDP. The enormous Russian bet on military power lost and communism fell. America emerged from the Cold War with a degree of military superiority greater than any country in modern history. It also emerged with a technologically driven economy that had no real competitor, with Russia close to ruin after the collapse of communism and China in an early stage of economic development.

But the most remarkable thing about America's golden age of public-private cooperation is this: every one of the inventions of the digital age started with a research grant from the Defense Department or NASA, but few of them turned out the way that researchers expected. We discovered things we never imagined we would discover.

- The internet began as a limited exercise in survivable military communications.
- The semiconductor laser—which made optical communication possible—began as a Pentagon project to illuminate battlefields at night.
- CMOS chip manufacturing—the technique which first mass-produced fast, light computer chips—began as an Air Force project to allow pilots to forecast weather from the cockpit.

The most glaring deficiency of the current policy approach is the decline of federal R & D spending relative to GDP. Overall R & D spending seems robust, but most R & D aims for incremental changes in existing products. Universities continue to conduct fundamental research, but they do so in an ivory tower. The combination of fundamental research by corporate laboratories with access to engineers and production facilities makes it possible to turn scientific discoveries into weapons systems, and eventually, consumer products. The policy initiatives that succeeded so brilliantly during the Cold War should provide a template for policymakers today. Renewing and improving defense R & D programs are not only essential to national security, but can also become a critical driver of innovation and economic growth.

The Role of Technology in Winning the Cold War

Although the American victory in the Cold War was decisive when it ultimately came, that does not mean that it was easy, let alone foreordained. Different policies might have spelled defeat. The Soviet Union sent the first satellite into space in 1957, and the first man into space in 1961. If the Eisenhower administration had not responded to Sputnik with massive funding for basic research and scientific education, or if John F. Kennedy had not proposed the moon shot after Yuri Gargarin's first flight into space, or if public funds had not been channeled into private research facilities to meet military needs, or if Ronald Reagan hadn't undertaken the Strategic Defense Initiative—we would be living in a different world.

During the 1970s, military analysts calculated rates of attrition of tanks and aircraft to determine who was likely to win a war. At the time, they reckoned that Russia would beat the West in a war of attrition, and conventional wisdom called for détente as a way of delaying an inevitable Soviet victory. Russian surface-to-air missiles and artillery as well as guided anti-tank weapons gave the advantage to Soviet-aligned Egypt in the largest air and tank battle since World War II, the 1973 Yom Kippur War between Israel and its neighbors. As former Deputy Secretary of Defense Bob Work said in a September 2016 speech:

> In 1973, the Yom Kippur War provided dramatic evidence of advances in surface-to-air missiles, and Israel's most advanced fighters...lost their superiority for at least three days due to a SAM belt. And Israeli armored forces were savaged by antitank guided munitions. U.S. analysts cranked their little models and extrapolated that the balloon went up in Europe's central front and we had suffered attrition rates comparable to the Israelis. U.S. tactical air power would be destroyed within seventeen days, and NATO would literally run out of tanks.[204]

Calculating men concluded that Russia would win an air and land war with the United States in Europe, which meant that Russia had the upper hand in the Cold War.

Then came the militarization of the microchip. During the Syrian collapse in June 1982, Israel deployed a combination of American and locally developed weapons systems and technologies, many in their first combat use, including F-15s and F-16s, AWACs, lookdown radar, and remotely piloted vehicles. Decoy drones drew fire from the Soviet-made SAM batteries, while Israeli fighters destroyed seventeen out of the Syrians' nineteen batteries. Superior command and control through faster computation and lookdown radar allowed Israeli F-4s, F-15s, and F-16s to destroy nearly one hundred Syrian planes over the Bekaa Valley while losing just one Israeli fighter.

Such a victory would have been impossible without the new fast and light microchips that enabled the American-made fighters to carry sufficient onboard computing capacity for the new radar systems. The CMOS chips that powered the F-15's lookdown radar—beginning in 1978—were manufactured for the first time only ten years earlier, and for entirely different reasons. Originally, the Defense Advanced Research Projects Agency (DARPA) commissioned RCA researchers to manufacture fast and light chips for weather analysis. In fact, the definitive inventions of late twentieth century technology—laser-powered optical networks, fast and light integrated circuits, and the internet—all came out of Defense Department projects whose originators could not have foreseen the impact of the new discoveries.

The "Bekaa Valley Turkey Shoot" of 1982, as it came to be called, marked a decisive shift in the Cold War. In less than a decade, the American military—with some contributions from Israel—reversed what had appeared to be a decisive Soviet advantage in air combat and established overwhelming American superiority. By 1984, as Deputy Secretary Work commented, "Soviet Marshall Ogarkov famously said that reconnaissance strike complexes, the Soviet and Russian term for battle networks, could achieve the same destructive effects as low-yield tactical nuclear weapons." The Soviet military concluded that it could never catch up to American avionics. That and the threat of the Strategic Defense Initiative persuaded Russia's leaders that America would win a conventional war, which set in motion the collapse of communism.

Despite the overall weakness of President Jimmy Carter's foreign policy, the Defense Department under Secretary Harold Brown achieved many of the technological breakthroughs that helped the Reagan administration win the Cold War during the 1980s. In collaboration with the national laboratories and several major corporate laboratories, DARPA made a revolution in war-fighting that for the first time brought massive computing power to bear in a practical way. All the elements of the modern digital economy—integrated circuits, laser-powered optical networks, sensors, and displays—were invented at the behest of NASA or the Defense Department.

In 2013, the director of RCA Labs who supervised their manufacture, Dr. Henry Kressel, and this writer described the impact of military-driven research and development in the American Interest:

> When DARPA set out to create a communications system with multiple pathways for national security reasons, no one had the slightest notion that this would create the Internet. When the Defense Department contracted RCA Labs in the 1970s to develop ways to illuminate night-time battlefields, no one could have foreseen that the semiconductor laser would revolutionize telecommunications. And when the Defense Department commissioned RCA Labs to develop light and energy-efficient information processors to analyze weather data in the cockpits of military aircraft, no one expected that the outcome would be mass production of inexpensive chips by the CMOS method.[205]

Kressel added:

> Companion technologies also sprang up that greatly expanded the ways in which lasers could be used. This led to their current status as not only the key to all fiber optic communication systems, including voice and data networks, but as the enabling technology of millions of instruments, DVD players, and a host of other devices.

Not one of the war-winning technologies funded by DARPA was employed for the purposes first envisioned by the Defense Department.

And no one in DARPA or the laboratories developing these technologies foresaw their transformative impact on the civilian economy. Private entrepreneurs adapted the technologies that arose from defense research, with remarkable speed. CMOS chip manufacturing was invented in 1963, at Fairchild Semiconductors, and the first CMOS chips were made at RCA Labs in 1968, under contract from DARPA. The first practical personal computers were on the market by the mid-1970s, and by the 1980s, the personal computing revolution was in full swing.

American technological advances gave America an unequalled edge in military as well as civilian technologies, and America dominated world economic life to a degree not achieved since the highpoint of the British Empire during the nineteenth century. Fast and cheap computing, optical data transmission, sensing, imaging, CAD/CAM manufacturing—all the technologies that have defined the economy of the past thirty years—were products of America's drive to win the Cold War.

New Challenges to American Technological Superiority

Conservative critics frequently compare the Obama administration to the Carter presidency by arguing that the United States experienced a decline in world influence under both presidents. In terms of defense fundamentals, however, the Obama presidency was incomparably worse. America's edge in defense technology has eroded, and even fallen behind its prospective adversaries in critical areas. Federal research and development spending has dropped to barely half of its 1978 level as a proportion of GDP. The national laboratories are hollowed out, and the major corporate laboratories—at IBM, the Bell System, General Electric, and RCA, among others—that contributed significantly to defense R & D during the Cold War no longer exist. Within the shrinking defense R & D budget, a disproportionate share has been squandered on the F-35, a poorly conceived and executed weapons system with the highest price tag in defense history.

America remains the world's strongest military power, but select Russian and Chinese advances already limit America's strategic freedom of action. Russia's S-400 air defense system, for example, can acquire one hundred separate targets at distances of up to four hundred kilometers. Moreover, the deployment of the S-400 in Syria made short work of American proposals for a no-fly zone in that country. U.S. commanders are not willing to risk stealth aircraft within the range of the S-400, because we do not know how close the Russians are to defeating stealth. The consensus is that Russia cannot defeat stealth yet, but they may be able to do so in the not too distant future.[206]

Many military breakthroughs—such as Israel's Iron Dome missile defense system—depend on the quality of algorithms and the speed of computation, rather than on changes in hardware. Defeating stealth is mainly a matter of computation—enhancing a small radar footprint quickly enough to acquire a target. At the end of 2018, China had the world's fastest and second-fastest supercomputers, made entirely with domestically produced integrated circuits.

Although China's military industry in many respects remains a generation or more behind its U.S. counterparts, China has made advances in technologies that represent a strategic threat to the West to which the United States has no obvious countermeasures. These developments include satellite-killer missiles and hypersonic weapons delivery vehicles.

There is no single, decisive, dramatic breakthrough in China comparable to Russia's 1957 launch of the first orbital satellite or the first manned space flight in 1961. Instead, there has been a steady accretion of technological advantages that, combined, pose a threat to American strategic superiority over a ten-to twenty-year horizon. It is important to understand how touch-and-go America's position was at many junctures of the Cold War, and the determination and commitment of resources that were required to restore America's technological advantage at moments when it was in jeopardy.

High-tech industrial production has been shifting away from the United States since the late 1990s. Until then, America ran a substantial surplus in high-tech goods. In the early 2000s, however, that surplus turned into a deficit, which is likely to exceed $100 billion this year. Most of America's trade deficit in high-tech goods consists of technologies invented in the United States, often supported by federally funded research sponsored by the Department of Defense and NASA. The seven technologies listed below constitute the basic elements of all modern electronics from computers to smartphones. In each case, their manufacture has migrated to Asia because Asian governments adopted the formerly American practice of supporting basic R & D. The economic benefits of the digital revolution that originated in the United States have shifted to Asia. America's share in the manufacture and distribution of its own inventions is relatively small.

The core digital technologies include the following:

Liquid crystal displays, which are employed in a wide variety of products, with $100 billion in annual sales. South Korea controls 35 percent of the market, Taiwan 25 percent, and China 20 percent.

Light-emitting diodes (LEDs) are produced mainly in China and Taiwan.

China and Taiwan dominate the production of semiconductor lasers, the energy source for fiber optic communications.

Solid-state sensors, which generate images in digital cameras and related devices, are produced mainly in Taiwan and Japan.

Flash memory is produced mainly in South Korea, Japan, and China, with only 10 percent of world output coming from the United States.

Integrated circuits are a $270 billion global industry. Most are produced in Taiwan and South Korea, and China has undertaken an aggressive investment program in the industry. Less than one-quarter of world output is produced in the United States.

Solar energy panels, a $30 billion industry, are dominated by China.

Venture capital commitments to the manufacturing industry have collapsed because American investors do not believe that American industry can stand up to Asian competition. Some of the Asian advantage is the result of the theft of intellectual property, but most of it stems from above-board collaboration of government and industry. Asian countries have licensed U.S. technologies and supported joint ventures with American companies in order to foster technology transfer, and they have made cheap capital available to their high-tech industry. Asian governments have also supported technical education. China now graduates twice as many STEM Ph.D. candidates as the United States does each year.

America developed many of the high technology products that are built by Asian manufacturing. But Asian dependence on American technology is starting to diminish. China's flagship high-tech manufacturer, Huawei, now employs tens of thousands of engineers, including thousands of Western researchers in several centers in Europe. A decade ago, Huawei was regularly accused of stealing Western technology. Now it is a vigorous defender of intellectual property rights, because it is committed to innovation of its own. Huawei now spends 14 percent of gross revenues on R & D—more than Microsoft, and the same level as Google.

A New R & D Policy Agenda

Is it too late for American high-tech manufacturing? No, but drastic policy changes are required. Tax incentives for exports and tax disincentives for imports may not be sufficient to turn the tide of Asian dominance. In many instances, the entire supply chain for tech projects has relocated to Asia, which leaves American manufacturers overwhelmingly dependent on Asian production for imports. The simplest and most direct response would be to require domestic production for all sensitive defense-related goods, including all computers, displays, integrated circuits, sensors, and other high-technology equipment used in defense applications. In other words, for certain important categories of security-related manufactures, the tariff should be infinite. This is the only reliable way to ensure that American manufacturers will bring production—including critical parts of the supply chain—back to the United States.

Russia's head start in the space race elicited a national effort to keep American technology in the forefront in the late 1950s and early 1960s. The real possibility that Russia might triumph in the Cold War motivated a comparable effort in the early 1980s. We need the same sense of urgency today. We have no guarantees that America will retain technological leadership. Britain dominated world industrial production in 1870, with one-third of total global output, but fell to one-seventh of the world total by World War I. In 2010, China edged out the United States to become the world's largest goods producer, with one-fifth of the global total.

Russian and Chinese advances in air defense, missile technology, submarine warfare, satellite interdiction and other critical areas pose a set of scientific problems comparable to the ones that DARPA addressed during the 1960s through the 1980s. Targets for future scientific research should include (but are not limited to):

- Defeating the current generation of Russian air defense systems
- Enhanced use of drones in place of manned aircraft
- Hardening of satellites against prospective enemy attack
- Cyber warfare
- New physical principles in computing (e.g., quantum computing)
- Quantum communications and encryption
- Detection of ultra-quiet submarines (the present generation of Chinese diesel-electric boats are practically undetectable, and submarine drones could be used to deliver nuclear weapons to coastal cities)
- Detection and defeat of the next generation of hypersonic missiles
- Countermeasures against anti-ship missiles (rail guns, laser cannon)

America succeeded in the Cold War because of "long ball" rather than "small ball" research and development. Usually, corporate R & D must be justified by relatively short-term improvements in revenues. Investigation of new physical principles cannot typically be justified by corporate planners. That is why military R & D plays such a unique role; to win wars, the United States has had no choice but to push the envelope of physical knowledge.

Federal R & D Spending and Productivity Growth

By one measure, the growth rate of labor productivity, the American economy is in its worst shape since the stagflation of the 1970s, and there is a close relationship between federal R & D spending and productivity growth. That is because research that leads to fundamental breakthroughs is more likely to be funded for defense and aerospace needs. "Long ball" R & D typically involves strategic objectives, while private R & D focuses on "small ball" requirements with specific product goals in sight. In many cases, federal R & D has led to innovations with enormous economic consequences that were unforeseen by the original sponsors; this is the nature of frontier research.[207]

The notion that defense and aerospace R & D fosters economic growth is not new. In 1976, NASA released a study by Chase Econometrics, stating that if a "sustained increase in NASA spending of $1 billion—in 1958 dollars—for the 1975–1984 period" were implemented, then "constant-dollar GNP would be $23 billion higher by 1984," versus a baseline of no increase in expenditures. Even so, conventional methods of economic estimation cannot begin to assess the revolutionary impact of breakthrough technologies on American productivity, because these technologies radically changed what economists call the investment opportunity set—the basic constituents of the economy itself. The civilian use of these defense technologies vastly outstripped the original objectives of their government sponsors. The demands of American defense pushed scientists to discover new physical processes—among them, solid-state semiconductors—and these discoveries transformed economic life.

Creating Unintended Consequences

Federal R & D is effective not merely because it is federal, however. On the contrary, governments frequently waste R & D funds on white elephant projects such as Solyndra, the California-based solar power venture that defaulted on a $535 million U.S. government loan. The F-35 and other poorly conceived acquisition programs also absorb large amounts of R & D funding. In contrast to these incremental projects, R & D that is focused on game-changing breakthroughs is the most productive. And the technological innovation it makes possible becomes transformative only when entrepreneurs effectively commercialize it. Kennedy's moon shot and Reagan's Strategic Defense Initiative had such lasting economic reverberations because they were accompanied by tax cuts and regulatory relief that made it easier for entrepreneurs to capitalize on basic scientific innovations. The Trump administration has already proposed aggressive fiscal and regulatory measures to improve incentives for investment. Neither innovation nor investment alone is enough, however; the innovations must turn into investment and employment in the United States.

There is a clear division of labor between the public sector and the private sector. Few, if any, of the game-changing inventions of the 1950s through the 1980s would have emerged—or emerged as early as they did—without federal R & D funding. Once the technology is invented, though, private investors must bear the brunt of the risk. Conventional industrial policy is the worst approach. It allows bureaucrats to create vested interests in existing industries, and it creates incentives to suppress new technologies that might threaten investments undertaken by political cronies. There is a strong case, however, for using government funds to seed new companies that can develop innovative technologies. In an ideal world, the venture capital community would assume this function. But in the real world, the requirements of defense R & D and production require public funding.

The unintended consequences of federally sponsored R & D vastly exceeded the expectations of the projects' initiators. The economic spinoffs of the technologies invented for urgent national security reasons had incalculable impacts on growth and productivity. None of this could have been pre-programmed. Innovation is unpredictable by definition. The greatest lesson we can draw from the Kennedy space program and the Reagan Strategic Defense Initiative is that the most productive investments are the ones that test the frontiers of physics. These projects enabled us to fight the next war, not the previous one.

Unlike the Russian space flights of 1957 and 1961, or the success of Russian air defenses in the Yom Kippur War, we can point to no single development to provoke a "Sputnik moment." Like a frog in a pot of cold water on a low flame, we do not notice the gradual increase in temperature. Circumstances, nonetheless, demand a sense of urgency comparable to that experienced at the peak of the Cold War. We can leapfrog our competitors. Or we may suffer the fate of a boiled frog.

We will never match China in absolute numbers of scientists and engineers. China's economy will be larger than ours in absolute terms. We have one decisive advantage, though, and that is America's genius for innovation. Industrial policy should focus on fostering innovation, as it did under the aegis of the Apollo Program and the Strategic Defense Initiative.

APPENDIX

CHINA TRIES TO REDEFINE THE WORLD—A DIALOGUE[15]

How do the Chinese view themselves? Here is an opportunity to eavesdrop on China's internal conversation. A prominent Chinese political commentator, Professor Wen Yang of Shanghai's Fudan University, responded at length to a summary of this book's thesis published on October 16, 2019, in the Swiss newspaper *Weltwoche*. The interview, conducted by *Weltwoche*'s foreign editor Urs Gehriger, appeared under the headline, "You can never be China's friend." It created a stir in China, and the leading Chinese news site guancha.cn published a full Chinese translation of the *Weltwoche* transcript. Professor Wen, a regular commentator for the popular site, then offered a lengthy response to the interview on the guancha.cn website. Asia Times then translated and published Professor Wen's commentary in a three-part series. In turn, I responded to Professor Wen's critique. What makes this exchange remarkable is that it was conducted on a major Chinese-language website for a Chinese audience. I have responded to Professor Wen.

Professor Wen's key statement is this: "Miracles can happen when the Chinese government and its people have the same goal; there will be a global impact when China tries to redefine the world." Wen dismisses the idea that the Chinese do not understand Western democracy. On the contrary, Chinese city-states exercised a democracy of sorts in the 1st

[15] Portions of this appendix first appeared in Die Weltwoche (Switzerland) and the website guancha.cn. They are used by permission.

millennium B.C.E., he claims, but transcended this primitive phase of political organization with the founding of the Qin Dynasty in the 3rd Century B.C.E. He writes:

> Goldman does not understand that the so-called 'public trust and subsidiarity' that's mentioned by Westerners is merely what Chinese political philosophy classifies as the 'city-state politics" of the pre-Qin period.' This sort of politics is not common. It has remained an orthodox concept that is popular only among small political systems with autonomy, or special groups of citizens.
>
> He is mistaken to think that 'the Chinese are completely unfamiliar with these concepts.' Rather, these concepts are completely outdated for the Chinese. From the city-state to the territorial state and from the territorial state to the empire, the Chinese people already completed the evolution of their civilization through dramatic social reforms and state mergers two thousand years ago.

Where democracy is concerned, Professor Wen avers, China has been there and done that, and gone on to better things—the wise and benevolent rule of a technocratic elite that knows what the people want better than the people do, and makes sure that they get it, whether they want it or not. Wen claims that China that has evolved a superior mode of social organization, and that it is prepared to "redefine the world."

"You Can Never be China's Friend" —Spengler

Interview with Urs Gehriger, Foreign Editor, Weltwoche (Switzerland). Reprinted by permission.

Asia specialist and distinguished columnist David P. Goldman is convinced that the US and Europe stand a chance against the Red Dragon—but the clock is ticking.

He was a phantom among journalists, using the mysterious nom de plume, "Spengler." Like his German philosopher namesake, the cultural critic returned again and again to his despairing theories of the decline of the West.

The work of "Spengler" drew from a deep and rich intellectual pool. And since the herald has revealed his true identity, we learn why. David P Goldman—philosopher, economist, mathematician, and musicologist—is a Renaissance man. A former investment banker for the Bank of America and Credit Suisse, the American is known for his widely read column for *Forbes* magazine and *Asia Times*.

Dutch writer Leon de Winter crowns Goldman's work as "among the most interesting in the world."

We meet at the noble Princeton Club in Midtown Manhattan, where Goldman is a member. He is intensively involved with China. Informed by close experience in the country and with its people, Goldman counsels caution toward the aggressive Asian empire. But before training a critical eye on the East, the keen observer sharply examines his own culture and the president for whom he voted in 2016.

Q: As we speak, the country is in turmoil. For the fourth time in US history, a president might be impeached. Your thoughts?

A: Trump's real liability isn't impeachment. It's China and the economy. What the Trump administration has been doing so far, vis-à-vis China, is an own goal.

Q: Why is it an own goal?

A: Because the effect of the tariffs on the US economy is at least as bad as the effect of the tariffs on the Chinese economy. American export orders are collapsing. We have the weakest industrial reading since June of 2009. We are in a manufacturing recession, according to the Federal Reserve. Factory output is contracting. Trump won in 2016, by carrying key manufacturing states like Pennsylvania, Ohio, Michigan, and Wisconsin. This blunder could lose him the election. This is much more dangerous than the impeachment masquerade. China's also suffering, but appears to be suffering less. And the big difference is Xi Jinping [China's president] doesn't have a presidential election in 2020, and Trump does.

Q: In fact, President Xi will never face an election. He is elected for life.

A: That is true. But all that can change if he fails to succeed.

Q: You have compared the situation that the US is facing toward China to the siege and conquest of Baghdad by the Mongols in 1258.

A: The Mongols, by themselves, did not have the capability to penetrate the twelve-foot-thick walls of the city of Baghdad. But they hired a thousand Chinese siege engineers. Within three weeks, the Chinese mercenaries breached the walls, at which point the Mongol horsemen went in and killed the entire population of Baghdad.

Q: Who are today's Chinese siege engineers who are breaching the American fortress?

A: Huawei very much is the spearhead, because in the Chinese model of economic expansion and the development of world economic power, broadband is the opener to everything else.

It's a company with a lot of very talented people. Ten years ago, if you asked people, *What Chinese products do you buy?* you wouldn't mention a single brand name. But everyone now knows Huawei. They produce the world's best smartphones. They certainly dominate 5G internet. But Huawei is not a Chinese company. It is an imperial company.

The Chinese empire is doing better than us because it's absorbed the talent of a very large number of others. Fifty percent of their engineers are foreign. They bankrupted their competition and hired their talent. They have fifty thousand foreign employees, and a very disproportionate amount of their research and development is conducted by foreign employees.

I've seen this personally. I worked for several years as an investment banker in Hong Kong for a Chinese-owned boutique. During that time, I collaborated with people from Huawei. I introduced them to foreign governments. Huawei was very clear about its objectives. They'd tell, for example, the government of Mexico, *Let us build a national broadband network. Once you get broadband, you get e-commerce and e-finance, and then we'll supply the logistics and the financing for that, and we'll integrate you into the world market.*

They've become one of the most connected societies on earth. China has, by far, the highest percentage of e-commerce of any society in the world. Electronic payment systems and electronic banking are much more advanced there than anywhere else.

Q: When I interviewed US Secretary of State Mike Pompeo during his visit to our country this summer, he strongly warned, "Switzerland should stay away from Huawei." Across Europe, the Americans are sending out the same message. How successful have they been so far, in stopping European partners from cooperating with Huawei?

A: As you say in Yiddish, "Soll ihr gor nischt helfen [it's completely useless]." The campaign has been a humiliating failure, and in fact, one of the most comprehensive policy failures that the United States has ever had.

A senior Cabinet-level US official told me recently that the Chinese were way ahead of us before we figured out what was going on, but now we're catching up. That statement is wrong on two grounds. First, they haven't figured out what is going on. Secondly, they're not catching up. Two years ago, the US Intelligence Community realized that what 5G would do is not only give China a great deal of economic power, which by itself is a national security concern, but it would also, within the next several years, eliminate America's advantage in signals intelligence.

Q: Can you explain how?

A: I actually broke the story in July, in the *Asia Times*. It's since been discussed in various other media. The Chinese have pioneered a communications technique called *quantum communications*, which uses the entanglement of electrons at a distance to create a communications signal. The quantum system is such that if you interfere with it in any way, the signal disappears. The quantum state is destroyed. So it's like a letter that disappears the moment you look at it. It's theoretically impossible to hack. The 5G bandwidth is so powerful that you can integrate quantum communications into ordinary 5G communications and make it standard.

We already know that the Chinese are using quantum communications for sensitive data transmission inside China through fiber optic cable. But there are a half-dozen major groups working on embedding quantum communications in 5G. SK Telecom is working on it. Toshiba is working on it. There's a group at the University of Bristol, which claims very good results. So the result is America's ability to eavesdrop on everyone else will disappear in two or three years.

It is one thing for the Americans to say, *Do not buy into 5G Huawei.* But eventually, customers in the West need 5G technology. Is there an alternative for Europeans, to Huawei?

Well, there isn't at present, which is what makes the American initiative so ineffective. A senior official of Huawei told me, "We don't understand why the Americans didn't have Cisco buy Ericsson and create a competitor." Of course, the answer is that would have brought down Cisco's equity prices, and we don't do anything in the United States that brings down stock prices.

Q: What would be the right policy?

A: The right policy would be to do exactly something like that. Have a merger of Cisco and Ericsson, or get Microsoft involved. Google. There are many American companies that could compete effectively. It might require some subsidies, tax subsidies, perhaps direct research and development subsidies. You'd have to bring the CEOs into the Oval Office and tell them, *Tell us what you need to make it happen.* I think that all of the European countries would be very happy to work with the United States as opposed to China, even if it involves some delay in the rollout of 5G. But as long as there's no American alternative, the Europeans are all over the place.

Q: I hear a lot of people say, *Americans have eavesdropped on the German Chancellor Merkel. They have stolen data from around the world, as we learnt from Edward Snowden. Why worry about Huawei when the Americans do exactly the same?* What do you say to this?

A: Well, [chuckles]. A former head of the Central Intelligence Agency told me it's a matter of whether we steal everybody's data, or the Chinese steal everybody's data. And don't you prefer having the Americans steal your data?

Q: Most would say, *We don't want anybody to penetrate our privacy.*

A: Well, I think this is a moot question anyway, because the development of cryptography—particularly quantum cryptography—will eliminate the US's ability to eavesdrop, in any case. I think all that has happened is the US intelligence agencies look for a way to delay the 5G rollout until they've figured out how to address this problem. They are basically floundering.

Remember, we spend $80 billion a year on our intelligence services. The vast majority goes for signals intelligence. ["SIGINT" is intelligence derived from electronic signals and systems used by foreign targets, such as communications systems, radars, and weapons systems.] All of a sudden, the screens will go dark at the National Security Agency. They will lose an enormous amount of power.

Q: When we learn about this vastly growing Chinese global influence, we start to wonder: What is China's grand strategy behind it?

A: China was the world's dominant manufacturing power for most of the last one thousand years. Then it dropped about two hundred years ago at the beginning of the Industrial Revolution. The Chinese view this as a temporary aberration, and they want to re-establish China's preeminence. They look at Chinese technological dominance, both in terms of innovation and in control of major world markets, as the key to Chinese power and prosperity.

Remember, China had dynasties which fell because of famine, plague, foreign invasions, and so forth. It really hasn't been a stable country. This is the first generation of Chinese that doesn't have to fear hunger. They've basically removed the main source of fragility of the Chinese system. And now, China is turning outward and asserting its power globally. The combination of telecommunications, logistics, e-finance, e-commerce, and the other applications of artificial intelligence, are the instruments of Chinese expansion.

The Chinese understanding is that every smartphone is a data gatherer. It'll gather data on health, on consumer transactions, on the environmental traffic patterns. All of this data can be uploaded to the Cloud. It can be processed by Chinese computers, and it can give China massive advantages in terms of industrial controls, health systems, the environment, urban planning, and of course, social and political control.

Since 800 A.D., the Chinese borders have stayed the same. I don't see any intention to expand—apart from the South China Sea.

Q: I agree. So what is their strategy? What do they want?

A: They want to have everybody in the world pay rent to the Chinese Empire. They want to control the key technologies, the finance and the logistics, and make everyone dependent on them. Basically, make everyone else a tenant farmer.

Q: How far have they gotten so far on this road?

A: Well, it's very preliminary, because basically what China wants to do is to transform other countries the way they transformed themselves. This is not easy to do. You have political obstacles, cultural obstacles. For example, in a country like Pakistan, where they've invested enormously, you have 50 percent illiteracy and a great deal of political instability, massive infrastructure deficits. No one is going to make Pakistan look like China anytime soon. A country like Brazil, for example, where China is building a national broadband network—that's a candidate. The whole of Southeast Asia—Vietnam, Malaysia, Cambodia, Thailand—these are candidates to be transformed into economic adjuncts of the Chinese Empire. If you include Indonesia, Southeast Asia is already six hundred million people.

Q: Once the Chinese achieve their goal, would they press their "tenant farmers" politically and ideologically?

A: I think the Chinese are not curious about how the barbarians govern themselves as long as they're subordinate to China, economically and technologically. The Chinese are the least ideological people in the world and the most pragmatic.

A lot of my American friends say the problem is the wicked Chinese Communist Party which is oppressing the good Chinese people. I think that's complete nonsense. I see the Communist Party as simply another manifestation of the Mandarin administrative cast which has ruled China since it was unified in the third century BC.

Compared to the Russians, with their schools for spies and their subsidies for local communist parties and so forth, the Chinese have no interest in such things. The ideological ambitions of the Chinese Communist Party are vastly exaggerated by authors like Michael Pillsbury [the American director of the Center on Chinese Strategy at the Hudson Institute in Washington DC] and other American critics. But that doesn't mean China is not dangerous, or that they're not a challenge to us.

Q: The most prominent expert on China in the western hemisphere is Henry Kissinger. In his book *On China*, he explains that the Chinese operate like in a kind of three-dimensional chess. Go, I think the game is called.

A: Exactly.

Q: This sounds like the Chinese have some sort of a super brain.

A: I think that can be exaggerated. What holds China together is the ambition of the Mandarin caste. China has always been a very disparate set of ethnicities and languages, and so forth. What holds it together is that the Chinese Empire has recruited, through the Mandarin system, the cleverest people from the provinces, and aligned their interests with the center.

Q: What, in your view, is the biggest misconception about China, in the West?

A: The single biggest misconception is that you have a wicked government and a good people. The Chinese have had three thousand years for the government and the people to shape each other. The institution in the West that most closely resembles the Chinese system is, in fact, the Sicilian mafia. You have a *capo di tutti capi*, who prevents the other *capi* from killing each other. Because they're natural anarchists, they don't like any form of government. They're loyal to their families. The emperor is nothing but a necessary evil. The idea of public trust and subsidiarity that's fundamental to democracy is unknown to the Chinese.

What holds a country of anarchists together, if not the emperor?

There's an old joke about [former American President] Eisenhower and [former Israeli Prime Minister] Ben Gurion, from the 1950's. Eisenhower tells Ben Gurion, "It's hard to be president to two hundred million Americans." And Ben Gurion says, "It's even harder to be prime minister of two million prime ministers."

Well, China is a country of 1.4 billion emperors. Everyone wants to be an emperor. Everyone strives for his own and his family's power. There's no sense of res publica. Certainly, no Augustinian sense of common love to hold a country together. What holds the country together is ambition. Therefore, it's critical that the meritocracy be fair.

Xi Jinping's daughter goes to Harvard, but no Chinese president can get his child into Peking University unless she gets the right score on the Gaokao, the university entrance exam.

Q: So all hope is not lost for the West when the Chinese "capo di tutti capi" is educating his offspring in one of America's Ivy League schools?

A: Well, the one thing that we're much better at than the Chinese is innovation. As I mentioned, Huawei is very much dependent on Western employees for innovation. I'm not saying the Chinese can't innovate. During the Tang dynasty (618 to 906 A.D.), which is considered a golden age of Chinese arts and culture, the Chinese invented the clock, the compass, gunpowder, printing, and virtually all of the elements of the beginning of the Industrial Revolution. However, the Chinese form of meritocracy, which is based on standardized exams, is the second-best way of running that meritocracy. Albert Einstein, who sat in the Swiss patent office because he couldn't get a university job—

Q: And then invented the theory of relativity at his private home…

A: Right. This is unimaginable in China. If you ask the Chinese what worries them the most, many will say, *How come we have no Nobel prizes?* Eight Chinese have won the Nobel prize in sciences, but they are all Chinese who lived in America.

The Chinese system is very bad at identifying those eccentrics, like an Einstein, who make fundamental contributions. We are much better at that. The Western idea of the divine spark in the individual simply doesn't exist in China. So I think we do have a chance against the Chinese.

Q: President Donald Trump has been saying all along, "We have to stop the Chinese from stealing our innovations and ideas." He is right, isn't he?

A: Well, I think there are good points and bad points to it. Certainly, the rise of China is a threat to the prosperity and security in the West, and he's right to call attention to it. Joe Biden as vice president appears to have been interested in China mainly to help his son. A few months ago, he said the Chinese are nothing to worry about. Now that's either a stupid statement or a corrupt one. Of course we need to worry about the Chinese. If the Chinese dominate the next wave of major industrial applications, we'll be poor, and we'll be less secure. We'll be dependent on them, and I don't like that.

I don't think the Chinese plan to invade us or establish an American Communist Party on the model of the Chinese Communist Party.

Q: You don't see any military confrontation emerging anytime soon?

A: No. If you look at the disposition of Chinese forces, it looks like a person with a gigantic head and tiny legs. The Chinese spend fifteen hundred dollars to equip a foot soldier. That's basically a rifle and a helmet and some boots. Americans spend eighteen thousand dollars to equip a foot soldier. We have enormous airlift capability. We have an enormous amount of technology applied to the infantry. The People's Liberation Army (PLA) infantry is one of the most poorly equipped and badly trained in the world. On the other hand, their missile forces, their satellite forces, their submarines, and so forth, are extremely good.

The entire Chinese military strategy is focused on controlling their borders. Especially control of the South China Sea. They have perhaps one hundred thousand Marines and mechanized infantry they could put in Taiwan pretty quickly. But apart from that, they've shown no interest. They have, of course, the base in Djibouti. One can expect the Chinese to put more resources into their Navy, because the United States is showing less interest in the security of the Persian Gulf. My view is more Chinese presence in the Persian Gulf is inevitable because of basic economic interests. But that's not the same as projecting a military empire. It's not the Soviet Union.

Q: Some people say that confrontation is the wrong strategy, that we should become friends. Do the Chinese have the same concept of friendship that we have?

A: The Chinese, as individuals, have no friends. China, as a country, all the less so.

Q: A peasant somewhere out in the Chinese countryside doesn't have friends?

A: It was explained to me by my Chinese colleagues while I worked there, that when you're in first grade in primary school, you look to your left and right and try to figure out whom you're going to walk over. In China, you have your family. Otherwise, you have inferiors and superiors. But there are no parallel institutions. There's no group of people coming together, spontaneously, to do something together as equals. You have a superior and you have inferiors. There's no concept of political friendship, in Aristotle's sense.

Q: No personal friendships?

A: People have personal friends, of a sort. But you don't have the Western idea of political friendship, which goes back to Aristotle. China only has interests; it has no friends. There's a term that was applied to southern Italy, called *amoral familism*, where you're completely amoral with dealings of the world except for your family, where you have different standards. That very much characterizes China.

Q: It is obviously in the Chinese interest to appear "friendly." They have launched a tremendous PR strategy buying space and time in Western media to propagate themselves as a friendly giant.

A: They do a very bad job, don't they?

Q: Why do you think?

A: Because the Chinese are tone-deaf to Western sensibility, they're very bad at conducting a dialogue in Western terms. The thing I'm least worried about is Chinese propaganda in the West. They're very good about generating influence through money and technology and so forth.

Q: But they are not winning hearts and minds?

A: No. I think the Chinese system is so alien to what Westerners want or expect that it will never look attractive to us.

Q: Kipling was not completely wrong when he wrote, "East is East, and West is West, and never the twain shall meet"?

A: You can never be China's friend. We obviously have to do business with China. You can't isolate 1.4 billion clever and industrious people. That's absurd. But one can only deal with them successfully from a position of strength.

Q: President Trump is pursuing a strategy of threats and demonstration of power. Does this impress the Chinese?

A: I don't think it does, at present, because the president makes a lot of threats that he doesn't execute. Iran is a good example. It's fine to say, *We're locked and loaded, ready to attack Iran.* We're not going to attack Iran. If we'd attacked Iran, we'd have a major interruption of oil supplies in the Persian Gulf. On the other hand, the Chinese are very paranoid about the United States. When Steve Bannon goes around talking about trying to destabilize the Chinese political system, I know a lot of Chinese in very senior positions who think that he's secretly speaking for President Trump, even though he was never really doing so.

Q: You have called Trump's strategy of economically confronting China a failure.

A: I think it has been a complete failure. Now, I voted for Trump. I will almost certainly vote for Trump again. I would like to see him re-elected. But I'm distressed that he may be his own worst enemy.

He ran on a platform of reviving American industry. American manufacturing is the weakest sector of the economy. And because his re-election depends on victory in several manufacturing states, I think his re-election is in greater jeopardy than it might have been. So I think the tariffs hurt.

And as I mentioned before, the attempt to persuade the rest of the world not to buy Huawei's 5G equipment has been a complete failure. Huawei will ship six hundred thousand 5G base stations this year, and it can now produce them with no American components.

The humiliating thing is we invented the semiconductor. We invented the displays. We invented the optical networks. Every single component to the digital economy was an American invention. Yet we produce very little of it, or, in some cases, none in the United States.

So for Trump to say, "It shouldn't be like this," is completely reasonable. But I think the methods that he's chosen have been ineffective, and even counterproductive.

Q: Has America lost? Or can you catch up?

A: Of course we can. But it's very hard to say exactly how it will happen. Under the Reagan administration, I consulted for the National Security Council. The United States spent, in direct federal subsidies for research and development, the equivalent of $300 billion in today's dollars—about one and a half percent of GDP. Every one of the major corporations had laboratories employing thousands of scientists. Every single invention that created our modern digital economy came from a Pentagon project. In many cases, the results were much more far reaching than anything we anticipated.

In 1976, the US Defense Department decided they wanted fighter pilots to be able to do weather forecasting in the cockpit. They asked for a fast and light computer chip. What they developed was immediately applied to "look down radar." Look down radar requires computer imaging, and the development of the chips at RCA labs made that possible. The Defense Department did anticipate that, but that was one of the technologies that gave us a decisive advantage over the Russians during the Cold War.

If we have the mobilization of resources that I would like to see, similar to what we've done in the past, I believe we'll get results greater than we anticipate. The important thing is to restore the culture of innovation, and mobilize human and corporate resources to do this.

Q: What would a winning strategy towards China look like?

A: I'll give you an example. Part of the single biggest Chinese investment is now in semiconductors. China is the largest importer of semiconductors. They import more than two-hundred-billion-dollars-worth of semiconductors. They'd like to produce most of that at home. So they're spending vast amounts on chip fabrication plants. Chip fabrication plants are extremely expensive. The latest one that Taiwan Semiconductor built cost thirty billion dollars for a single plant. There are new physical techniques for creating semiconductors. They can be grown as opposed to pressed.

Let's say we were to take some of these experimental technologies and make them work. Then we would wipe out one-hundred-billion-dollars-worth of Chinese investment in semiconductor fabrication plants. I would try to target critical technologies where innovation can make radical changes and wipe out the value of existing Chinese investments.

Q: Where do you see China's weak spots that could cause substantial problems for their future?

A: China has a set of weak spots. First, they've got a very rapidly aging population. Like all countries with aging populations, they need to export capital and employ young people and other countries to pay for the pensions of their own people. Germany does this, too. That's part of the motivation for China's strategy. They will have an enormous burden supporting the aged in the future. They're hoping to deal with that through automation, through more efficient healthcare.

Their biggest problem is the ambitions of their young people. The Chinese created a generation of which ten million people each year take the Gaokao (university) exam. A third of them study engineering. They expect opportunities.

If China loses its edge in technology, if they fall behind the West, if the Communist Party is seen to have failed in competing with the West, I think that will be a significant threat to its power.

You can't effect that by complaining about human rights in China. China's violation of human rights is repugnant to us. Of course, we will complain. But that doesn't really do anything. The Chinese only respect power, and our power is in innovation. If we show that we can out-innovate the Chinese and leave them behind in critical sectors of technology, I think that will undermine the credibility of the present government.

Response from Professor Wen Yang of Fudan University (Shanghai), on the Chinese news Website Guancha.com

David Goldman could have learned more about China.[208]

Parts of "You can never be China's friend" are only partly correct, while most other parts are completely wrong.

A Chinese translation by Guanfang Translation of an interview with David Paul Goldman, the American philosopher, economist, mathematician, and music critic, has drawn a lot of attention and inspired discussions among readers.

The article was published in English on October 16, 2019, in Switzerland. Goldman, according to the translator, Kris, is co-owner of Hong Kong's English-language news organization *Asia Times*—where the interview article was republished—and often writes about the Western world's crisis, using the pen name "Spengler," which is borrowed from Oswald Spengler, author of *The Decline of the West.*

This article was translated into Chinese because Kris wants to present an interesting perspective on how a smart, decent opponent sees China.

In terms of his views on China, Goldman is a smart person. In the interview, he talked about the Sino-US trade war, Huawei Technologies, 5G and quantum communication, and also matters related to China's history, political system, strategy and military capabilities. He talked about China's weaknesses and problems, mentioning a lot of good points as well.

Author Wen Yang, Fudan University professor said:

Goldman is indeed a "decent opponent" with some of his assertions, such as, "They want to have everybody in the world pay rent to The Chinese Empire," and "I see the Communist Party as simply another manifestation of the Mandarin administrative cast that has ruled China since its unification in the third century BC."

These points, whether right or wrong, are not matters that can be raised by mediocre observers.

But that's it. Even if Goldman is smarter and more decent, he is still a "Western media person." The reality is that the popular critics in the Western media are unlikely to be experts on China affairs at the same time. These two roles are fundamentally contradictory. There is no need to say the reason.

Thus, some of Goldman's remarks are only partly correct, while most other parts are completely wrong.

China's Systems

Unlike most Western media critics—who have no sense of history, do not understand what a big country is, and like to judge China freely—Goldman understands that "contemporary China is the continuation and development of historical China." It doesn't represent a sudden change and a mutation. This is a correct point that he has made.

This is why he pointed out that the biggest misunderstanding of the West about China is to regard China as an evil government that oppresses its good people.

He concluded that "the government and people of China have been shaping each other for three thousand years." With this knowledge, he at least could understand the unique and ancient "home-state-empire" conceptual structure of the Chinese people, and the fact that there is no such structure in the Western civilization. And of course, in the Western world, there was no similar history in which the government and the people were shaping each other.

From these, he should have reached some deeper conclusions—for example, *miracles can happen when the Chinese government and its people have the same goal; there will be a global impact when China tries to redefine the world* [emphasis added]. Unfortunately, he obviously lacks this kind of analytical knowledge, and falls into the quagmire of fallacy with his narrow Western centralist standpoints before he can get close to the truth.

For example, the following paragraph is full of logical confusion and cognitive errors:

"The institution in the West that most closely resembles the Chinese system is, in fact, the Sicilian mafia. You have a capo di tutti capi who prevents the other capi from killing each other. Because they're natural anarchists, they don't like any form of government. They're loyal to their families. The emperor is nothing but a necessary evil. The idea of public trust and subsidiarity that's fundamental to democracy is unknown to the Chinese."

Goldman is unlikely to be familiar with China's history from the Western Zhou Dynasty to the Qin and Han Dynasties, so he does not understand how many major issues need to be resolved from the transition between city-state politics and empire politics.

By using the Western civilization as a standard, he rashly believes that the Chinese have "no Augustinian sense of common love to hold a country together;" that we "don't have the Western idea of political friendship, which goes back to Aristotle;" and that the Chinese system is similar to the Sicilian mafia, with a Chinese society similar to the "amoral familism" in southern Italy.

This is ridiculous. I don't know if he realizes that when he judges China with these Western concepts of China, his points of reference are the history and geographical scope of several small city-states on the northern shore of the Mediterranean that were only equivalent to small ducal states including Qi, Lu, Wei, and Song in the early period of the Western Zhou Dynasty.

The evolution of Chinese history is iterative. The aristocratic politics of the city-states basically gave way to empire politics since the Qin and Han dynasties. Even though in the pre-Qin period, what we could call "Western concepts" similar to Plato's and Aristotle's political philosophies had appeared in China, they disappeared quickly. It is meaningless to use these examples as historical references to compare with the political reality in newer eras.

In 719 BC, there was a coup d'état in ancient China's Wei nation. Vệ Châu Dụ, who killed the leader Huan Gong and declared himself the new leader, was not accepted by the nation's people. With the help of some senior officials, people chose a different new leader, Xuan Gong, who was the younger brother of Huan Gong.

Referring to the political theory of ancient Greece, this can be regarded as the political practice "classical democracy." It happened two centuries earlier than the Athenian great uprising in 510 BC, to overthrow the Hipparchus.

There is a huge quantity of ancient and modern documents related to ancient Greek democracy, but much less documentation of the historical record of the democracy of the Wei nation.

There are not enough documents to show how the people of the Wei nation collectively negotiated and chose their new leader. And regardless of the historical background of that incident, one thing is worth being highlighted: such a political practice, which is available only in small countries, became outdated after the rise of many larger states.

The officials who recorded history were, thus, not interested in this small event as they turned to focus on key issues in the larger states and empire.

After the Qin nation conquered the six neighboring nations, China's territory had reached more than three million square kilometers, equivalent to the size of a dozen Italian peninsulas, or more than twenty Greek peninsulas.

Since then, China had entered an era of empire politics. It outgrew the coverage of Aristotle's political theory or Sicilian political reality. In the Qin Dynasty (221 to 206 BC), China was a territory with the Central Plain as the center. It then expanded to the "forest cultural circle" in the northeast, the "grassland cultural circle" in the north, the "western cultural circle" in the northwest, the "highland cultural circle" in the southwest, and the "maritime cultural circle" in the southeast. Each region covered about three million square kilometers.

During the golden era in the middle of the Qing Dynasty (1644 to 1911), the Chinese empire had a territory size of 13.8 million square kilometers, with people of heterogeneous cultures and different ethnicities. Can this be understood by the western political philosophy originated from the ancient city-state politics?

Goldman deserves recognition, as he is somewhat aware of the depth and breadth of things Chinese. He pointed out that "China has always been a very disparate set of ethnicities and languages, and so forth. What holds it together is that the Chinese Empire has recruited, through the Mandarin system, the cleverest people from the provinces and aligned their interests with the center."

Speaking so, he appeared to be a China expert. But, after all, he isn't. He is a western commentator and can never get rid of some old concepts. He will never get the right answer by measuring China, which is a giant, against the small rulers of the times of Aristotle and Augustine, and against Sicily in Italy.

Long-term Strategies

Goldman's comparison of China's challenges against the United States to the Mongolians' conquest of Baghdad in 1258 is almost nonsense.

Today, the United States is a superpower that plays the role of "world police." It has nothing in common with the peaceful and prosperous city Baghdad in the 13th century. Also, China, a developing country working hard for the reunification of the motherland and national rejuvenation, has nothing in common with the Mongolian Army that conquered the entire known world at that time.

It remains unclear whether there was any evidence for the "historical fact," cited by Goldman, that the Mongols had hired thousands of Chinese siege engineers to break through the twelve-feet-thick castle wall in Baghdad within three weeks.

Judging by common sense, it was unlikely that the Arabs in the 13th century could distinguish whether the Asians who fought for the Mongols were people from Song Dynasty, Khitan, Western Xia, or Khwarazm. People from Asia could not be simply categorized as "Chinese siege engineers."

In addition, the leaders of the Mongolian Army that attacked West Asia at the time were Hulagu Khan, fifth brother of Kublai Khan, and General Kitbuqa Noyan. Their troops went from Central Asia to West

Asia and swiftly conquered many cities like lightning. It remained doubtful whether a team of siege engineers exclusively from China had followed.

If Goldman's arguments were not correct, his comparison was not providing new insights, but creating an ancient fear—the Yellow Peril.

By saying "Huawei very much is the spearhead," Goldman described Huawei Technologies, a Shenzhen-based company, as the pioneer of siege. What he meant was that the Western world is facing a much bigger crisis than Europe in the 13th century, as the "Yellow Peril" that historically made the Europeans tremble, now owns unstoppable technology.

However, no matter how scary Goldman's historical comparison was, he still couldn't find any real evidence to characterize today's China as an expansionist country similar to Mongolia in the Middle Ages and Russia in modern times.

He acknowledged that "China is not the Soviet Union." He also pointed out that the key goal of China's military strategy was to protect its territorial integrity—"but apart from that, they've shown no interest."

This is why he believed that there won't be any military confrontation between China and the United States.

When talking about China's military capabilities, he compared the equipment carried by the Chinese and American soldiers. He said the technical content of equipment used by an American infantry was very high. The cost of equipment for an American infantry is more than ten times of that for a Chinese infantry. The United States army also has a strong capability in air transport, and can send its troops across a long distance.

"The People's Liberation Army (PLA) infantry is one of the most poorly equipped and badly trained in the world," he wrote, adding that the PLA's strengths are mainly in the areas of missiles, satellites, and submarines. This comparison also shows that the Chinese Army is defensive, while the U.S. Army is invasive.

When an army that frequently invades the territory of other countries is often surrounded by local soldiers and civilians, it has to equip its soldiers with a complete set of advanced equipment.

On the contrary, the Chinese Army, which adopts a proactive defense strategy, mainly develops deterrent weapons and equipment with strong counterattack capabilities.

Goldman knew it clearly, but he did not express it. The belligerence and aggressiveness of the United States are collective taboos of Western media people, and can never be pointed out directly.

Therefore, Goldman's arguments showed a dilemma in logic. If the United States is peace-loving, even like the passively defensive Baghdad City in 1258, and China has never been an expansionist country, who now corresponds to the ancient Mongolians? Where does the "Yellow Peril" come from? What's to feel nervous about?

Because of this logical dilemma, Goldman was asked about what China's strategy is and what China wants. He talked through his hat with an answer that raised a hot debate online:

The Chinese "want to have everybody in the world pay rent to the Chinese Empire. They want to control the key technologies, the finance and the logistics, and make everyone dependent on them. Basically, make everyone else a tenant farmer."

This is a shocking comment. It showed that he did not really know about China. It also revealed his Jewish mindset that everything is commercial. For a long time in the past, Jews did not have their own country. After each "Diaspora," the entire nation can only live in different countries as small Jewish communities. They relied on doing business. With no political support at all, the most successful parasitic business model of the Jews was nothing else but to "control the key technologies, the finance and the logistics, and make everyone dependent on them. Basically, make everyone else a tenant farmer."

Goldman must take it for granted that as China is not a Western-style hegemonic country or a Russian-style expansionist country, it must be a Jewish commercialist country. He could not figure out another way in Western history that can control the world.

In the matter, Goldman's comments reflected the boundary of Western strategic mindsets. This is why many people in the West have taken a skeptical and even hostile stance towards China's proposal of the Belt and Road Initiative, the principle of "wide consultation, joint contribution, and shared benefits" and the vision of "building a community with a shared future for mankind."

After all, according to westerners' mindsets, any global initiative that does not seek control, exploit and pursue self-interest, is incomprehensible. David Goldman is the same. Even if he knows China better than many others, he is still the "Western media person" and cannot get rid of the narrowness and limitations of Western centralism. Although this interview has a lot of impressive comments, they are basically some sort of self-talk with a Western mindset.

The duty of understanding and presenting China accurately falls on Chinese scholars.

Does China Still Need to be Cruel? My Response to Professor Wen

Mutual understanding is not necessarily conducive to peace; the European statesmen of 1914 understood each other all too well, as did the Athenians and Spartans before the Peloponnesian War. Unlike the Germans and French of 1914, or the Athenians and Spartans of 431 B.C.E., though, China and America have scant reason to go to war, and better understanding may prevent miscalculations. I am the first to say that the consensus American view of China is terribly distorted, and I have heard equally distorted views from prominent Chinese analysts. This sort of dialogue, therefore, may be of great benefit, all the more so because the public can listen in and participate.

Professor Wen writes that China "is not a Western-style hegemonic country." China did not create the winner-take-all world of technology business, in which there is room for only one Microsoft, one Facebook, one Google—or one Huawei. By attributing to China the goal of collecting rent from the rest of the world, I simply referred to a basic economic definition: monopolies exact rent. That is true of the American technology monopolies, and China hopes that it will be true of Huawei as well. Of course, Huawei's spearhead in telecommunications is the first step towards dominance in artificial intelligence, with applications in manufacturing, mining, healthcare, supply chain management, urban planning, and a dozen other fields. It was America who created the first generation of great technology monopolies. China hopes to leapfrog America and dominate the next generation, and on a global scale. This surely is not the Yellow Peril of the comic strips, but it is a formidable challenge to American preeminence, and as an American I have urged my compatriots to meet the challenge. I want China to be prosperous, secure, and weaker than the United States.

For five thousand years, China has adapted to its unique geography by building a centralized state with the resources to control its floods and irrigate its fertile plains. Only a centralized state could command the labor required to wrangle with China's unruly rivers and uncertain climate. By no means do I believe that geography is destiny, but China's political model, from the Xia dynasty of legend to the Qin dynasty of historical record and beyond, was founded on a massive riparian infrastructure that was the true wonder of the ancient world, compared to which the irrigation canals of Egypt and Mesopotamia seem like child's play in a sandbox. I briefly reviewed this history in chapter one of this book. This imperial system suited Chinese circumstances so well that the Chinese have reconstructed it countless times after it dissolved into apparent chaos. Like the ancient empires of the West, all of China's dynasties fell. But unlike the Western empires, the Chinese recreated them in the same form. That fact is sufficient to dispel the notion that China's political system arose by accident. But Chinese governance has also been tragically cruel, from the days of Qin Shi Huang to Mao Zedong.

I ask Professor Wen: Is it not time to break the tragic cycle and put such cruelty behind you? Chinese history validates Luo Guanzhong's cyclical pessimism in *The Romance of Three Kingdoms*—the celebrated saying that what is long divided must unite, and what is long united must divide. Western writers speak of the supposed "end of history." One might say, by contrast, that Chinese history is just beginning. This is the first generation of Chinese that need not fear mass destruction of life through famine, flood, or earthquake. Technology has improved to the point that Green Revolution crop yields ensure an adequate food supply, and civil engineering can mitigate floods. China no longer needs a Qin Shi Huang to unify warring kingdoms, or even a Li Bing to conscript tens of thousands of workers to divert rivers through hand-hewn channels through mountains. The imperial model with its disregard for the lives of individual Chinese may have been justified by historical circumstances. These circumstances are no longer present. China persists in its ancient model updated with new technology, and its people accept the ancient model because they do not know any other.

Professor Wen refereed caustically to my "Jewish style of business thinking." He is beguiled by the perception sadly common in China that Jews have a special capacity to make money.[209] As journalist Clarissa Seabag-Montefiore wrote, "Most Chinese will think Jews are smart, clever or good at making money, and that they have achieved a great deal."

Professor Xu Xin, director of the Institute of Jewish Studies at Nanjing University—one of over half a dozen centers in China dedicated to studying Judaism—told me, "Revelations of Jewish People's Wisdom, an account on China's largest microblog site, Sina Weibo, has nearly one-and-a-half-million fans. Its revelations include, 'Make a fortune under adverse circumstances.' This logic—that the Jews are admired for their success despite their small numbers and historical oppression—has also led to a burgeoning industry of self-help books that use Jewish culture and the Talmud to preach business tips."

This says less about the Jews than it does about the materialism of the Chinese, who consider a small people whose spiritual and intellectual influence on the world has vastly exceeded their tiny numbers, and focus only on pecuniary success. But there is a particular way in which the Jews are good at money, although it is not what Professor Wen seems to believe.

Jews have a talent for finance, and several reasons are cited for it. During the Middle Ages, Jews lent money when the Church forbade usury. Jews were outsiders—often forbidden to own land—who had to develop other means of making a living. In his 2010 book, *Capitalism and the Jews*, Jerry Z. Muller observes that Jews had a towering advantage in international trade during the Middle Ages because they had international law: a judgment issued by a rabbinical court in Yemen would be valid for Jewish merchants on the Rhine.

Something more fundamental, though, explains Jewish success in finance. Like overseas Chinese in Asia or Greeks and Armenians in the old Levant, Jewish immigrants developed trading skills that became embedded in their culture and countless jokes (ask a Jewish first grader to add two and two, and he'll reply, "Is that buying or selling?"). But there is nothing uniquely Jewish about this. The same jokes are told about Greeks and Armenians.

Jews distinguished themselves in finance in an entirely different way during the Industrial Revolution. They played a central role in the new government debt markets that followed the Napoleonic Wars, and made a modern economy possible. Jewish bankers like the Rothschild, Mendelssohn, Bleichroeder, Warburg, and Seligman families pioneered the new capital markets. Bonds issued by European governments provided a secure long-term store of value, and set a precedent for financing the great projects of the era: railways, canals, and other infrastructure basic to modern industrial society. This was not the mercantile economy of the preceding two centuries, where the basic unit of capital was the bill of exchange in trade, but an industrial economy that required long-term investment to achieve lasting gains in productivity.

Something other than mere trading skills was required for an investment-driven economy, and that was long-term credit, a concept that derives from the Latin *credere*, "to believe." It is not an exchange of one peasant's eggs for another peasant's barley, or Mexican silver for Chinese tea or silk, but rather a commitment of the savings of whole populations to grand ventures that would pay interest because they drove growth.

Moreover, capital markets create a kind of democracy. If the whole of society relies on the public debt as a store of value, the value of all the savings of society is gauged directly or indirectly against the benchmark of public debt. But that also puts power in the hands of the market—the market has the power to tell the government whether it is doing well or badly, by selling or buying the public debt. It is not simply that the government creates a market that provides convenience and advantages to the people; it becomes dependent on the people's faith in its policies. When that faith is shaken, and confidence flees the government debt market, the result can be catastrophic. Free capital markets require governments to win the faith of the people.

Capital markets require belief in the viability of investments, trust among counterparties, and faith in the future. It is fitting that Jews created capital markets because the Jews invented faith. The secret of Jewish success in public finance is to be found in the Jewish encounter with the divine. The gods of the pagan world did not require faith. The gods simply were there, as much as the natural world which they personified. The god-infested world of the pagans was simply the natural world as it presented itself to man, with all its arbitrariness and cruelty. To the extent that gods demanded loyalty, it was in their capacity as the patrons of a particular policy protected by that god, for example, Athena in the case of Athens.

Nowhere in the pagan world, though, do we encounter a God who could instruct the Hebrew patriarch Abraham to leave his homeland and his father's house, and betake himself to a place which God would later show him. Never do we meet a God who offers his laws (the Torah) to a people, as the Lord did at Mount Sinai, and ask that people's free assent to accept these laws. In no other instance do we hear of a single universal creator God who enters into a covenant of mutual obligations with humans. That is the origin of faith, *emunah* in Hebrew, meaning loyalty as well as belief. The Jewish concept of *emunah* implies not only that we conceive something to be true, but that we also must be steadfast in acting according to that truth.

That is the Jewish genius: to be able to inspire faith—or what is usually called "confidence" in markets—to make possible long-term investments in capital markets involving millions of participants. The investors in a bond or stock issue are not linked by ties of family or personal loyalty, but rather by contract, law, and custom. Their obligations extend beyond the ancient loyalties of family and clan. That may seem obvious on first reflection. But most countries in the world lack functioning capital markets because faith is absent. The public does not trust the government to enforce contracts, or the management of a company not to steal money. That is emphatically true in China, which is struggling to create modern capital markets, rather than depend on state banks and shadow financing. In backward countries, trust is inconceivable outside the narrow circle of blood relations. Firms remain small because trust is restricted to family members.

That is what Chinese can learn from Jews about business. The Jews have no special aptitude for trading. But we have a special gift for promoting the rule of law and public and private institutions which promote credit—that is, faith in future outcomes and the fair treatment of market participants. In the absence of faith, there never will be enough lawyers to enforce contracts, or policemen to arrest embezzlers, or watchdogs to extirpate government corruption. Something more fundamental is required: a sense that the law is sacred. And if any of us breaks the public trust, all of us are damaged.

Adam Smith's invisible hand isn't enough. Capital markets require more than the interaction of self-interested individuals; they require a common sense of the sanctity of covenant, of mutual obligations between government and people, and between one individual and the next. That is why the United States of America is the most successful nation in economic history. It was founded by devout Christians who hoped to construct a new nation in emulation of ancient Israel.

Jews are no longer particularly prominent in banking. Israelis are more interested in the frontiers of technology than in financial markets. The paranoid perception of a Jewish banking conspiracy has faded because so few of the old Jewish banking houses are still in business. The ones that remain, like Rothschild, have little influence. But the Jewish idea that contributed to modern banking remains as powerful as it was in the past. That should be of special interest to the Chinese.[210]

China's government understands that it must reform its capital markets. Housing makes up 79 percent of urban and 61 percent of rural household wealth.[211] By contrast, real estate is roughly one-quarter of US household wealth. The average Chinese home costs nine times the average annual income of Chinese households,[212] and the Chinese Academy of Social Sciences warned in 2019, that any further increase would harm economic growth.[213] By contrast, the average US home costs only four times the average annual income in the United States. Stocks comprise only 8 percent of Chinese household wealth, versus one-third in the United States. This reflects the Chinese people's lack of trust in capital markets and corporate management. As a result, China depends far too much on inefficient state-owned banks to make credit decisions. All of these distortions arise from lack of trust.

Many Chinese understand the Jews better than does Professor Wen. I serve on the advisory board of an Israeli non-governmental organization called SIGNAL, which arranges cultural and intellectual exchanges between Israel and China.[214] In that capacity, I have visited China numerous times and had the privilege to meet some of China's most influential thinkers. In November 2019, I spent several days with a group of Chinese scholars in Tel Aviv.

Over dinner, I asked the senior member of the Chinese delegation why six million Israeli Jews command the attention of representatives of 1.4 billion Chinese. The Chinese education system, he said, is very good at teaching students to memorize answers, but it is not as good at fostering the highest level of creativity. For example, Jews earned one in five Nobel Prizes, although they comprise less than one-five-hundredth of the world population. Eight Israelis have won Nobel Prizes in science, while not a single Nobel Prize in the sciences has been awarded to a Mainland Chinese, except for an award to a practitioner of Chinese traditional healing. Five scientists of Chinese descent have won the prize, but for work done in North America.

What makes the Jews so creative? My Chinese interlocutor wanted to know. I'm not sure I can explain it, I told him, but I can show you.

After the conference, we went to Jerusalem, and our first stop was Yad Vashem, the Israeli memorial to the victims of the Holocaust. After viewing some of the historical exhibits, we went to the Children's Memorial, a tunnel through the living rock where a single memorial candle is reflected through a system of mirrors to become an infinity of lights. The first time I saw it many years ago, I broke down and sobbed. The names and ages of the million and a half murdered Jewish children are pronounced quietly as the visitors pass through. The secret of Jewish creativity, I told them, is that we regard every individual human being as an entire universe. The value of each human being is infinite; the worth of one life is commensurable with the worth of all lives. By the same token, one creative mind can transform the lives of the whole of humanity. Of course, not everyone will do so. But the Jews are predisposed to the possibility. Talent is everywhere. The hard part is to avoid crushing it before it has a chance to flourish.

It is not my job to instruct China as to how to run its affairs. I do not think the West will gain much by lecturing China about violations of human rights, although this Chinese government—like every Chinese government of the past—takes actions which horrify Western opinion. My question is: Is all the sacrifice of the individual to the collective, the frequent cruelty of the Chinese state, the ruthless suppression of minorities—is it all still necessary?

ENDNOTES

1 David P. Goldman, "China suppressed Covid-19 with AI and Big Data," *Asia Times*, March 3, 2020. https://asiatimes.com/2020/03/china-suppressed-covid-19-with-ai-and-big-data/

2 Pillsbury, Michael. *The Hundred Year Marathon*. (Henry Holt, 2015).

3 Graham, Allison, *Destined for War: Can America and China Escape Thucydides' Trap?* (Houghton Mifflin, 2017).

4 Gingrich, Newt. *Trump vs. China*. (Center Street, 2019).

5 Spalding, Robert. *Stealth War: How China Took Over While America's Elite Slept*. Penguin, 2019.

6 Gertz, Bill, *Deceiving the Sky*, (Encounter Books, 2019).

7 https://www.whitehouse.gov/briefings-statements/remarks-president-trump-state-union-address-2/.

8 Gertz, Bill, *Deceiving the Sky*, p. 169-171.

9 David P. Goldman and Henry Kressel, "Prosperity, Security and Markets," *The American Interest*, October 2013.

10 Center for Business and Economic Research, Ball State University, November 4, 2018, https://commentaries.cberdata.org/975/china-is-a-poor-and-backward-nation.

11 Dougherty Edward R. "The Decline of American Science and Engineering," in *Journal of American Affairs* Vol. III No. 1 (Spring 2019), https://americanaffairsjournal.org/2019/02/the-decline-of-american-science-and-engineering/.

12 https://www.timeshighereducation.com/world-university-rankings/2019/subject-ranking/engineering-and-IT#!/page/0/length/25/sort_by/rank/sort_order/asc/cols/scores.

13 Arthur, Herman. "The Quantum Computing Threat to American Security," *The Wall Street Journal*, November 10, 2019, https://www.wsj.com/articles/the-quantum-computing-threat-to-american-security-11573411715.

14 Davenport, Thomas. "China is Overtaking the US as the Leader in Artificial Intelligence," MarketWatch, March 7, 2019, https://www.marketwatch.com/story/china-is-overtaking-the-us-as-the-leader-in-artificial-intelligence-2019-02-27.

15 https://www.scmp.com/business/banking-finance/article/3040476/chinas-tsunami-bond-defaults-topped-us17-billion-november.

16 Goldman, David P. "A different way to look at China's debt," *Asia Times*, October 18, 2017.
https://www.asiatimes.com/2017/10/article/different-way-look-chinas-debt/.

17 US Treasury Press Release, "Treasury Designates China as a Currency Manipulator," August 5, 2019, https://home.treasury.gov/news/press-releases/sm751.

18 Roundtable before the Congressional-Executive Commission on China, May 22, 2009, https://www.govinfo.gov/content/pkg/CHRG-111hhrg51188/html/CHRG-111hhrg51188.htm.

19 Lovell, Julia, *The Great Wall: China against the world 1000 BC–2000 AD*. Sydney: Picador Pan (Macmillan, 2006).

20 https://www.screendaily.com/the-mummy-3-has-strong-opening-in-mainland-china/4040623.article.

21 Sage, Steven, *Ancient Sichuan and the Unification of China,* (SUNY Press, 1992), p. 156.

22 Middleton, Nick, *Rivers: A Very Short Introduction*, (Oxford University Press 2012), p. 93.

23 Steven I. Dutch, *"The Largest Act of Environmental Warfare in History," Environmental & Engineering Geoscience, 15 (4): 287–297, November 2009.*

24 Muscolino, Micah S., "Violence Against People and the Land: The Environment and Refugee Migration from China's Henan Province, 1938–1945," Environment and History (17), p 294, (2011).

25 http://bmcr.brynmawr.edu/2006/2006-11-14.html.

26 Hasting, Adrian, *The Construction of Nationhood*, (Cambridge University Press, 1997).

27 Qiu, Xigui (2000), *Chinese Writing*, Translated by Gilbert L. Mattos, Jerry Norman. Berkeley: Society for the Study of Early China and The Institute of East Asian Studies, University of California, p. 148.

28 Yu, Jiyuan, *The Ethics of Confucius and Aristotle: Mirrors of Virtue* (Routledge, 2007).

29 Sisci, Francesco, *A Brave New China: The Big Change,* (2014)

30 Rahe, Paul, *The Spartan Regime: Its Character, Origins and Grand Strategy*. Yale Library of Military History, 2016.

31 https://www.scmp.com/economy/china-economy/article/2168189/chinas-middle-class-spend-less-they-scrimp-and-save-their.

32 https://www.scmp.com/news/china/society/article/2176377/chinese-parents-spend-us43500-year-after-school-classes-their.

33 https://www.nytimes.com/2016/07/10/business/international/steinways-grand-ambitions-in-china.html.

34 https://www.businessinsider.com/china-facial-recognition-video-games-2018-12.

35 *The Moral Basis of a Backward Society*, by Edward Banfield (Free Press, 1958).

36 Sisci, op. cit.

37 Book XII, A Summary Account of Sacrifices, https://oll.libertyfund.org/titles/school-the-sacred-books-of-china-the-texts-of-confucianism-part-iv-the-li-ki-xi-xlvi.

38 https://www.scmp.com/news/china/society/article/2183049/3-billion-trips-40-days-china-begins-lunar-new-year-mass.

39 Cotterell, Yong Yap, Cotterell, Arthur, *The Early Civilization of China*, (G.P.Putnam's Sons, 1975), p. 30.

40 Feng, Li, *Early China: A Social and Cultural History*, (Cambridge University Press, 2012), p. 48.

41 Liu, Bin, Ningyuan Wang, Minghui Chen, Xiaohong Wu, Duowen Mo, Jianguo Liu, Shijin Xu, and Yijie Zhuang, "Earliest Hydraulic Enterprise in China, 5,100 Years Ago," PNAS, December 26, 2017, 114 (52), 13637-13642

42 Yanko-Hombach, V., Mudie, P., and Gilbert, A. S., 2011, *Was the Black Sea Catastrophically Flooded During the Post-Glacial? Geological Evidence and Impacts*, Benjamin, J. et al. (eds.), *Underwater Archaeology and the Submerged Prehistory of Europe*: Oxbow Books, p. 245–262.

43 Sage, Steven, *Ancient Sichuan and the Unification of China*, (SUNY Press, 1992) p. 150.

44 Sima, Qian, *The First Emperor. Selections from the Historical Records*, (Oxford: Oxford University Press, 2007), p. 102.

45 Victor Davis Hanson, *The Other Greeks: The Family Farm and the Agrarian Roots of Western Civilization* (University of California Press, 1995).

46 Brian Perkins-Ward, *The Fall of Rome and the End of Civilization,* (Oxford University Press, 2016), p. 41.

47 Goldhill, Simon, *Being Greek Under Rome: Cultural Identity, the Second Sophistic and the Development of Empire*, (Cambridge University Press, 2006).

48 Cui Kai and Sharon P. Shoemaker, "A look at food security in China," in NPJ Science of Food, Article number 4 (2018). https://www.nature.com/articles/s41538-018-0012-x.

49 BMJ. 2006 Aug 19; 333 (7564): 362–363.

50 https://www.reuters.com/article/us-china-languages-idUSTRE62B0EW20100312.

51 Raymond Zhong, "Who Owns Huawei? The Company Tried to Explain. It Got Complicated," https://www.nytimes.com/2019/04/25/technology/who-owns-huawei.html.

52 https://www.androidheadlines.com/2019/06/10000-huawei-workers-eliminate-us-partner-reliance.html

53 "5G: The Chance to Lead for a Decade." Deloitte research report. https://www2.deloitte.com/content/dam/Deloitte/us/Documents/technology-media-telecommunications/us-tmt-5g-deployment-imperative.pdf.

54 https://www.wsj.com/articles/israel-prepares-to-unleash-ai-on-health-care-11568599261.

55 https://www.mobihealthnews.com/11453/official-google-health-shuts-down-because-it-couldnt-scale.

56 https://ehrintelligence.com/news/ehr-adoption-interoperability-brought-google-back-to-healthcare.

57 https://www.theverge.com/2018/11/27/18115077/amazon-electronic-health-records-software-text-analysis-medical.

58 https://www.fiercehealthcare.com/tech/google-patent-indicates-work-doctor-facing-interface-to-provide-predictions-clinical-outcomes.

59 https://www.youtube.com/watch?v=mv69ZxKOFSw.

60 https://www.huawei.com/us/press-events/news/2018/11/huawei-ascend-310-world-internet-conference-2018-award.

61 https://asia.nikkei.com/Business/China-tech/Huawei-closes-technology-gap-with-Apple-on-chip-design.

62 https://www.scmp.com/video/china/2181656/china-completes-worlds-first-5g-remote-surgery-test-animal.

63 https://www.healthcareglobal.com/technology/huawei-and-phillips-will-collaborate-new-cloud-based-healthcare-solution.

64 https://asia.nikkei.com/Spotlight/Asia-Insight/Huawei-plays-star-role-in-new-China-Russia-AI-partnership.

65 https://www.theatlantic.com/international/archive/2018/02/china-surveillance/552203/.

66 https://www.statista.com/statistics/734070/mobile-data-traffic-per-capita-in-mexico-since-2010/.

67 https://www.bloomberg.com/news/articles/2019-01-08/guess-who-s-behind-latin-america-s-tech-boom-china-of-course.

68 https://www.huawei.com/minisite/gci/en/country-profile-eg.html.

69 Suwatchai Songwanich, "China's Race to a Cashless Society," http://www.bangkokbank.com/BangkokBankThai/Documents/Site%20Documents/China%20Articles/Update/2016/Chinaweek2016_17.pdf.

70 http://bkm.com.tr/wp-content/uploads/2017/05/cashless-2023.pdf.

71 Morgan Stanley Research Report, "Inside China's Plan to Create a Modern Silk Road," March 14, 2018. https://www.morganstanley.com/ideas/china-belt-and-road.

72 Andrew Chatzky and James McBride, "China's Massive Belt and Road Initiative, Backgrounder for the Council on Foreign Relations," May 21, 2019, https://www.cfr.org/backgrounder/chinas-massive-belt-and-road-initiative

73 https://www.morganstanley.com/ideas/china-belt-and-road.

74 Keynote Address at CERAWeek, "U.S. Foreign Policy in the New Age of Discovery," https://www.state.gov/keynote-address-at-ceraweek/.

75 "US Secretary Mike Pompeo 'Saddened' as Italy Signs up for China's Belt and Road Project," *South China Morning Post*, March 28, 2019. https://www.scmp.com/news/china/diplomacy/article/3003610/us-secretary-state-mike-pompeo-saddened-italy-signs-chinas.

76 https://nsarchive2.gwu.edu/NSAEBB/NSAEBB114/chipak-26.pdf.

77 https://asia.nikkei.com/Politics/International-relations/India-and-Japan-to-cement-relations-with-new-security-deal.

78 Andrew Small, *The China Pakistan Axis: Asia's New Geopolitics,* Telegraph India, November 15, 2015, https://www.telegraphindia.com/7-days/how-china-helped-pakistan-build-the-bomb/cid/1313752.

79 https://www.reuters.com/article/us-china-pakistan-defence/china-says-military-ties-backbone-to-relations-with-pakistan-idUSKCN1LZ03P.

80 Saaed Shah, "China's Belt-and-Road Initiative Puts a Squeeze on Pakistan," *The Wall Street Journal*, April 3, 2019, https://www.wsj.com/articles/chinas-belt-and-road-initiative-puts-a-squeeze-on-pakistan-11554289201.

81 Dr. James M. Dorsey, "Is China Engaging in Debt Trap Diplomacy?," The Begin-Sadat Center for Strategic Studies, December 27, 2017, https://besacenter.org/perspectives-papers/china-debt-trap-diplomacy/

82 https://www.reuters.com/article/us-china-silkroad-malaysia/china-malaysia-restart-massive-belt-and-road-project-after-hiccups-idUSKCN1UK0DG.

83 Kinling Lo, "Sri Lanka Wants its Debt Trap Hambantota Port Back. But Will China Listen?," *South China Morning Post*, December 7, 2019, https://www.scmp.com/news/china/diplomacy/article/3040982/sri-lanka-wants-its-debt-trap-hambantota-port-back-will-china.

84 John Hurley, Scott Morris, and Gailyn Portelance, "Examining the Debt Implications of the Belt and Road Initiative from a Policy Perspective," The Center for Global Development, March 2018. https://www.cgdev.org/sites/default/files/examining-debt-implications-belt-and-road-initiative-policy-perspective.pdf.

85 David P. Goldman, "A Path Out of the Trade and Savings Trap," *Journal of American Affairs* (Fall 2017, Vol. 1, Number 3).

86 https://theaseanpost.com/article/us-using-opic-counter-chinas-bri.

87 Efe Udin, "Huawei's 5G to be used in over 20 European countries," in Gizchina, December 15, 2019, https://www.gizchina.com/2019/12/15/over-20-european-countries-have-chosen-huaweis-5g/.

88 Asa Fitch and Dan Strumpf, "Huawei Manages to Make Smartphones Without American Chips," *The Wall Street Journal*, December, 1 2019, https://www.wsj.com/articles/huawei-manages-to-make-smartphones-without-american-chips-11575196201.

89 Sijia Jiang, "Huawei says it Has Begun Producing 5G Base Stations Without US Parts," Reuters, September, 26, 2019. https://www.reuters.com/article/us-usa-china-huawei-tech/huawei-says-it-has-begun-producing-5g-base-stations-without-u-s-parts-idUSKBN1WB0YD.

90 Cheng, Ting-Fang and Lauly Li, "Inside Huawei's Secret Plan to Beat American Trade War Sanctions," Nikkei Asian Review, Sept. 11, 2019, https://asia.nikkei.com/Spotlight/Cover-Story/Inside-Huawei-s-secret-plan-to-beat-American-trade-war-sanctions.

91 Stu Woo and Kate O'Keefe, "Washington Asks Allies to Drop Huawei," *The Wall Street Journal*, November 23, 2018, https://www.wsj.com/articles/washington-asks-allies-to-drop-huawei-1542965105?tesla=y.

92 Bob Davis, "Pentagon Blocks Clampdown on Huawei Sales," *The Wall Street Journal*, January 24, 2020.

93 Bob Davis and Drew Fitzgerald, "US Pushing Effort to Develop 5G Alternative to Huawei," *The Wall Street Journal*, Febuary 5, 2020. https://www.wsj.com/articles/u-s-pushing-effort-to-develop-5g-alternative-to-huawei-11580831592.

94 https://www.cnbc.com/2018/02/13/chinas-hauwei-top-us-intelligence-chiefs-caution-americans-away.html.

95 https://www.state.gov/interview-with-maria-bartiromo-of-mornings-with-maria-on-fox-business-network-5/.

96 https://www.nytimes.com/2019/05/08/technology/pompeo-huawei-britain.html.

97 https://wikileaks.org/ciav7p1/.

98 https://techcrunch.com/2019/06/26/nsa-improper-phone-records-collection/.

99 https://www.nsa.gov/news-features/press-room/Article/1618691/nsa-reports-data-deletion/.

100 Chris Mills Rodrigo, "Pompeo Warns US May Not Share Intel with UK if it Lets Huawei into 5G Network," thehill.com, May 8, 2019, https://thehill.com/policy/technology/442817-pompeo-warns-us-may-not-share-intel-with-uk-if-it-lets-huawei-into-5g.

101 "U.S. National Security Adviser Warns UK About Allowing Huawei in 5G-FT," *The New York Times*, December 24, 2019, https://www.nytimes.com/reuters/2019/12/24/business/24reuters-usa-china-huawei-tech-britain.html.

102 Andy Greenberg, "This 'Demonically Clever' Backdoor Hides In a Tiny Slice of Computer Chip," wired.com, June 1, 2016. https://www.wired.com/2016/06/demonically-clever-backdoor-hides-inside-computer-chip/.

103 Dan Nidess, "Don't Trust the Chinese to Make Microchips for the Military," *The Wall Street Journal*, October 26 2017, https://www.wsj.com/articles/dont-trust-the-chinese-to-make-microchips-for-the-military-1509059023.

104 Stu Woo and Dustin Volz, "US Considers Requiring 5G Equipment for Domestic Use Be Made Outside China," *The Wall Street Journal*, June 23, 2019. https://www.wsj.com/articles/u-s-considers-requiring-5g-equipment-for-domestic-use-be-made-outside-china-11561313072.

105 Anna Isaac, "Nokia and Ericsson Plan Emergency Break-up Over Trade War and Security Fears," The Telegraph, June 8, 2019, https://www.telegraph.co.uk/business/2019/06/08/exclusive-nokia-andericsson-plan-emergency-break-up-trade-war/.

106 "Ericsson Automated Smart Factory Operational in China," Ericsson press release, September 17, 2019. https://www.ericsson.com/en/press-releases/2019/9/ericsson-automated-smart-factory-operational-in-china.

107 https://www.reuters.com/article/us-france-huawei-minister/france-will-not-exclude-chinas-huawei-from-5g-rollout-minister-idUSKBN1XZ1U9.

108 https://www.huawei.com/en/press-events/news/2017/11/Huawei-GroupePSA-Partnership-Connected-Cars.

109 Lingling Wei, "China Cancels Trade Talks With U.S. Amid Escalation in Tariff Threats," *The Wall Street Journal*, September 22, 2018, https://www.wsj.com/articles/china-cancels-trade-talks-with-u-s-amid-escalation-of-tariff-threats-1537581226.

110 https://www.businesstoday.in/top-story/trump-didnt-know-about-arrest-of-huawei-cfo-meng-wanzhou-white-house-official/story/298221.html.

111 Dan Managan, "National Security Advisor John Bolton Says, 'I Knew in Advance' About Arrest of Huawei Executive—Trump Reportedly Did Not,'" CNBC, December 6, 2018, https://www.cnbc.com/2018/12/06/national-security-advisor-bolton-knew-before-huawei-executive-arrest.html.

112 "Secretary Ross Announces $1.4 Billion ZTE Settlement," Commerce Department press release, June 7, 2018, https://www.commerce.gov/news/press-releases/2018/06/secretary-ross-announces-14-billion-zte-settlement-zte-board-management.

113 https://www.anandtech.com/show/13687/qualcomm-snapdragon-8cx-wafer-on-7nm.

114 https://www.huawei.com/en/press-events/news/2019/8/Huawei-Ascend-910-most-powerful-AI-processor.

115 Debby Wu, "TSMC to Keep Supplying Huawei, Quashes Talk of US Pressure," Bloomberg News, November 3, 2019, https://www.bloomberg.com/news/articles/2019-11-04/tsmc-to-keep-supplying-huawei-quashes-talk-of-u-s-pressre.

116 Juan Pedro Tomás, "US Semiconductor Industry Urges Trump to Approve Huawei Licenses," rcrwireless.com, September 16, 2019, https://www.rcrwireless.com/20190916/chips/us-semiconductor-industry-urges-trump-approve-huawei-licenses.

117 https://www.hindustantimes.com/tech/huawei-turns-to-india-build-an-ecosystem-to-rival-google-s-applications/story-1Tq3WTqZszM8qqz72dV3FM.html.

118 Efe Udin, "TSMC Can Still Supply Huawei 7NM Chips," Bizchina, December 23, 2019. https://www.gizchina.com/2019/12/23/tsmc-can-still-supply-huawei-7nm-chips-may-face-issues-with-14nm-chips/.

119 Scott Foster, "Huawei Appeals to Japan as the US Miscalculates," *Asia Times*, December 6, 2019, https://www.asiatimes.com/2019/12/article/huawei-appeals-to-japan-america-miscalculates/.

120 "Britain's ARM to continue supplying chip technology to Huawei," October 25, 2019, https://www.reuters.com/article/us-china-usa-huawei-arm/britains-arm-to-continue-supplying-chip-technology-to-huawei-idUSKBN1X40YU.

121 Shuhei Yamada, "Cutting off ARM: China Leads Exodus from Top Chip Architect," Nikkei Asian Review, Oct. 28, 2019, https://asia.nikkei.com/Business/China-tech/Cutting-off-Arm-China-leads-exodus-from-top-chip-architect.

122 Kensaku Ihara, "Taiwan Loses 3,000 Chip Engineers to 'Made in China 2025,'" *Nikkei Asian Review*, December 3, 2019, https://asia.nikkei.com/Business/China-tech/Taiwan-loses-3-000-chip-engineers-to-Made-in-China-2025.

123 "5G: The Chance to Lead for a Decade." Deloitte research report, p. 6., https://www2.deloitte.com/content/dam/Deloitte/us/Documents/technology-media-telecommunications/us-tmt-5g-deployment-imperative.pdf.

124 Gingrich, Newt, Christensen Claire, *Trump vs. China*, (Center Street, 2019), pp. 122-123.

125 Ibid., p. 127.

126 Bob Davis and Drew Fitzgerald, "US Pushing Effort to Develop 5G Alternative to Huawei," *The Wall Street Journal*, February 5, 2020, https://www.wsj.com/articles/u-s-pushing-effort-to-develop-5g-alternative-to-huawei-11580831592.

127 Susan Miller, "DARPA's Plan For a US-Friendly 5G Network," defensesystems.com, February 5, 2020, https://defensesystems.com/articles/2020/02/05/darpa-secure-5g.aspx?m=1.

128 Office of the Director of National Intelligence press release, "DNI Releases Budget Figure for FY 2018 Appropriations Requested for the National Intelligence Program," June 12, 2017, https://www.dni.gov/index.php/newsroom/press-releases/item/1767-dni-

releases-budget-figure-for-fy-2018-appropriations-requested-for-the-national-intelligence-program.

129 Shorrock, Rim, *Spies for Hire,* (Simon and Shuster, 2008).

130 Grace Wyler, "One-Fifth of the US's $52 billion 'Black Budget' Is Dedicated to Code Breaking," vice.com, August 30, 2013, https://www.vice.com/en_us/article/nzza5m/one-fifth-of-the-uss-52-billion-black-budget-goes-towards-code-breaking.

131 Gabriel Popkin, "China's Quantum Satellite Achieves 'Spooky Action' at Record Distance," Science Magazine, June 15, 2017, https://www.sciencemag.org/news/2017/06/china-s-quantum-satellite-achieves-spooky-action-record-distance.

132 "Telefónica, Huawei and UPM Perform a Groundbreaking Field Trial Applying Quantum Cryptography on Commercial Optical Networks to Provide Secure Communications Services," Huawei press release, June 14, 2018,
https://www.huawei.com/en/press-events/news/2018/6/Telefonica-Huawei-UPM-Field-Trial.

133 "SK Telecom Continues to Protect its 5G Network with Quantum Cryptography Technologie,." IDQ Press release March 18, 2019, https://www.idquantique.com/sk-telecom-continues-to-protect-its-5g-network-with-quantum-cryptography-technologies/.

134 Andrew Shields, "Quantum Cryptography: The Next Generation of Secure Data Transmission," Information Age, December 16, 2018, https://www.information-age.com/quantum-cryptography-123477496/.

135 Glenn Greenwald, "NSA Collecting Phone Records of Millions of Verizon Customers Daily," *The Guardian*, June 6, 2013, https://www.theguardian.com/world/2013/jun/06/nsa-phone-records-verizon-court-order.

136 Glenn Greenwald and Ewen MacAskill, "NSA Prism Program Taps in to User Data of Apple, Google and Others," *The Guardian*, June 7, 2013, https://www.theguardian.com/world/2013/jun/06/us-tech-giants-nsa-data.

137 Wikipedia entry, "Edward Snowden."

138 Lucas Matney, "Uncovering Echelon: The Top-Secet NSA/GCHQ Program That Has been Watching You're your Enitire Life," Techcrunch, August 3, 2015, https://techcrunch.com/2015/08/03/uncovering-echelon-the-top-secret-nsa-program-that-has-been-watching-you-your-entire-life/.

139 Dina Temple-Raston, "How the US Hacked ISIS," National Public Radio, September 26, 2019, https://www.npr.org/transcripts/763545811.

140 https://www.thelocal.de/20160223/nsa-eavesdropped-on-merkels-intimate-conversations.

141 Allison, Graham, *Destined for War: Can America and China Escape Thucydides' Trap*?, (Houghton Miflin: New York, 2017).

142 https://www.ussc.edu.au/analysis/averting-crisis-american-strategy-military-spending-and-collective-defence-in-the-indo-pacific.

143 https://www.defensenews.com/pentagon/2018/03/06/hypersonics-highest-technical-priority-for-pentagon-rd-head/.

144 https://nationalinterest.org/blog/buzz/hypersonic-weapons-are-literally-unstoppable-america-cant-stop-them-57642.

145 https://web.archive.org/web/20070128075259/http://www.aviationweek.com/aw/generic/story_channel.jsp?channel=space&id=news%2FCHI01177.xml.

146 https://steveblank.com/2010/01/28/balloon-wars/.

147 https://www.theguardian.com/us-news/2019/aug/02/pentagon-balloons-surveillance-midwest.

148 Mark Harris, "Ghost Ships, Crop Circles and Soft Gold: A GPS Mystery in Shanghai," MIT Technology Review, November 19, 2019, https://www.technologyreview.com/s/614689/ghost-ships-crop-circles-and-soft-gold-a-gps-mystery-in-shanghai/.

149 https://www.scmp.com/news/china/article/2021235/end-stealth-new-chinese-radar-capable-detecting-invisible-targets-100km.

150 https://nationalinterest.org/blog/buzz/quantum-radars-chinas-new-weapon-take-out-us-stealth-fighters-f-22-44652.

151 According to analyst Erica Downs writing on the website of the research organization CNA in December 2019:

"With gas beginning to flow through the Power of Siberia, Russia is poised to become China's most important supplier of energy. In crude oil, Russia displaced Saudi Arabia as China's biggest supplier on an annual basis in 2016, due in large part to the construction of Russia's East Siberia Pacific Ocean pipeline and its spur to China, which began crude deliveries in 2011. Russia exported 1.4 million barrels per day of crude oil to China in 2018, accounting for 15 percent of China's crude oil imports. In natural gas, Russia was already supplying China with small volumes of liquefied natural gas (LNG), delivered by ship, accounting for one percent of China's LNG imports in 2018. Now the Power of Siberia pipeline is likely to make Russia one of China's largest—if not the largest—natural gas supplier after the pipeline ramps up to its full annual capacity of 38 billion cubic meters (bcm), which is targeted for 2024. For comparison, the 34 bcm of natural gas Turkmenistan delivered to China in 2018 was the most of any supplier in that year." https://www.cna.org/news/InDepth/article?ID=25

152 https://nationalinterest.org/blog/buzz/chinas-military-cant-conquer-taiwan-just-yet-pentagon-report-55927.

153 "In the end, the ZTZ-99A is likely a lethal threat for the older tanks in the American tank fleet and the majority of the Russian tank fleet, but both the latest versions of American and Russian tanks are likely to beat it in a fight. The constant flux of basic turret and hull designs being manufactured suggests that China is not really sure what its requirements for a tank are, and thus the ZTZ-99A is probably fairly developmentally immature, at least in contrast to the latest American and Russian tanks." https://nationalinterest.org/blog/buzz/chinas-ztz-96-main-battle-tank-any-good-81081

154 "US Special Operations Forces: Background and Issues for Congress," The Congressional Research Service, March 28, 2019, https://fas.org/sgp/crs/natsec/RS21048.pdf.

155 Hanson, Victor Davis, *A War Like No Other,* (Random House: New York, 2005), p. 8.

156 Allison op. cit, p. 36.

157 Allison p. 34.

158 Warner Rex, *Thucydides, History of the Peloponnesian War,* (Penguin Classics, 1974), p. 382.

159 David P. Goldman (Spengler), "The 30% Solution: When War Without War Ends," *Asia Times,* March 13, 2016. https://www.globalstrikemedia.com/uploads/3/7/7/4/37740703/the_30__solution_--_when_war_without_end_ends__spengler_%7C_asia_times.pdf.

160 David, Paul A., Gutman, Herbert, Sutch, Richard, Temin, Peter, and Wright, Gavin, *Reckoning with Slavery: A Critical Study in the Quantitative History of American Slavery,* (New York: Oxford University Press, 1976).

161 Clark, Christopher, *The Sleepwalkers: How Europe Went to War in 1914* (2012), p. 509.

162 Clark op. cit., p. 481.

163 Gertz, Bill, *Deceiving the Sky: Inside Communist China's Drive for Global Supremacy,* (Encounter Books, 2019).

164 Gertz, p. 196.

165 Gertz, pp. 45-46.

166 "TSMC will build a 12" Fab in China," Anysilicon.com, April 6, 2016, https://anysilicon.com/tsmc-will-build-12-fab-china/.

167 Catherine Wong, "China's Three Gorges Dam 'can survive nuclear attack," *South China Morning Post*, March 22, 2016, https://www.scmp.com/news/china/society/article/1928774/chinas-three-gorges-dam-can-survive-nuclear-attack-says-nations.

168 David P. Goldman, "The Digital Age Produces Binary Outcomes," American Affairs Journal, https://americanaffairsjournal.org/2017/02/digital-age-produces-binary-outcomes/.

169 Annual Report to Congress: Military and Security Developments Involving the People's Republic of China 2019 (Office of the Secretary of Defense).

170 http://eng.chinamil.com.cn/view/2019-05/10/content_9500318.htm.

171 https://nationalinterest.org/blog/buzz/air-force-testing-secret-weapon-drone-swarms-86896.

172 David P. Goldman, "A Pax Sinica in the Middle East?," The Middle East Forum, October 28, 2013,

173 https://www.hoover.org/research/us-middle-east-policy-must-contend-new-power-block.

174 https://besacenter.org/perspectives-papers/china-player-middle-east/.

175 Minnie Chan, "Chinese Navy Set to Build Fourth Aircraft Carrier, But Plans for a More Advanced Ship Are Put on Hold," *South China Morning Post*, November 28, 2019. https://www.scmp.com/news/china/military/article/3039653/chinese-navy-set-build-fourth-aircraft-carrier-plans-more.

176 Sasha Gong, "Steve Bannon, Two Chinese Military Officers and the Book That Made Him a China Hawk," *South China Morning Post*, October 4, 2018, https://www.scmp.com/news/china/diplomacy/article/2166982/steve-bannon-two-chinese-military-officers-and-book-made-him.

177 Henry Holt (2015).

178 Liao and Wang, pp. 22-23.

179 Ibid, p. 128.

180 "9/11 Congressional Report Faults FBI-CIA Lapses, *The New York Times*, July 24, 2003. https://www.nytimes.com/2003/07/24/us/9-11-congressional-report-faults-fbi-cia-lapses.html.

181 https://www.c4i.org/unrestricted.pdf, p. 181.

182 Liao and Wang, p. 153 et. Seq.

183 Michael Kugelman, "Masood Azhar is China's Favorite Terrorist," Foreign Policy, March 21, 2019. https://foreignpolicy.com/2019/03/21/masood-azhar-is-chinas-favorite-terrorist/.

184 https://www.judicialwatch.org/wp-content/uploads/2015/05/Pg.-291-Pgs.-287-293-JW-v-DOD-and-State-14-812-DOD-Release-2015-04-10-final-version11.pdf.

185 https://pjmedia.com/spengler/2014/11/21/book-review-why-we-lost-by-gen-daniel-p-bolger/.

186 Andrew Jacobs and Chris Buckley, "China Blames Xinjiang Separatists for Stabbing Rampage at Train Station," in The New York Times, March 2, 2014. https://www.nytimes.com/2014/03/03/world/asia/china.html.

187 Author's notes.

188 Ben Blanchard, "China says 13,000 'terrorists' Arrested in Xinjiang Since 2014," *The New York Times*, March 17, 2019.

189 Dawn Murphy, China's Approach to International Terrorism. Peace Brief by the United States Institute of Peace, October 2, 2017, https://www.usip.org/publications/2017/10/chinas-approach-international-terrorism.

190 Gingrich, Newt, *Trump vs. China*, (Center Street, 2019), p. 197.

191 Jimmy Lai, "There's Hope for Freedom, Even in China," *The Wall Street Journal*, September 30, 2019. https://www.wsj.com/articles/theres-hope-for-freedom-even-in-china-11569885399.

192 Almen Chui, "More violence as Hong Kong Protests Continue," *Asia Times*, October 14, 2019, https://www.asiatimes.com/2019/10/article/more-violence-as-hong-kong-protests-continue/.

193 Jeff Pao, "Hong Kong Man, 70, Dies After Clash With Protesters," *Asia Times,* November 15, 2019. https://www.asiatimes.com/2019/11/article/hong-kong-man-70-dies-after-clash-with-protesters/.

194 "Death Toll in Chile Protests Since October Rises to 27," National Public Radio, December 28, 2019. https://www.pbs.org/newshour/world/death-toll-in-chile-protests-since-october-rises-to-27.

195 "'Hong Kong Mob'—How mainland Chinese See the Democracy Movement," Deutsche Welle, August 19, 2019, https://www.dw.com/

en/hong-kong-mob-how-mainland-chinese-see-the-democracy-movement/a-50084621.

196 Peter Stein, "Did British Blunder Cause Hong Kong's Handover?," *The Wall Street Journal*, May 15, 1997, https://www.wsj.com/articles/SB863631108450656500.

197 Gwynn Guilford, "The Secret History of Hong Kong's Democratic Stalemate," *The Atlantic*, October 14, 2014, https://www.theatlantic.com/international/archive/2014/10/the-secret-history-of-hong-kongs-democratic-stalemate/381424/.

198 Marco Rubio, "American Industrial Policy and the Rise of China," The American Mind, December 10, 2019, https://americanmind.org/essays/american-industrial-policy-and-the-rise-of-china/.

199 Gingrich, Newt, *Trump vs. China*, (Hachette Book Group, 2019).

200 "The US Can't Use Cold War Tactics to Engage with China, Says Former NSA Head Michael Rogers," CNBC interview, December 13, 2019, https://www.cnbc.com/2019/12/03/michael-rogers-former-nsa-chief-on-china-tech-and-cold-war-tactics.html.

201 Arthur Herman, "America Needs an Industrial Policy," *Journal of American Affairs,* Vol III, No. 4 (Winter 2019).

202 https://www.wsj.com/articles/silicon-not-steel-will-win-the-next-war-11545598669.

203 Chuin-Wei Yap, "State Support Helped Fuel Huawei's Global Rise," *The Wall Street Journal*, December 25, 2019. https://www.wsj.com/articles/state-support-helped-fuel-huaweis-global-rise-11577280736.

204 Bob Work, "Remarks to the Air Force Association," Sept. 21, 2016, https://www.defense.gov/News/Speeches/Speech-View/Article/973907/remarks-to-the-air-force-association.

205 David P. Goldman and Henry Kressel, "Prosperity, Security and Markets," American Interest, October 10, 2013, http://www.the-american-interest.com/2013/10/10/prosperity-security-and-markets/.

206 Dave Majumdar, "America's F-22 and F-35 Stealth Fighters vs. Russia's S-300, S-400 and S-500: Who Wins?," National Interest, August 18, 2006, http://nationalinterest.org/blog/the-buzz/americas-f-22-f-35-stealth-fighters-vs-russias-s-300-s-400-s-17394.

207 David P. Goldman and Henry Kressel, "Prosperity, Security and Markets," The American Interest, October 2013.

208 Translation published in *Asia Times*, December 7, 2019, Professor Wen Yang's response appeared in Chinese language at guancha.cn on October 28, 2019, https://www.asiatimes.com/2019/12/article/more-about-china-that-goldman-could-have-learned/ and https://www.guancha.cn/WenYang/2019_10_29_523123_s.shtml.

209 Clarissa Sebag-Montefiore, "Oh, To Be Jewish in China," *The New York Times*, October 2, 2012. https://latitude.blogs.nytimes.com/2012/10/02/oh-to-be-jewish-in-china/.

210 "Why Jews are Good at Money," PJ Media, February 12, 2015, https://pjmedia.com/spengler/2015/2/12/why-jews-are-good-at-money-crossposted-from-asia-times/

211 Yu Xie and Yongai Jin, "Household Wealth in China," China Sociology Review, 2015, 47(3) 203-229, https://www.ncbi.nlm.nih.gov/pmc/articles/PMC4589866/.

212 "China's Housing Price to Income Ratio Hits 9.3," China Banking News, http://www.chinabankingnews.com/2019/07/01/chinas-housing-price-to-income-ratio-hits-9-3-cass-frets-over-economic-impacts/.

213 http://www.chinabankingnews.com/2019/07/01/chinas-housing-price-to-income-ratio-hits-9-3-cass-frets-over-economic-impacts/.

214 http://en.sino-israel.org/about/board-of-advisors/david-goldman/.

ACKNOWLEDGMENTS

Too many people aided my understanding of China to thank individually, but I should like to mention several to whom I am greatly indebted. Dr. Francesco Sisci, an eminent sinologist and author, has been a friend and colleague since we worked together at *Asia Times* in its original incarnation as a print newspaper in the 1990s; with his kind consent, I cite his book *A Brave New China* in several instances. Dr. Uwe von Parpart, the Editor of *Asia Times*, has given me the benefit of his vast knowledge of Asia and keen understanding of China over many years. Carice Witte, the executive director of SIGNAL (Sino-Israel Government Network & Academic Leadership) asked me to advise her organization in 2014, in which capacity I had the privilege of many background discussions with Chinese policymakers and scholars.

Dr. Henry Kressel, a distinguished physicist, inventor, and venture capitalist, gave me an education in the origins of the digital age and the nature of America's technology war with China. Dr. Kressel and I collaborated on several articles on the topic, and those ideas were incorporated into this book. The late Dr. Andrew Marshall, the director of the Defense Department's Office of Net Assessment, gave me many insights into Chinese military aims and capabilities. Dr. Norman A. Bailey, for whom I consulted at the National Security Council during the first Reagan administration, first asked me to look into the civilian spinoffs of high-tech military R&D in 1983, and in a sense, set this book in motion. Paul Scanlan, the Chief Technology Officer of Huawei Technologies, generously explained Huawei's view of the world and ambitions in an October 2019 interview.

Editors at several publications encouraged me to write about China and helped me clarify many of the ideas contained in the following pages, including James Taranto at *The Wall Street Journal*, Charles Kesler at *Claremont Review of Books*, David Samuels at *Tablet* magazine, Matthew Peterson at *The American Mind*, Adam Garfinkle at *The National Interest*, Robert Reinsch at *Law & Liberty*, and R.R. Reno at *First Things*. Urs Gehriger of *Die Weltwoche* (Switzerland) and Laure Mandeville-Tostain of Le Figaro (France) interviewed me on the subject of China and helped me focus my thinking. I also should like to thank Hillsdale College President Larry Arnn, Jean-Guillaume de Tocqueville of the Tocqueville Foundation, Robert Reilly of the Westminster Institute, Arthur Milikh of The Heritage Foundation, Yoram Hazony of the Edmund Burke Foundation, and David Horowitz of the Horowitz Freedom Center for inviting me to lecture on China and develop my ideas before a critical audience.

Finally, I should like to thank Prof. Wen Yang of Fudan University, who responded at length to my discussion of China in *Weltwoche*, and kindly allowed *Asia Times* to translate his remarks in full. These and my response form the Appendix to this book.

ABOUT THE AUTHOR

David P. Goldman has written the "Spengler" column for *Asia Times* for twenty years. An award-winning Wall Street strategist, he has advised the US National Security Council, the Department of Defense, and institutional investors globally. He is president of Macrostrategy LLC, a senior fellow at the London Center for Policy Research, a past fellow of the Jewish Institute for National Security Affairs and the Middle East Forum, among other institutions. His book *How Civilizations Die* appeared in 2011.

Printed in Great Britain
by Amazon

53702408R00156